THE DIARY OF A SUFFOLK FARMER'S

Also by Sheila Hardy

PAGES FROM THE PAST
STORIES OF EDWARDIAN CHILDREN
1804 – THAT WAS THE YEAR . . .
THE STORY OF ANNE CANDLER . . .
THE VILLAGE SCHOOL

The Diary of a Suffolk Farmer's Wife, 1854–69

A Woman of her Time

Sheila Hardy

Foreword by Ronald Blythe

Consultant Editor
Jo Campling

© Sheila Hardy 1992
Foreword © Ronald Blythe 1992

All rights reserved. No reproduction, copy or transmission of
this publication may be made without written permission.

No paragraph of this publication may be reproduced, copied or
transmitted save with written permission or in accordance with
the provisions of the Copyright, Designs and Patents Act 1988,
or under the terms of any licence permitting limited copying
issued by the Copyright Licensing Agency, 90 Tottenham Court
Road, London W1P 9HE.

Any person who does any unauthorised act in relation to this
publication may be liable to criminal prosecution and civil
claims for damages.

First published 1992 by
THE MACMILLAN PRESS LTD
Houndmills, Basingstoke, Hampshire RG21 2XS
and London
Companies and representatives
throughout the world

ISBN 0–333–52408–X hardcover
ISBN 0–333–52409–8 paperback

A catalogue record for this book is available
from the British Library

Printed in Great Britain by
Antony Rowe Ltd
Chippenham, Wilts

Reprinted 1992

For Mitzi Tyler and Tony Copsey,
without whom none of this would have been possible

Contents

List of Plates

Acknowledgements

I have received invaluable assistance from many sources during the research for this work. My often rather strange requests for information met with unfailing courtesy and generosity. To each of the following who became involved with me in unravelling the life of Elizabeth Cotton, I offer my very sincere and grateful thanks: Lord Tollemache; Lord Walsingham; M.A. Holding, HM Consul General, Naples; Dr Patrick Moore CBE FRAS; G.E. Hamilton, Head of Newspaper Library, Colindale; Wallace Morfey; the Clowes family; Neil Clayton; Patricia Burnham; Michael Haxell; Mr and Mrs Peter Haxell (for permission to quote from *A Scramble through London and Brighton*); Christine Favell (for permission to quote from the Cotton farm ledgers); Louise Abbott; Pat Bryant; Robyn Buchanan; Simon Catterick; F.G. Coniam, Ilfracombe Publicity Department, Devon; Jill Freestone; Brenda Gamlin; Frank Jowett (New Zealand); J.A. Kendrick; Denise Morcom; Richard Pipe; Miss M. Powell, Derbyshire Dales District Council; Sue Rodwell; Richard G.A. Rope; Ipswich Public Library Service; The Kennel Club; The Law Society; the Record Offices of Essex, Norfolk and Lancashire. The Suffolk Record Office deserves a very special mention, as does my long-suffering family.

Foreword

In spite of all the self-exposure, a diarist remains an enigmatic being. 'All' is not told. The imbalance between what happens and what is put down, day after day, is one of the first things one notices when reading a diary. Why put so much about this in, why leave out all reference to that? Historians and novelists are frequently tempted to fill-in the gaps. What is never mentioned becomes so terribly eloquent; what is passed over in a sentence or two remains tantalising.

The diary that Elizabeth Cotton kept between 1854 and 1869 is no mere outline, yet there are the usual intriguing spaces. And again one is reminded of those colouring-in books which one had as a child, and in which the pictures remained vague until they were correctly completed. But who best qualifies to write between the lines of somebody else's diary? The social historian? The novelist? In this instance it is a neighbour in the same locality as the diarist, but from another century, someone who not only knows every twist of the road where Elizabeth Cotton walked, but who is natively familiar with all the twists and turns of her Suffolk thinking. It was this possession of a shared territory that Sheila Hardy saw as her authorisation to interpret in more detail what the wife of a Victorian farmer was often no more than just tentatively mentioning, during those decades which we now like to think of as one of the 'golden ages' of British agriculture. The hungry forties were past, the great 'coming down time' was still way over the horizon. For the Cottons it was a kind of 'bright morning' when the rural middle class could feel stability, if not the wilder forms of prosperity. There was confidence and comfort. Elizabeth was in her mid-thirties, her husband his mid-fifties. Nothing in her diary suggests that they were other than well suited, though not according to our stereotypical view of Victorian marriage. One of the reasons why Sheila Hardy has opened this diary a little wider than Elizabeth intended is to throw light on a scene which we have darkened with our popular myths about the old countryside, and especially about its classic drudge, the farmer's wife.

The Suffolk Farmer's Wife is not at all the woman we think we know, the forever toiling, breeding, isolated creature with her old saws and customs. She exists, most interestingly and quite unselfconsciously, in a cultivated world between that of what used to be called the 'working farmer' and that of the 'lady', and an intelligent and vital world it was, and a far remove from our dull and stuffy notions of it. In fact, Mrs Herbert Cotton of Amor Hall, Washbrook, a village just outside Ipswich, is far more like the independent-minded countrywoman of today than ever we could have imagined, given our fancifulness about those days. Elizabeth inherited her poise and taste from her family the Nelsons and the Haxells, who between them were innkeepers and stage-coach proprietors extraordinary in London, East Anglia and indeed all over England. One of the family inns was the Great White Horse at Ipswich which was so vilified by the youthful Dickens in *Pickwick Papers* that he was very nearly sued for defamation and libel.

Sheila Hardy begins her fascinating book with an exciting account of the last years of the coaching trade – by the time Elizabeth had become mistress of Amor Hall and was writing her diary, the railways had taken over – and ends it with an equally absorbing description of the intense religious drama of the period, when Elizabeth falls for the teachings of the saintly and beautiful Father Ignatius, a young deacon to whom Low Church East Anglia was to give such a rough ride that he eventually forsook hostile Suffolk and Norfolk for the Black Mountains in Wales, there to set up his Benedictine order. People often forget that the Tractarian or Oxford Movement actually originated in Suffolk at the Hadleigh Conference. The diarist's full involvement in its local consequences was courageous as well as spiritual, and again shows her as a woman intelligent enough to live her own life and not be browbeaten by what 'they' said. No less a person than John Mason Neale, the brilliant hymnologist, assisted Father Ignatius in his attempt to found a sisterhood in Suffolk, and Elizabeth's diary gives a village glimpse of the movement which would transform the Church of England.

What the diary does not do is offer any kind of picture of mid-nineteenth-century farming, and rightly. Elizabeth plays in the meadows with her children, cares for her servants and labourers and their families and does her duty, and with none of the so-called charity of the day. She writes, not to leave behind her a social record of Amor Hall, but to create the type of diary now known as a Book of the Self. She wants to see herself existing beyond the commonplaces of marriage, having babies and being mistress of a sizeable house, so we have reading, music, holidays and religion. She buys plants and makes a garden. She joins in the famous Victorian fern craze. With her hotelier relations in the capital, there is much going up to London. Nor is she culturally on her own at all in Suffolk; there are many friends in the Ipswich area who share her interests.

Sheila Hardy's method has been to follow each of Elizabeth's references through, and to integrate them into a single well-told story. It is filled out, both factually and imaginatively, with learning and with great understanding of Elizabeth's personality. The diarist, who left such a generous scattering of clues as to her existence and selected activities, is satisfyingly traced. One has the feeling that she would have been pleased and amused, and would have approved being presented with such clarity. A self-sketch has been made the basis of a finished portrait. A better analogy might be a photographic one, the recovery of the subject of some wonderful but now indistinct picture taken long ago by an early camera. It is good to see the Suffolk grass growing under Elizabeth's feet and all the character in her face.

RONALD BLYTHE

1

Introduction

I send you a diary for you at least to note down dates . . . or else your life will pass without anything to look back to – and when you wish to refer to what you did in such and such a year – you will remember nothing – all will be in one cloud of confusion . . . what events occur from day to day. Thus 'saw so and so, gave a dinner'. 'Heard of such and such an event.'

Dearest Child – The Private Correspondence of Queen Victoria and the Crown Princess of Prussia, 1851–61 – R. Fulford (ed.)

That the habit of keeping an account of one's daily life, recommended by Queen Victoria, was followed by many of her subjects is evident from the number of diaries which have survived. The reasons for keeping a personal record of one's life were probably as varied as the books in which they were inscribed. To some it may have been a discipline, a time set aside for reflection on how much, or how little, had been achieved in a day; for others, a chance to release pent-up emotional response to a particular event, which would allow the diarist to return later to review the experience in a more tranquil mood. Was it also an attempt to create for oneself some order out of the chaos of life, to be able to see a pattern emerging? The rapid changes of the nineteenth century may have led to this need for a feeling of personal stability, a desire to free oneself from the 'cloud of confusion' all around.

The value of personal diaries from the past has long been recognised as source material for our understanding of those times. The voices of statesmen and politicians, famous and infamous, cross time to give us their interpretation of the events they influenced, but often it is the insignificant, even trivial comment that illuminates a particular aspect of a life about which we know little. Important though it is to be given insight into how a decision which had major impact on the course of history was reached, for many of us there is more interest in finding out how people like ourselves coped with everyday living; their problems with housing, jobs and family relationships; their attitudes towards the arts, sciences, religion and politics; their hopes and fears for their own lives and those of their children. Perhaps by reading of another's life revealed in a personal diary from the past we are better able to make sense of our own.

For me, having spent much of my life reading and teaching literature, diaries have the advantage of adding authenticity to knowledge that has been acquired from fiction. Thus to meet with a woman who was living at the time George Eliot, for example, was writing, who had actually heard Thackeray lecture and met Mrs Wordsworth, was remarkable. Even more so when one realised that the woman concerned was neither of the rank which gave patronage nor a member of the literary world. She was just an ordinary middle-class woman whose life spanned most of the nineteenth century; the wife of a farmer, living in a Suffolk village, who followed the fashion of keeping a diary.

Asked to describe how they imagined life to have been for a farmer's wife in Victorian times, groups of present-day women produced very similar pictures. They saw her as hardworking, spending the majority of her time in the kitchen producing an endless stream of meals for her own large family – she would have at least twelve children – as well as for all the farm labourers. Her long day would involve her in bread-making, butter-churning, feeding fowls and egg-collecting, huge amounts of washing and ironing in addition to the general care of her children. When she did sit down in the evening it would be to take up her sewing, either making clothes or repairing them. Additionally, it was thought she would occasionally undertake field work, especially at harvest time. Her only escape from this routine would be the weekly visit to the local market to sell her surplus produce and buy necessities. On Sundays she would go to church, probably twice, and on rare occasions she would entertain family and friends or be entertained by them; it was even possible she might attend social functions connected with the church. The consensus of opinion was that for a Victorian countrywoman life after marriage was one of drudgery, relieved only a little as the older daughters were able to share some of the household burdens.

How had these ideas been formed? Immediately it became apparent that the term 'Victorian' was part of the problem. Many of those questioned stated they had gleaned information passed to them from grandmothers and great aunts who were Victorians. These were, in fact, women born at the very end of the nineteenth century who would have grown up in the Edwardian era. Other information had been absorbed from novels and films set in the period. Closer questioning revealed that the groups tended to be selective in what they remembered, choosing to retain images of the harsher side of life. When, for example, the novels of Thomas Hardy were mentioned, few recalled that in *Far From the Madding Crowd* Bathsheba Everdene's lifestyle as a working farmer was quite comfortable, as was that of the Melburys in *The Woodlanders*, preferring to dwell rather on those like Gabriel Oak or Giles Winter-bourne who had fallen on hard times.

From school history lessons had come information about the lives of the wealthy and the very poor, but little about those in between who, for want of a better title, we label as the middle classes. As we talked it was revealed that for most, the idea of a comfortable, leisured way of life in the past was equated to a very large income. It was difficult for the group to conceive that people in quite modest circumstances similar to their own could possibly have led a life that was in any way comparable to, or even better than, that which they were now living.

It was their and my own lack of understanding that made me embark on this book. I had never felt particularly drawn to the Victorian age, it seemed a dull, claustrophobic time. School history lessons had emphasised the horrors of industrialisation, the grinding down of the poor by the exploitation of insensitive employers exemplified in Dickens's *Hard Times*. Then there was all that false morality, the prudery which masked festering unnatural practices; a dark, brooding, sinister lifestyle which must eventually erupt – all these aspects came together in the rapidly expanding middle classes. The upholders of all that was dreary; the comfortably-off families living their neat restricted lives in which father went off to his place of business leaving wife and children at home in the pleasant house he was able to maintain as a result of his business expertise – and at the expense of his ill-paid workers. There were servants worked to death to attend to the needs of the household and to look after the children. The mistress of the house regulated the workers under her control but, apart from the inconvenience of frequent child-birth, had little to do but an idle round of visiting and pottering with the accepted feminine pursuits of embroidery and music. Of her children she saw little; they remained in the nursery except for being 'brought down' to spend an hour or so with their parents in a totally artificial atmosphere. Discipline was firm, often stern. Parents were to be respected and obeyed implicitly. What education the children received (before going to school if they were boys) was given by the downtrodden governess, a figure who looms large in the novels of the period. Girls were kept isolated in this world of the schoolroom, taught little which would exercise their minds, the main requisite being to fit them to be graceful hostesses and pliant wives to their future husbands.

Such were the ideas I held. What possible interest then could there be in reading about the daily activities of someone who had lived in such a dull time? Furthermore, a middle-class farmer's wife, living in a small village outside a medium-sized country market town hardly seemed likely to provide anything to whet the appetite. What could this woman have to impart that would provide either interest to the general reader or fresh information for the serious student? She had not made her mark on the history of England as a leader like Queen Victoria, as a great reformer or innovator like Florence Nightingale or a talented novelist like George Eliot, all of whom were born in the same year as herself.

My immediate reaction when I read Elizabeth Cotton's diary of

1854–63, however, was to seek to share it with the world as it stood, but it was suggested that the world might not share my enthusiasm for reading it in its entirety and that a thematic approach might be preferable since it did contain some valuable insights into everyday life. Mrs Cotton had obviously been an inveterate diary-keeper for some years, so the volume I had been given simply took up a life she had consistently recorded. Hers is not an introspective journal with long entries; she simply recorded, often very briefly, her daily activities and those of her family. It was her habit to write the date on Sundays and then follow this with a note of the main events for each day of the week. When nothing was worthy of mention she would write 'Rest of the week at home'. For no apparent reason she changed to daily recording in April 1860.

Mundane though many of the entries are she manages to present not only the life of her family but also that of those with whom she came into contact. Far from the received picture of the farmer's wife whose life revolved around the farm kitchen, Elizabeth Cotton spent much of her time engaged in the social activities available in nearby Ipswich and the surrounding area. Her scrupulous dating of each concert or lecture she attended made it easy to check the event with the local newspapers and I have drawn upon both the *Ipswich Journal* and the *Suffolk Chronicle* to explain or to reinforce some of her comments. However, we are not limited to the provincial scene; we move outside the area with her, in particular to London where lived most of the members of her large family with whom she maintained a close relationship.

I am not a social historian, so I am not able to draw all the conclusions that a professional would from the material at my disposal. I was primarily interested in the woman herself: what made her behave as she did, what influences shaped her character. For this reason, I felt it necessary to research her background as fully as I could. It was while seeking information about her father's business that I had one of the many chance encounters which have been a feature of my time spent on this research. Unable to help with that particular line of enquiry, my contact disclosed that he possessed Mrs Cotton's diary for 1864 onwards. He generously offered me the use not only of that but also the unpublished diary of George Ranson, a farming neighbour of the Cottons. Later, a listener to a lecture I had given about the first diary, having heard my mention of the date of death of Elizabeth's last surviving child, furnished me with a copy of the will which cleared up the mystery of where Elizabeth was buried. A further demonstration that truth can indeed be stranger than fiction occurred when I was given 'just for your interest' some old newspapers which had been found in a local barn. Ranging in date from 1856 to 1914, it was a random selection and apart from the one that commemorated the accession of Edward

VII, there seemed no logical reason for their having been kept. Among them was a double sheet containing pages three to six of the *News of the World* for 21 October 1860. Curious to see if the journal bore any resemblance to its modern counterpart, I was stunned when on turning to page four, I found myself reading a court case which referred to the activities in London of one of Elizabeth Cotton's brothers. Here, by the most amazing coincidence, I had found one of the secrets which the diary had not revealed.

Since for the lay person much of historical knowledge is based on generalisations, it is extremely difficult to say if one individual can be taken as typical of a group. My belief is that Elizabeth was not an unusual woman for her time. Had she been so out of step with the rest of her kind, she would not have had the wide circle of friends and acquaintances she did have. The very fact that she and her women friends took part in the social life offered them in the immediate locality and in the town suggests that this was 'typical' behaviour. How far Ipswich was typical of other market towns expanded by industrialisation, the reader must decide. Since her roots were so firmly set in the Ipswich area, it is inevitable that much of what follows is relative to that town. Nonetheless, I do not think this lessens the value of the diaries' information.

While this is not an in-depth academic study of the period, I hope that by using Elizabeth's diaries and those of some of her contemporaries, plus relevant extracts from other sources, I can share with the general reader as well as the student of history, a picture of the life that was led by countless other ordinary women and their families, members of the middle class during the middle years of the nineteenth century.

2

Family Background

'That 'ere your governor's luggage, Sammy?' inquired Mr. Weller . . . as he entered the yard of the Bull Inn, Whitechapel . . . and away went the Ipswich coach up Whitechapel to the admiration of the whole population. '. . . a thousand things may have happened by the time you next hear news o' the celebrated Mr. Veller o' the Bell Savage.'

Pickwick Papers – Charles Dickens

THE COACHING BUSINESS

For most readers there is an added dimension to a novel which mentions places with which they are familiar. An exact location helps not only to make the story more alive to them at the time of reading, it can also make them recall it every time they pass that particular spot. Even today, more than 150 years after the young journalist Charles Dickens came to Ipswich to cover the parliamentary elections in the county of Suffolk for the *Morning Chronicle*, the Great White Horse is still recalled as the setting for Mr Pickwick's unnerving encounter with the lady in the yellow curl-papers.

However, there was more than that to catch the attention of Elizabeth Cotton, née Haxell, for not only was she brought up amid the busy and exciting background of the coaching business in Ipswich, but the two London inns mentioned in the quotation above were of special significance to her; the Bull, in particular, playing an important part in her life.

Elizabeth's maternal forebears had been in the innkeeping and transport business for several generations. Her grandmother, Ann Nelson, made her home at the Bull, Whitechapel Road, Aldgate, but had interests in several other city hostelries and was in partnership with various coaching businesses. She was, by 1812, a widow, but like so many women of that era and those that preceded it, found this no bar to carrying on a successful business enterprise. She is described in Charles Hooper's *Road Book* as 'one of those stern, dignified, magisterial women of business, who were quite remarkable and a feature of the coaching age, who saw their husbands off to an early grave and alone carried on the peculiarly exacting double business of inn-keeping and coach proprietorship and did so with success'. From her inns coaches ran all over the country. At one time Ann Nelson held the monopoly of the route into East Anglia, no mean feat in a cut-throat business where men vied with each other to take possession of the valuable trade; where the ability to run a new service that knocked even half an hour off the journey time was enough to kill the one already in existence.

A possibly partial view of Ann and her business is contained in a little book written in the 1880s, thirty years after her death, by her grandson, Edward Haxell.

> I see her now dressed as in the fashion of full one hundred years since, the high-heeled black velvet shoes, with red heels and silver buckles, a snow white mob-cap and spotless India muslin kerchief. In summer days Dame Ann adorned her regal form with the choicest black bombazine, which was changed in winter for black velvet worn to the last day of her long and meritorious life in loving remembrance of her fondly loved husband. For years, unaided, she alone held possession of this Eastern Road, different friends and members of her family residing at the principal towns along its route. Hers, however, was the one mind that defeated those well organised plans of opposition, hers the courage that never saw danger, her indomitable energy and will enabling her to surmount and crush all competing interests, finally establishing herself at the very head of one of the largest carrying establishments of the age, reigning indeed supreme, until the business itself was submerged by the great railway wave that swept away not only the coaching period but changed the very age itself.
>
> Born with a gigantic mind, eminently handsome, her eyes black and searching . . . and a courage unknown – speaking generally – to the ladies of the present day, she would under different circumstances equally well have filled the throne of Elizabeth of England or graced the coronet of Sarah, Duchess of Marlborough.

As we shall see later, this grandson had a great love of both the theatre and amateur dramatics, so we may allow that this account is somewhat flamboyantly narrated. Nonetheless, it does give us some idea of the forceful woman who was Elizabeth Cotton's grandmother.

Ann had three sons and a daughter who survived to adulthood. Robert took over the coach business which operated from the Belle Sauvage (Mr Weller's Bell Savage), a large galleried inn, part of which abutted the infamous Fleet prison. From here coaches left south-westwards to Bath, Bristol, Exeter and Plymouth, and west, north and east to Oxford, Gloucester, Coventry, Carlisle, Manchester and Norwich.

John assisted his mother at the Bull, taking over on her death. Ann was still holding sway there in 1826 when Dr Jonas Asplin of Prittlewell in Essex joined the 4 a.m. coach for London which 'reached The Bull Inn, Whitechapel about half past 9. Breakfasted there. Mrs. Nelson still keeps the house'.

The 1822 timetable issued by Nelson's General Coach and Waggon office at the Bull showed that a countrywide service operated from there too. This gave not only the destination of each coach and the duration of its journey but also the promise of link services further afield. For example the Independent New Post coach took twenty-four hours to reach Manchester from where it was possible to make connections to Liverpool, all parts of Cumberland and Scotland.

The Bath and Bristol Express offered the opportunity to go on to Wales and parts of Ireland, while the Independent Safe Coach took ten hours to reach Southampton for connections to the Isle of Wight and the Channel Islands.

In Chapter 53 of the *Pickwick Papers*, Mr Weller tells his son, 'I have come to the determination o' driving the Safety and puttin' up vunce more at the Bell Savage, vich is my natural born element, Sammy.'

Among the many drawings and etchings by Elizabeth Cotton is one for a bill-head for the King's Head Inn, Ipswich, which shows the Independent Safe Coach. To those of us brought up on Christmas card pictures of coaches where the outside passengers sat atop the vehicle necessitating the injunction given by Tony Weller to 'Take care o' the archway, gen'l'm'n. "Heads," as the pieman says', the design of the Safe Coach shows how it earned that name for the outside travellers sat in front of the closed portion in much the same way as they would have driven in a private open carriage.

The scale of coaching business can be imagined from a report in 1830 which stated there were fifteen hundred opportunities for a person to leave London in the course of twenty-four hours. Apart from the main routes to principal towns and cities, there were smaller services to outlying districts. It was probably to safeguard the Ipswich end of her Great Eastern route and to develop the cross-country services that Ann Nelson set up her daughter Rebecca and son-in-law, James Haxell, following their marriage at Grey Friars, Newgate, in January 1812.

Beyond the fact of his baptism in a Suffolk village in 1782, nothing is known of James's early life or what brought him to London, but his later career shows that he was knowledgeable about horses. Possibly he started work as a horse-keeper or ostler at a London inn, working his way up to become yard porter, a position responsible for finding the business to keep the stables filled as well as ensuring that the horses were correctly fed and tended. In addition the yard porter superintended the maintenance of the vehicles. In the golden days of coaching it was a prestigious position that brought large tips from grateful customers.

Since neither of the first two children of the marriage appear in the baptismal records in Ipswich, it may be that Rebecca and James served an apprenticeship to the business in London first, although Ann Nelson would have made sure that her daughter had been brought up fully conversant with all aspects of the business. By 1817, however, Rebecca and James Haxell had become established in Ipswich, initially perhaps to supply the horses needed for the coaches. To that end they were installed at a farm called New Place on the outskirts of the town where the land adjoined the main London road.

A coach proprietor, or a syndicate of owners, was only as successful as the quality of the horses used to pull the vehicles. Since it was necessary to change horses every five to fifteen miles along the route according to the difficulty of the terrain, it was essential to enter into contract with reliable suppliers along the road. Most proprietors owned only those horses which were used for the first stage out and the last in of their chosen route. Few could afford to support establishments like that of William Chaplin who, in the 1830s, was running sixty coaches from his five London yards, employing two thousand workers and maintaining thirteen hundred horses. With the cost of each horse at a conservative estimate of £30–40, plus the daily expenses for food, stabling and general maintenance, it is easy to see why it was necessary to use contractors along the way. A minimum of four horses was required for each coach, so with several vehicles plying up and down a route there was a constant demand for good animals. It was reckoned that a slow coach-horse had a working life of six years while that of a fast one was three years, not only half as much, but it had to be rested every fifth day. And it was not long into the 1830s when there was an even greater demand for fast horses.

In 1832 Israel Alexander put the Quicksilver company coaches on the Ipswich road in an attempt to break the Nelson-Haxell monopoly. The Quicksilver had for some time been running on the Brighton road, so Nelson-Haxell retaliated by putting one of their Dark Blues, the Dart, on that route. The battle for control of the route was described later by Edward Haxell, recalling his first trip to Brighton in 1836:

how well I remember being hoisted up to the front seat of the Dart, for little fellow that I was, climbing was out of the question, so I was literally lifted on with about as much consideration as would be shown to a barrel of oysters, or a more than usually fragile parcel legibly endorsed, "Perishable, with care," "This side up." . . . My fellow schoolboys turned out and heralded my Hegira from the Bull Inn . . . With the exception of myself and Sir Henry Peyton, a great patron and friend to our family, there was no one on the dark Blue, excepting, of course, the coachman and guard . . . both very powerful men, the former indeed possessing an amount of decision and obstinate determination of will that I have never seen in any other man. Scarcely had we reached the Elephant and Castle, the last halting place in London, when we came up with the opposition coach – opposite in every sense of the word, for ours was painted a deep blue, with four of the finest dappled grey horses it was possible to couple together, with simply the letter N painted on the horses' blinkers and pads, while the opposing coach was painted a staring red, its name Quicksilver, in huge golden letters, and its horses, four grand pie-balds, were in harness redolent of brass, the collars, pads and front-lets being also of a bright red. In an instant, without any sign more perceptible than a slight shake of the reins, we were off, our horses broke into a swinging gallop and succeeded in obtaining the lead. We were, however, pluckily followed by the Quicksilver. At this time the coaching business, was conducted with a species of recklessness altogether unknown to any other; it was simply a question of ruin, and nothing less than ruin, to the contending parties, the longest purse carried the day. . . . In the face of every opposition the regular fares of 12/- out and 20/- in were invariably dropped to 5/- and 10/- and for one week passengers, if any could be found bold enough to ride, were carried for nothing and in addition provided with a good dinner at Reigate.

As this was known to be a life and death struggle in which the victors would not only destroy that coach, the nominal cause of the dispute, but would retain possession of the entire traffic of the Great Eastern Road, the real cause of the opposing interests, and would certainly frighten others from similar attempts, accordingly the most strenuous exertions were made on either side. Stables were built at six mile distances, thorough-bred horses alone were used, pairs of leaders stationed at every steep gradient – with boy in saddle and two men to hook on the leader traces almost before the coach stopped; while at the six mile changes the fresh horses were drawn out the moment the coaches were sighted, when on stopping four men sprang to the used-up team, as many more adjusted the fresh ones, the cloths were drawn, the coachman never leaving his box, the reins were thrown at him, the guard scrambled up as only guards could. One minute and a half only was allowed for the changes, and then both were off again on their mad career.

In one stage we met the fish vans, that then galloped every inch of the distance from Brighton to London. In other moments we were challenged, and for a time even headed, by the costermongers who then travelled in light carts drawn by eight or ten powerful dogs. . . . Just at this moment I heard Sir Henry Peyton say to the coachman, "Upon my soul, I think they're off." "There ain't no thought about it," was the reply, "They've been off these ten minutes, and what's more I'm d--d if I can stop 'em; for the Lord's sake, Sir Henry, you take the leaders, keep 'em straight, that's all I ask, I'll pull at the wheelers." And so we sped on and on; here, an opening was made in the ranks of some friendly hay and market carts en route to town – for Nelson & Co. were ever popular on the roads – only to be closed again on our antagonist making its approach; there, a horse fell or staggered, and was instantly recovered; now we were a few yards ahead, again neck and neck with the Quicksilver, the horses covered with foam, and we almost blinded with dust, and so we raced on. Our last six mile change was done, the Quicksilver then a few feet only ahead, and so we raced until the Steyne was in sight. In the narrowest part of this road, there was a meeting of two old road wagons their summits as high as the neighbouring second floor windows, drawn by some twelve or fourteen horses, the tires of their wheels some two feet wide, and the two drivers were conversing together, with a carriage way of some twelve feet, or possibly less, between them. I remember our coachman saying to Sir Henry, "I am going to drive at those wagons, if you've the nerve to sit by; hold fast. By God, I'll go at that fellow, and either get through fust or knock us both over." . . . One wild shout – a flash of the whip – and we were off at a fearful speed. Instantly the other coach was caught, and for a moment we were both driving at the narrow opening left by the wagons. For a second or so it was impending death to all, in the next the driver of the Quicksilver fairly cowed drew on one side, and I may add, disappeared altogether both from this and the Eastern Road e'er many more weeks. We dashed ahead, and a very few minutes more saw us, our horses a sheet of foam, before the door of number four Castle Square.

With the ability to describe so graphically this dramatic event from his childhood, it seems a pity that Edward Nelson Haxell should have confined his literary output to *A Scramble Through London and Brighton* which is little more than a tourist's guide. And however much the story may have been embellished in the telling, we can imagine its impact on his brothers and sisters when he related it immediately after the event.

The presence of Sir Henry Peyton was in keeping with the early nineteenth-century fashion when aristocratic young gentlemen paid highly for the thrill and excitement of being allowed to drive a fast coach. A close intimacy often grew up between the well-born young man and the coachman, leading George Borrow in *Romany Rye* to attribute the ill-mannered and self-opinionated behaviour of coachmen in general to this unnatural mixing of the social classes.

Edward calls himself a child in his account and insists he was too small to reach the driving-box unaided, but unless he was mistaken in the date of 1836, this emphasis on size must be for dramatic effect, since he was in that year almost fourteen. Reason tells us that his uncle would hardly have allowed a small child to embark on such a journey. Since he also states that his school fellows turned out to see him off, it looks as if he had made his home in London with his maternal relations, as perhaps did his brothers. There is no doubt that the Nelson influence was very strong upon all the Haxell children, each of whom bore the maternal surname in front of that of their father. As the coach company was known as Nelson-Haxell & Co., it is likely that the importance of the former name would stand them in good stead in later life ensuring them an entrée into business circles. It is further possible that both George and John Nelson, being childless, took on a financial responsibility for the growing number of nephews and nieces who flourished in Ipswich.

By 1832 there were ten little Haxells. Following James and Ann came, in close succession, Rebecca, Susanna, Elizabeth (b. 26 December 1819), Edward, Arthur, Catherine, George and Margaret. The older children were brought up on the farm, but by 1822 they had moved to the coach office with its adjoining house and stables in Brook Street in the town centre. The farm was retained to supply the needs of the precious horses, but James needed to be in the centre of things, supervising the bookings for departures, providing the on-the-spot horses for the change-over which took place when the coaches clattered into either the Coach and Horses next door or the Great White Horse a few yards up the road; negotiating deals with the coach builders who supplied the Dark Blue vehicles which were the Nelson-Haxell trademark and opening up the cross-country services.

It was amid this bustling atmosphere that Elizabeth grew up, in the heart of a small but flourishing town. The ancient borough of Ipswich enjoyed many advantages. Set fourteen miles upstream from the North Sea, the river Orwell provided not only navigable access to the inland port but a safe haven for ships to lie at anchor. With a hinterland that was almost totally agricultural, the town was a natural market town. During the heyday of the medieval woollen industry, Ipswich had flourished in its export trade with the continent. Easy access to London by both highway and water had added to its importance. At various times its industries had included fishing, in the North Sea and as far afield as Greenland for whaling, and shipbuilding. Although the fortunes of the town had fluctuated throughout history it had never been so dependent on any one trade or industry that it had either grown greatly or declined totally. In a county not famous for its heights, the town nestled in the flat land around the head of the river encircled by small hills on most of which stood the windmills which provided the flour needed to feed the ever-growing population. A plentiful supply of good water provided not only for everyday needs, but laid the foundations of the eighteenth-century brewing industry.

The various wars of the eighteenth century, culminating in that against Napoleon, were to prove favourable to the town's prosperity. Not only was a large contingent of the military quartered there, the navy too used the estuary for anchorage.

In addition, Suffolk became a fashionable – and reasonably cheap – area in which to live. The fall in land prices in the mid-eighteenth century led to many wealthy tradesmen buying up property which they then either rebuilt or modernised. The villages in the immediate vicinity of Ipswich abounded in large Places, Parks, Halls or Houses surrounded by carefully landscaped acres. Admirals and Captains, whose fortunes had been made by lucrative bounties of war, built themselves fine country estates overlooking the Orwell, settling down to become country squires who entertained the rich and famous for shooting parties. Thus in 1823, for example, the populace of Ipswich was informed by its local newspaper that at Wherstead Lodge the Duke of Wellington and the Count and Countess Lieven were among those staying for the shooting. For those, less affluent, who were finding it hard to meet the very high rents charged in London and were faced with a down-grading in their social status if they moved to cheaper areas of the City a move to Ipswich provided a satisfactory alternative. There they could find a 'good' property well within their means and still be able to get up to Town to engage in their business, a situation which was paralleled during the boom in house prices in 1987–8.

All this led to Ipswich being filled with a vast number of extra people all of whom required basic necessities as well as entertainment and leisure pursuits. The town was quick to respond to those needs. The prosperity of the local tradespeople in the town is reflected in its numerous and varied shops which by the 1850s were catering for an increasing middle- and upper-class population, a consumer society which was demanding such items as 'Hot air and other stoves, suitable for warming Churches, Chapels, Shops, Conservatories, Harness Rooms and Water Closets'. Ready-made and fashionable clothes came from large shops which were established then and were to remain as landmarks in the town until most of them became swallowed up by the mid-twentieth-century conglomerates. There were shops to provide shoes for dancing and evening wear, trunks, portmanteaux and carpet bags for the traveller; watchmakers and jewellers; hairdressers and perfumers; chemists with their abundance of patent remedies; retailers of cheap but well-made furniture upholstered in rich materials; grocers who imported high-class food and wines; specialist pastrycooks and confectioners who undertook outside catering for bridal breakfasts, luncheons, ball suppers, or simply offered a take-away service of soups and made-up dishes for small occasions: 'Mock turtle soup 2/6 per quart sent to any part of town or country'.

The advertisements in local newspapers provide more than fascinating and amusing reading, they are a guide to the tastes and fashion of an era. From them we learn of the growing passion of the Victorian middle classes to adorn their homes with wallpaper and carpets, china and glass, carvings and gildings. Nurserymen abounded, to supply the needs of the family garden and the fashionable conservatory. Portrait painters and photographers met the ever-increasing desire to surround the family with mementoes of the past. Bookshops and subscription libraries encouraged the thirst for literature among those who had the leisure to read. For those with musical inclinations there were pianos and harmoniums for sale or hire from one of several warehouses, a term used with pride since it indicated a very large establishment, thus distinguishing it from the shop which had been carved out of the ground floor rooms of a house.

The desire for entertainment was met in various ways. Ipswich had long had a theatre, and the Assembly Rooms for dancing. The Corn Exchange hall was used for musical entertainments until the Public Hall came into being. Then followed the Museum, a lecture hall and other places where the public might meet together for entertainment or educational purposes. The old informal racecourse was reorganised and developed. Opportunities for an infinite variety of social activities were available outside the home, while indoors, if tired of making one's own amusement around the piano, there was the Victorian equivalent of the modern video recording. Shopkeepers then, as now, often diversified their stock:

Mrs Root – Milliner and Straw Bonnet Manufacturer, Princes Street. On Hire: Dissolving View and Phantasmagoria apparatus, first class moonlights, landscapes, interiors, moveable slides, comic scenes etc. adapted for evening parties.

Schulen & Co. Consulting and Manufacturing Optician – Magic Lanterns for hire.

Although the commerce of the town had since medieval times depended upon the docks and agriculture, there were also several small industries – those allied to shipbuilding, like rope-making; factories making silk, pottery, paper and cigars; but the great impetus to industrialisation came in the early nineteenth century with the establishment of ironwork engineering along the banks of the river. Neither coal nor iron ore are found anywhere near Suffolk but both could be easily transported by water to the town, where a plentiful labour force was available following the cutback in agricultural work. The coming of the railways assisted in developing Ransome's as a major engineering company. It is significant that when the railway reached Ipswich, the original station was situated close to the iron works.

This industrialisation led to a radical change in the town which had stayed within its original boundaries for centuries. Building had tended to take place within its confines on land which had once been very sizeable gardens and orchards. Now, however, housing was spreading outwards in all directions. Along the river to the south streets of small terrace houses provided homes for the employees of the ironworks and railway, while within the town itself further narrow streets were carved out to provide homes for workers in the smaller foundries and factories. This led many of the middle classes to leave their inner-town properties to 'move up' in the world, quite literally, for the better-class homes were built on the hills leading up from the town.

One victim of the advance of the railways was Elizabeth Cotton's father, James Haxell. By 1843, the railway from London had reached Colchester, some eighteen miles from Ipswich. The reaction to this much faster mode of travel was varied. W. Wire, watchmaker and postman of Colchester, noted in his diary the economic effects: '*27 May 1843* The Wellington coach is taken off the London road in consequence of its not paying, after having run from this town to London for many years.'

But for young George Ranson of Sproughton it opened up a whole new way of life. Accustomed to travelling to and from London by either coach or the Orwell Steamer, a journey which would have taken the best part of a day, he describes his first journey by train after having spent the day at Colchester market: '*24 July 1843* Monday. Left Colchester station at 1/2 past six, arrived in town at 1/2 past eight.' This gave him time for a leisurely supper before retiring, leaving him refreshed to spend the next two days amusing himself before returning home on Wednesday evening: Left London at 1/2 past six in the evening and in bed by 11. I like this travelling by railroad much.' After collecting his horse in Colchester, the short ride home would have taken him as long as the train journey had.

James Haxell would hardly have shared his enthusiasm. To compensate for the loss of the long-distance trade, Haxell responded to market forces by timing his Ipswich coaches to link up with the Colchester trains, and by 1846, when the railway reached Ipswich, his business was mainly in cross-country services. The development of the Ipswich railway line had even more impact on Haxell when it was decided to build the new station and develop the line beyond the town, for the route went right through his farm land. A court case for trespass gives details of Haxell's property and the extent of his business. The plaintiffs in the case alleged that they had the right to use an ancient footpath which had been built over by the railway. The *Suffolk Chronicle* devoted much space to the meticulous, if somewhat garrulous, testimony of George Green:

[The ancient path] then went through the centre of the site of the Railway station into a road across the line for a distance of 50 yards, ending in a road about 300 yards long opposite the gate leading to Haxell's farm. This was a carriage road, and at that time the only one from Ipswich to the above farm; along it the manure from the stables . . . in Brook Street was brought, whilst the hay and corn produced there were taken to the coaching stables, in which upwards of 100 horses were stabled. . . . Next was a meadow of about nine acres upon which the coach-horses, which required rest, were turned, with a number of thoroughbreds, of which a great number was bred for racing purposes. Those not suitable for those purposes were used in the coaches which ran to London and other places. On the left hand side the cart road turned slightly to the left, passing through the cloakroom of the station; the footpath, slightly diverging to the right, went . . . through the centre of the refreshment rooms and continued through the fields to the London road.

No such details exist for the early lives of Elizabeth and her brothers and sisters. From later evidence it is possible to deduce that the maternal relations exercised a very strong influence on the upbringing of the children. Edward's earlier reference to his school-fellows watching him leave the Bull at Aldgate, suggests that all the sons received at least part of their education in London and certainly three of the four later had their business in the City. The eldest, James, chose, or had chosen for him, the trade of auctioneer. This was quite unlike anything done by the rest of the family, and perhaps it was this in addition to being so much older than the others that led to his not maintaining the close relationship that they kept up. Although they started out in different trades, Edward as a wine merchant and Arthur in the leather business, both eventually returned to the family tradition of providing hospitality to the traveller; Edward was the proprietor of the Royal Exeter Hotel in the Strand and Haxell's Hotel, Marine Parade, Brighton, while Arthur had the Shakespeare Hotel in Dover.

From a family bred on travel, George was the most adventurous of the sons and like many young men of that era (among them, Trollope's John Caldigate), he set out at the age of twenty-four to make his fortune in Australia where he arrived in May 1853, to become a squatter in Victoria. His decision to emigrate was encouraged by Westrop Waller who had kept the neighbouring Coach and Horses in Brook Street. It can hardly have been mere coincidence that Waller and his family arrived in Melbourne just two months before George. In 1859 George and Waller went into partnership leasing vast tracts of land in the Melbourne area. Since we know from Elizabeth's diary that George made a return visit to England in 1858 it is possible that he came home to raise additional funds from the family for this venture. The partnership between George and Waller was further sealed by George's marriage to one of Waller's daughters. However, agricultural life was not to be his for long and he became a draper, first in Geelong, then in a partnership trading in what is nowadays the centre of Melbourne. This too failed to satisfy George, and almost as if it were inborn in him, he, as other members of the family, ended up in the inn trade, holding the licences of a number of hotels in both Australia and New Zealand.

Neither did all the girls remain at home as might have been expected of unmarried daughters. When we first meet them in the pages of Elizabeth's diary in 1854 only Susanna has remained with her father, acting as his housekeeper. Apart from Elizabeth only Rea was married, to Henry Page, a leather merchant who employed at least sixteen men in his London factory. The Pages had started their married life in the city, but following fashionable trends they moved out to a large house in its own grounds in Dulwich Park. A lodge in the grounds housed Henry's personal coachman and his family, a daughter acting as laundrymaid to the Pages.

The eldest unmarried daughter would usually take on the role of housekeeper to her widowed father, but, as we shall find throughout this examination of Elizabeth's diary, things are often not as we expect them. Anne, the eldest Miss Haxell, and the youngest, Margaret, had made their home with their uncle John at the Bull Inn. The most likely explanation for this is that Anne became housekeeper for her uncle following her grandmother's death. Unmarried sisters frequently took over the management of their brothers' bachelor establishments, as mid-Victorian literature shows only too clearly. George Ranson of Sproughton had his sister to keep house for him until she married his old friend. Nieces too, often took charge of the domestic arrangements of uncles – probably the best-documented case being that of Parson Woodforde and his niece Nancy. It is difficult to define exactly what Anne's role was, for the 1861 census assigns the title 'housekeeper' to a paid servant. Possibly Anne was very much the mistress of John's private domestic quarters, leading the life of a middle-class lady quite unlike that of her grandmother some thirty or forty years before. Between Anne and her sister Margaret there was an age gap of nearly twenty years which must have resulted in almost a mother/daughter relationship. There is no clue as to when Margaret joined her sister in London. If their mother died while Margaret was small, this would account for her being taken under her sister's wing in London. It must also be recognised that marriage prospects were likely to be better in London where Margaret had the opportunity to mix in the social circles provided by her uncles, her brother Edward and his wife Arabella, her sister Rea Page at Dulwich and her other sister, Kate.

Catherine Haxell was also living in London at the commencement of Elizabeth's diary. On her marriage in 1855 her place of residence is given, as is her husband's, as the parish of St Marylebone. Kate married her cousin James Nelson, son of their uncle Robert, who had prospered in the coaching business during the 1830s even more than his brother John. Married, with several children, Robert was very comfortably off even when the coach business declined in favour of the railway, for he still had interests in various hotels and inns. Elizabeth tells us that as children the Haxells and Robert Nelsons had played together and been on visiting terms, but that she had lost touch with them as they grew older. It is possible that on the death of her mother Kate was offered a home with her London relations and that is how she came to marry her cousin James. In all families there is a wide range of emotional attachments between the members. From her diary we are able to see which of her brothers and sisters Elizabeth is particularly fond of. Kate seems to occupy a peripheral position to the rest, not aided by what appears to be a natural antipathy of the others to cousin James.

All these different members of the family are to feature in Elizabeth's account of her life during the period 1854–69, but the most mysterious is Susanna. The nearest sister in age to Elizabeth, there are numerous references to her when the diary opens. She spends the day with Elizabeth at her home; Elizabeth visits and walks with Susanna; Susanna sends for Elizabeth when Father is taken ill. Immediately following their father's death, Elizabeth records that she went to say goodbye to Susanna who was leaving the following day for London. Thereafter she is never again mentioned. For such a close-knit family who exchanged news often on quite trivial matters, this seems very strange. The only piece of evidence relating to Susanna that has come to light is the fact that when she died in 1898 she had been residing in Genoa. So what possible explanation can be found for her not keeping in touch with the family? I considered the possibility of her having joined Miss Nightingale's team of nurses in the Crimea or one of the Sisterhoods which were so popular at that time, yet if she had, Elizabeth would surely have recorded this information among all the rest she gives. Neither of these courses would have prevented the exchange of letters. Neither was there any hint of a family rift, so why did this thirty-four-year-old woman disappear from her family's circle? A fertile imagination can supply several answers, one being that finally freed from domestic ties, she took her inheritance and moved to the continent to pursue her own life; another, more mundane, that she became a travelling companion to a wealthy lady. But in either case, would she not have written to her family, at least occasionally, to let them know all was well with her, and would she not have wanted to share in the family news of births, deaths and marriages? The ultimate conclusion which could account for what looks like total family ostracism is that Susanna offended against the moral code of the time and eloped, perhaps with a married man. Of such stuff are romantic novels made – the reality may be much more dull, but since it seems Susanna took her secret to the grave with her, we may never know.

For details of the girls' early upbringing, we must rely on what is revealed in the local newspapers and in Elizabeth's diary. Certainly all the girls had received a formal education at one of the many schools in Ipswich. Whatever deficiencies these early nineteenth-century schools for young ladies were reputed to have, we do know from her diary that Elizabeth was taught to write a 'a good hand' and that she had the ability to express herself clearly with only the very occasional lapse in spelling and punctuation. Her tuition had included French and German, for she tells us that she translates from both, and she has sufficient knowledge of Latin to be able to help her sons with their homework. Music too, had formed part of her education as had 'instruction in drawing' – that necessary requirement for all genteel young ladies. In Elizabeth's case the formal training developed a very real talent coupled with a genuine love of art. Living in an area which had produced Constable and Gainsborough, it is not surprising that art should be so important to young Suffolk ladies, but Elizabeth had an even closer role-model. The Ipswich artist, George Frost, much of whose work conveys a lively pictorial record of the everyday life of the town at the end of the eighteenth and the beginning of the nineteenth century, had for many years been the booking clerk at the Coach House. Although Frost died in 1821, his work certainly influenced her. When, in her sixties, the widowed Elizabeth was living in Ipswich, she spent a great deal of her time doing as Frost had done, wandering through the streets searching for noteworthy or suitably interesting places to draw. Figure drawing she found more difficult, but there is a delightful head of her son at the age of eighteen months and a sketch of a young woman who might be one of her sisters or even a self portrait. Looking at the little sketch book which contains work from the years before her marriage, it is as if all the heroines of early nineteenth-century novels come alive; the young ladies of Austen, Brontë and Eliot are showing their work.

HERBERT COTTON

Herbert Cotton was comfortably off as the tenant of Amor Hall, the largest farm in the village of Washbrook, with about 400 acres three miles out of Ipswich on the London road.

Descended from a branch of a well-established Suffolk family whose pedigree included a seventeenth-century Lord Mayor of London knighted for his services, Herbert's line came from younger sons who had gone into farming. His grandfather had died leaving his widow with three small children in the village of Lawford on the Essex/Suffolk border. In the adjoining village of Mistley lived the Mulleys who had become quite affluent from the inheritance of property throughout Essex. The two families were on friendly terms, the sons of each attending school together, and eventually Herbert Cotton (our Herbert's father) married Elizabeth Mulley in one of those typical Suffolk marriages which took place immediately it had been established that the bride-to-be was fertile. The Mulleys had moved into Suffolk to take the tenancy of Amor Hall and when the young couple married, Herbert Cotton had become tenant of Grange Farm, a much smaller holding in the village. It was here that Herbert junior was born and brought up, following his father into farming, and taking over on his parent's decease. He bought some land of his own locally, inherited property from his grandparents and by 1841 was installed as the tenant of Amor Hall. Past the age of forty when he achieved his modest fortune, perhaps he felt he should cast about for a wife and start a family to continue the Cotton name.

When we meet Herbert in the diary he is 54 years of age and his pattern of life has been set, so it is hard to tell what he was like as a very young man. Apart from his agricultural pursuits, he appears interested in art, literature and the theatre. He had been accustomed to spending his time with people older than himself, and showed very strong loyalty to his old friends. Among these were his farming neighbours, but his particular friend was Thomas Leath. Leath, like Herbert, was a bachelor, but ten years the elder. Before coming to Ipswich where he held a position in the Customs and Excise office as a 'permit writer' Leath had spent time in the East India service. He had sufficient private means or a pension to be assigned the title 'gentleman' in local directories. Thomas lived very comfortably in a modern house just outside the commercial area of the town with his sister Louisa, a maiden lady some fifteen years his senior. We can imagine that after Herbert had finished his business at market on a Tuesday he and Thomas met for dinner and an evening's entertainment. Frequently they would have visited the theatre, attended concerts, lectures and exhibitions, dined at the homes of friends, played cards, gone racing – all those activities which Ipswich had to offer to two unattached gentlemen. Leath no doubt felt equally at home at Amor Hall where he spent weekends and holidays. Here the two could indulge in country sports and long evenings of conversation assisted by food and good wine. It must have come as a shock to Leath when his old friend embarked on matrimony and it says much for the three parties involved that the friendship remained intact, as the diary proves.

For a researcher who likes all the facts cut and dried, it is frustrating not to know how Herbert came to meet Elizabeth and what it was about her that led him to relinquish his comfortable bachelor life. He certainly was not looking for a housekeeper as such, for he already had one, and other domestic staff to minister to his needs. Had he been in the marrying frame of mind earlier, there were a number of suitable young women he could choose from among the daughters and sisters of his farming friends and neighbours. And if we ask why he chose her, we must similarly ask what Herbert had to offer Elizabeth? Why did she marry a man twenty years her senior and settle for the rural life when she could, like her sisters, have gone to live in London?

There can have been no pressing need for her to marry at twenty-three. She had the example of her unmarried sisters living comfortably in London. From among the large circle of acquaintances provided by the extended family, she might have taken her pick. Unless a girl 'had her head turned' by a member of the Army or Navy, marriage partners tended to come from the brothers and sisters of close friends, relations or business contacts of the family. For example, George Ranson of Sproughton records in his diary the frequent visits from his old friend, a publisher in London. In spite of the notes George makes, it is obvious that they did not spend all their time pursuing foxes and rabbits, for it was not long before George's sister Sarah who acted as his housekeeper married his friend. George Ranson's diary starts in 1842, the year when Herbert Cotton may well have become Elizabeth Haxell's suitor. Although George was much younger than his neighbour Herbert, they were both farmers and had many acquaintances in common. From George we obtain a picture of the life of a tenant farmer at work and play:

26 *January 1842.* Wednesday. Sisters, brother and myself went to a Ball at the Assembly Rooms, Ipswich; in celebration of the Christening of the Prince of Wales. There were about 130 persons present.

24 *February 1842.* Thursday. Brother John and myself went to the Quadrille party at the Assembly Rooms; about 100 persons present.

5 *January 1843.* Thursday. . . . to a dance at Mr Walton Turner's of Ipswich. Spent a very pleasant evening.

At these public and private gatherings, to which, we can see, unattached men went, it is possible that Elizabeth and Herbert had the opportunity to further a relationship which might have come about through Herbert's business dealings with James Haxell. The connection may have been made through the supply of corn and animal foodstuffs or through the supply of horses or even the training of a racehorse, for Herbert was very fond of racing. Yet again, the original introduction may have come from a mutual acquaintance, perhaps the Walton Turner mentioned by George Ranson. This gentleman, (whose family feature greatly in the pages of Elizabeth's diary,) had a flourishing tannery and leather manufacturing business in the town. Most farmers would have had dealings with the business either on the retail side in the purchase of saddles and harness equipment or the wholesale with the selling of the skins of deadstock. It is also significant that Elizabeth's brother Arthur started out in the leather trade – perhaps with Walton Turner, and that Elizabeth's brother-in-law in London was also in the leather business.

In the absence of Herbert Cotton's diary, or Elizabeth's for 1843, we must make do with George Ranson to provide us with a picture of courtship for the period. However, what George reveals as the norm for himself and his brothers and sisters would not necessarily have been so for Elizabeth and Herbert. George's pattern was a series of visits exchanged between the couple, presumably once the suitor had declared his intentions and been accepted in that role: '25 July 1846. Saturday. Drove over to Thorndon to see Mary Woodward, my first visit and a very pleasant one.' Thorndon was a considerable distance from George's home, being in the north of the county, so how, one might ask, did George come to meet Miss Woodward. The answer follows the typical pattern of the time. Mary was related to neighbours of the Ranson family and no doubt it was while she was staying with Mr and Mrs Charles Woodward at Copdock Hall that she met George. Charles would be able to reassure Mary's parents as to the suitability of the young man as well as encouraging his friend in his suit.

8 August. To Thorndon. . . . *20 August.* To Thorndon. . . . *21 August.* Returned with Mary Woodward to pay a visit to my Father and Mother. Mary, myself and two sisters went to a concert, Mr. Foster's at the Theatre, Ipswich . . . *28August.* A party of us went to Harwich by the River Queen, a delightful afternoon. Myself, Mary Woodward and sister Mary were too late for the steamer at coming home, she was just off when we went down to the jetty, made a mistake of the times. I felt annoyed but managed very well. I ordered a boat and went across to Shotley Gate, went up to Mr Alderton's, borrowed his chaise, after having a good tea, arrived home very comfortably about 11 o'clock . . . *29August*. Drove Mary home to Thorndon.

Throughout the next three months, George was spending weekends at Mary's home, joining her father on shoots and accompanying Mary and her parents to dinner parties among their circle of friends. Mary, in turn, came back to spend another few days with George's parents, and the whole affair culminated with:

9 December. Myself, Father, Mother and Ellen had a fly and went over to Thorndon . . . *10 December*. Thursday. Married this morning at Thorndon Church to Mary Elizabeth Woodward, only daughter of Mr George A. Woodward.

There was much coming and going of young men and women in the senior Ransons' household as the various offspring brought prospective sons- and daughters-in-law to get to know the family and Mrs Ranson was kept busy accompanying daughters to distant parts of her county and the next for week-long visits to the families they were to join. But in Herbert's case there were no parents to welcome – and possibly instruct – his bride-to-be, and no mother on her side to chaperone her. The pair would have had to rely on the good offices of their mutual friends to assist in their courtship. Perhaps when Elizabeth visited her prospective home at Amor Hall for the day she was accompanied by one of her married friends, her sister Susanna or her very close friend Charlotte Brooks and her mother. This was the family who had lived at the Great White Horse during Elizabeth's youth. Just a stone's throw from her own home, one can imagine that the hotel was very much a second home to Elizabeth and Mrs Brooks perhaps supplied some of the affectionate motherly advice she lacked at home. Certainly she maintained for many years her close contact with the family and records Mrs Brooks's death with sadness. Elizabeth's loyalty to the family was tested by none other than the celebrated Charles Dickens.

Apparently, it was not so much the criticism of the building, in Chapter 22 of *Pickwick Papers* – 'Never was such labyrinths of uncarpeted passages, such clusters of mouldy ill lighted rooms, such huge numbers of small dens for eating or sleeping in' – that incensed William Brooks, the licensee, as the imputation contained in: 'After the lapse of an hour, a bit of fish and a steak was served up to the travellers, and when the dinner cleared away, Mr Pickwick and Mr Peter Magnus drew their chairs up to the fire (a dirty grate in which a small fire was making a wretched attempt to be cheerful but was fast sinking) and having ordered a bottle of the worst possible port wine, at the highest possible price, for the good of the house, drank brandy-and-water for their own.'

This was not even the thinly-veiled fictionalising as at Eatanswill, this was blatant personal comment on real people in a real place and likely to do real harm to those involved. This is Dickens the newspaper reporter exercising the journalistic right, as it is held today in some of the tabloid press, to make or break a reputation. Brooks was persuaded to drop his libel charge, but, although Elizabeth read Dickens's works as they were published, she studiously avoided joining those who gave him acclaim at his public readings in Ipswich. On the two dates in question, Elizabeth, who attended most of the public lectures and concerts held in the town, remained firmly at home. On neither occasion had she any other engagement which would have prevented her attending. The Brooks had long gone from the Great White Horse, but Elizabeth's loyalty remained steadfast.

However they met and whatever form their courtship took, Herbert Cotton married Elizabeth Haxell on 20 September 1843 at a ceremony witnessed by her father and brother Edward. We can assume that the wedding took place during the morning, as most did at that time, and that close friends and relations attended the bridal breakfast provided by James Haxell at the Coach House. The wedding would not have been the lavish affair which has become standard in the second half of the twentieth century. The mid-week, mid-morning celebrations sometimes did not even involve quite close members of the family. Again it is to George Ranson we turn for a description of a contemporary wedding and the priorities of such an occasion:

> 21 September 1846. Brother Henry married this morning to Charlotte Weatherly, niece of Mr F. Harcourt; at the same time Mr William Williams of Trimley to Miss Mary Anne Harcourt. Father, Mother, Henry and myself went to Church in a cab; it rained in torrents all the forenoon, cleared off about 12 o'clock. We had a sumptuous Breakfast at Mr Harcourt's. Father & myself afterwards drove to Melton Bullock Fair, everything very dear. Henry and his wife went off to London, has taken lodgings there.

Henry Ranson also chose late September for his wedding; he like Herbert was a farmer, and by then harvest would be well out of the way. And like Henry, Herbert probably took his bride to London for their short honeymoon, providing him with the opportunity to get to know better those members of the family of which he was now part. If London was not the destination, then one of the coastal resorts along the east coast, Felixstowe perhaps, or Aldeborough might have given them their first taste of life together. But wherever they went, it was not long before Elizabeth Cotton was installed at Amor Hall, Washbrook, ready to fulfil her role as wife and mother.

3

Wife and Mother

Useless doll and clinging parasite.
Victorian Wives – Katharine Moore

WIFE

The week before we first meet Elizabeth Cotton on 1 January 1854 she had celebrated her thirty-fourth birthday. She was entering the eleventh year of marriage and had had four children: Alice was nine, Bertie, six, Allan, five and the baby Evelyn would have her first birthday in the coming March. The popularly held notion that Victorian women produced a baby every year with monotonous regularity is not borne out here. Unlike Queen Victoria who more than once regretted pregnancy so early in her married life, Elizabeth's first child was not conceived immediately, for Alice did not arrive until fourteen months after the wedding. There may have been miscarriages during the years which elapsed before the birth of Evelyn, but certainly there is no record of any live births followed by early death. Although two more children were to come, this lack of fecundity may be due to the twenty years' age difference between husband and wife and Herbert's occasional bouts of ill health. Herbert came from a family which was not known for producing large families and although Elizabeth was one of ten, only two of her brothers fathered more than six children. By Victorian standards the rest of her siblings produced very small families of two or three.

After ten years of marriage we would expect to see any cracks in the relationship. Many adjustments would have had to be made on both sides initially. Herbert had been his own man until his forties, he had been brought up in the confines of a close-knit rural community with friends of his own age or older. The twenty-three-year-old Elizabeth, surrounded by younger brothers and sisters, must have found it difficult at first to settle into what could have seemed a staid routine with a husband who was but five years younger than her uncle John. Conversely, Herbert may have been somewhat overwhelmed when he became part of the large Nelson-Haxell extended family which embraced not only in-laws, but uncles, aunts and cousins, and he discovered he had a wife who was given to making and exchanging frequent visits with those many relations who lived in London.

If one were writing a nineteenth-century novel, given this scenario

25

one would expect that the exuberant young wife would eventually be worn down to conform to the pattern imposed by her older dominant husband, submissive to his demands, suppressing her own desires, ageing rapidly beyond her years, worn out by the cares of motherhood until she faded into insignificance. Alternatively, our heroine, having endured the submission until it became intolerable, might decide to withdraw from the situation either by running off with another man or to live her own life giving free rein to all her frustrated emotions and latent talents. Should the husband be the hero of this hypothetical novel, he might find himself unable to cope with his vivacious young wife, she might turn out to be the dominant one, filling his house with her numerous relations, holding parties on the least pretext, using him merely as the provider for her selfish whims, or worse, becoming a caustic-tongued shrew. He would be forced more and more to seek solace outside the home, with his old friends, most of whom would not be able to resist reminding him of the joys of bachelordom.

This, however, is not a novel, and what we are given is a picture of two well-adjusted people, who have learned to live with each other in mutual love and respect. Each has a clearly-defined role to play in life, yet within their marriage there is a strong sense of equality and inter-dependence.

Davidoff and Hall in *Family Fortunes* describe the major change to the way of life of the prosperous middle classes during the first half of the nineteenth century. Where once the family of those engaged in business and trade had tended to have their home 'over the shop', increasing affluence in early Victorian times led to a divorce between home and business. The family was moved to live in modest splendour on the outskirts of town with the father leaving each morning to spend his day at his place of work. This was the situation of Elizabeth's sister Rea who had moved from central London to Dulwich from where her husband commuted daily in his own carriage to his city business. Such moves meant that the wife, who in earlier times would have assisted her husband in the running of the business, now found herself with only the domestic arrangements to superintend. Thus husband and wife came together only in the evenings and at weekends – the accepted pattern of the present time. For Elizabeth, as for all farmers' wives, life was very different: she still lived in the workplace. However much she might try to 'gentrify' her home, it still contained Herbert's office where the daily business of the farm was conducted. Farming associates and agricultural representatives were frequent callers whom she would be expected to entertain. Her kitchen would be open to the farm labourers, the dairy was under her nominal supervision. She would know all those working on the farm, be involved in their lives, and when Herbert was absent she was in charge.

Although Elizabeth does not confide any of the intimate details of her married life to the diary, it is possible to feel the sense of togetherness in their relationship. She carefully records not only their joint activities but also Herbert's movements throughout the week. We feel with her a genuine concern for his well-being and his for her and the children. Unlike her contemporary Isabella Brett of Ipswich who formally records in her diary the comings and goings of 'Mr Brett', Elizabeth always uses her husband's first name. Instinctively one recognises a close intimacy that exists in one family but not in the other.

A conventional picture of the dutiful and submissive Victorian wife could be assumed from the following two extracts. The very first entry reads:

> *1 January 1854.* Sunday. To Washbrook Church with Herbert, Alice and Bertie. Evening read to Herbert. During the week I walked with the children when the weather would allow and read as usual in the evenings to Herbert. While in November 1858, she writes: 'Finished reading 'Guy Livingstone'. Began 'Deerbrook'. . . . Monday began reading 'Monte Cristo' instead of 'Deerbrook' which Herbert does not like.

But Herbert does not fit into the stereotype role of the conventional Victorian husband. Perhaps because he was that much older and had grown up during the Regency period, he had a more liberal outlook on a wife's place. Certainly he did not appear to impose any restrictions on Elizabeth's movements and she was free to travel wherever she wished. She records with some amusement an occasion while they were on a visit to London:

> *17 May 1857*, Monday   In the evening with Herbert to a Musical and Dramatic entertainment by Mr and Mrs Gorman Reed at the Gallery of Illustration. Returning from here Herbert called for Arthur to accompany him to Evan's Supper Rooms and I went home to the York [hotel] rather to the hostess Miss Law's surprise, alone.

In the same way, on their frequent holiday tours, Herbert seems to have recognised her ability to take care of herself when she went off alone on long walks, and when she stayed in London she and her sisters walked quite freely. Similarly, he left the management of the household entirely to her and delegated to her the responsibility of choosing the children's schools and paying the school fees. It was Elizabeth too, who sorted out the problems the children had at school and it was left to her to take the doctor to task for apparent dereliction of duty.

Herbert was far too busy with the management of the farm to concern himself with the domestic arrangements as well. As we shall see later, he was obviously quite content to allow Elizabeth a free hand to carry out improvements to the house and garden. Yet it is also obvious that he did not see her sphere to be entirely domestic, and neither did she. There must have been a mutual understanding between them.

February 1856. Mr Drake the agent for the Buildings Improvement Company and Mr Smith the builder of *our* new farming premises, looked over them.

May, 1856. A sale of materials of *our* old farm buildings here on Wednesday. Mr Turner the Auctioneer and Mr Cooper-Clark dined here and Mr Clark stayed the evening. [My italics.]

September 1857. One of the labourers, Gouty, run over by horses with cart. I went to Ipswich for a surgeon and called to see him.

December 1860. [Herbert is away in London for the Cattle Show] *14th.* Wrote to Herbert. One of our horses very ill . . . *15th.* At home. Had men keep with the horse day and night.

These extracts not only show that Elizabeth saw her own role as one of sharing in the life and work of the farm, but also echo the girl who had been brought up to know and understand the value of horses.

She seems to have accompanied Herbert happily to the round of horticultural and agricultural shows which dominated the farming calendar, accepting that on occasions she must return home alone in order that Herbert may attend the men-only dinner that sometimes followed such an event. Often she went with him to market in another part of the county using the opportunity to meet friends, visit nursery gardens or do some sketching. Their mutual decision-making is shown on one such visit: '*February 1858.* Thursday. With Herbert to Woodbridge. Bought a secondhand phaeton for the children and ordered plants.'

Special celebrations were held to mark the birthday of each member of the family, but it is only for Herbert that we are given details of the gifts she so carefully chose for him. These give clues to his particular interests: '*21 April 1856.* Herbert's birthday. I gave him a silver mug.' And the following year. '*7 April 1857,* Tuesday. To Ipswich. Called for the children and took them with me to see a statuette of Rebekah. Ordered one like it of Mr Bowar's to give Herbert upon his birthday. *21 April.* Herbert's birthday. The statuette which came home yesterday, he likes.' This presents a very happy family picture of Elizabeth involving the children in the selection of the present. In other years she gave him Morris's *British Birds* and a silver flask, no doubt to take with him on his shooting excursions.

Of her own birthday gifts Elizabeth makes no mention until many years later, but Herbert was quite likely to buy her a present for no specified reason, although I do wonder if the item referred to here was a token to mark the fact that Elizabeth was again pregnant.: *'July 1854. Friday with Herbert to Horticultural Fete at Colchester held in Mr Round's grounds. Herbert bought me a gold and coral brooch. Lunch and dinner at Cups Hotel.'*

When the older children were settled at school and the younger were still in the nursery stage, the couple's life together settled into a routine which took them to Ipswich every Tuesday for Herbert to attend the markets while Elizabeth shopped and called upon her friends before they met together to dine in the late afternoon at the Great White Horse.

The social activities the Cottons attended together will be dealt with more fully, but they, like many modern couples, often went for a quiet weekend away. Elizabeth frequently accompanied Herbert to the Orford area where he engaged in shooting water birds. There is no hint of compulsion in these excursions, in fact Elizabeth seems to enjoy very much being, 'on the water with Herbert, who shot some birds, all day'.

Herbert not only tolerated his wife's enthusiasm for various pursuits, he supported her even if he did not join her. For example, although he did not follow her and the older children in their search for the Truth as revealed by Father Ignatius, he did not attempt to play the dominant husband and domineering father and prevent them, whatever he may have thought privately about the disturbing movements within the established Church of England to which he was a solid adherent. His attitude probably laid him open to ridicule from some of his neighbours that he was unable to control his wife and family and the charge that he was tantamount to a traitor to the Church. Even when Elizabeth is actively flirting with the Roman Catholic faith, he makes no attempt to stop her. The second diary contains so much about Elizabeth's religious activities that a later chapter will be devoted to the subject. If differences of religious opinion caused disagreement between husband and wife, no hint of it is revealed in the diaries. On the contrary, Herbert seems to have welcomed the assortment of priests, nuns and other fervently religious acquaintances into his home.

That mutual toleration existed is demonstrated by the fact that Elizabeth accepted that she shared Herbert with his old friends. For several years she records that every Sunday 'Mr Martin spent the evening with Herbert'. This elderly neighbour also joined them on Christmas Day, probably continuing a habit formed in Herbert's bachelor days. In the same way Mr Leath came for days at a time on a number of occasions throughout the year. His inclusion in special celebrations within the family shows a relationship that may have provided Herbert with the brother he lacked. That his visits were regarded as informal is shown when he comes to keep Herbert company almost immediately after one of Elizabeth's confinements. There is no record of an exchange of visits with Leath and no mention of his sister until Elizabeth calls upon her when sick. The diaries tell us that Herbert attended the occasional exclusive male-only affairs, such as the annual tithe dinner for the tenant farmers of the area, the agricultural association and those which followed race meetings. Once a year too, he had a week away on his own shooting water fowl in Norfolk with another friend, a relation of his landlord.

Reading through the diaries, particularly the earlier one, one is conscious that Herbert and Elizabeth spent far more time together than might be expected, certainly more than their modern counterparts, and that they enjoyed each other's company. Elizabeth depicts a man who is kind and gentle, indulgent to a degree, but not dotingly so. That she was a forceful character there is no doubt, but I do not see him as a weak husband who gave in to pressure. They were mutually supportive, he recognising his wife's competence and strength. Thus, during the years 1864–9 as advancing years and ill health came upon him, he was content to let her assume even more responsibility for the family. Herbert inspired in his wife both deep affection and respect, so much so that blame could never be attached to him.

> *December 1857.* When returning home from the market this evening Herbert's horse ran away and came into violent collision with the chaise Mr Allen was driving. Herbert was greatly bruised and Mr Allen slightly hurt. Our chaise was destroyed, that of Mr Allen's broken and our horse cut in the leg. The incident was caused by Mr Martin's noisy behaviour.

Here Elizabeth follows the fashionable expectation of the dutiful wife as exemplified by Trollope in *Framley Parsonage* where Lady Lufton says to Mrs Roberts, '. . . there is no duty which any woman owes to any other human being at all equal to that which she owes her husband, and therefore you were right to stand up for Mr Roberts this morning.'

The restrained use of 'noisy behaviour' on the part of Herbert's passenger, Mr Martin, suggests that he had been drinking. Since the incident took place on the way home from market it is likely that all those involved had imbibed liberally. The local newspapers record frequent incidents of road traffic mishaps to farmers following a day at market. Although Elizabeth never once suggests that Herbert overindulged, there are a number of occasions when, following an overnight visit from one of his old friends, she records that he is 'sadly'. This delightfully descriptive word for a temporary upset in health seems to have disappeared from the modern vocabulary being replaced by 'poorly'. The word may have had class associations for in the later diary, when moving in slightly different circles, she uses the term only once, when under great emotional stress.

MOTHER

If Elizabeth was fiercely protective of her husband's well-being, she was even more so where her children were concerned. Although she had the assistance of a living-in housekeeper, the invaluable Mrs Marskall, and a succession of nursery maids, Elizabeth and Herbert were very much involved with the upbringing of their children. Theirs were not children who were daily paraded in their best clothes for the obligatory hour with Mama and Papa before bedtime. They were very much part of Elizabeth's everyday life. It is clear that she took her role of motherhood as seriously as everything else she did. And, perhaps more importantly, she enjoyed being a mother and gained pleasure from being with her children. Again, perhaps it was having been part of a large family herself that made her at ease with children, for certainly, over the years, her home was increasingly filled with young people.

If we define Elizabeth as a member of the middle class the question follows, to which section of that class did she belong. Generalisations would have it that the wealthy middle classes educated their children at home, with tradespeople and the lower middle class being more likely to opt for the meagre education offered by small 'academies for Young Ladies or Young Gentlemen'. Herbert's income and social position within the village should have led to their having a governess, yet all the children went instead to school.

Possibly it was the feeling that Alice needed the companionship of girls her own age that led to the decision to send her to Mrs Shalders's boarding school in Elm Street, Ipswich. It is not known at what age she first went, but at the end of January 1854, when she was nine, she was returning to school. It might be a popular notion that young children were packed off to school to be out of the way but this was certainly not Elizabeth's idea. It was probably more convenient to have Alice boarding rather than taking her daily to Ipswich, but her mother had no intention of losing close contact with her daughter. One wonders how many others did as she did – and how Mrs Shalders reacted to the frequent visits she made to the school. Often on her Tuesday visit to the town she would 'call to see Alice'. On other occasions she arrived bringing Bertie and Allan with her, or if one of the aunts was staying at Washbrook, then she too would be taken to 'see at Alice at school'. When there were family reunions at James Haxell's home, then Alice came from school to 'pass the evening with her grandfather'. He obviously kept an eye on her too, for it is from a visit from her father that

Elizabeth learns that Alice is ill which sends her hot foot to Ipswich not just that day, but every day for the next two weeks before she finally takes drastic action:

> *21 May 1854*. Monday. My father called to say that he had heard from Mrs Shalders that Alice was ill. I went to see her, then called to speak to Mr Hammond [the doctor] who refuses to authorise her being taken home. I went each day to see her until the following Saturday week the 3rd. of June, when as Mr Hammond still refused giving leave for her removing and believing the child was taking unnecessary medicine, I sent for a warm carriage and took her home with me, leaving a note for Mr Hammond to say what I had done.

When not visiting Alice, Elizabeth, in those early years, was busy with the other children. Like most mid-nineteenth-century mothers she was a firm believer in fresh air and exercise and she walked with the children a great deal, regardless of the weather. Both her attitude to 'unnecessary medicine' and the need for fresh air in the nurture of children found expression in the very popular *Peveril of the Peak* by Sir Walter Scott. We can imagine Elizabeth agreeing wholeheartedly with:

> The lady was the more ready to undertake this charge [of bringing up an orphan], that she herself had lost two infant children; and that she attributed the preservation of the third, to Julian's being subjected to rather a different course of diet and treatment than was generally practised. She resolved to follow the same regimen . . . a more sparing use of medicine, a bolder admission of fresh air, a firm, yet cautious attention to encourage rather than supersede the exertions of nature.

'*14 December 1855*. When fine enough we walked and when the weather would not allow us to do so, we took exercise in the passages of the farm buildings.' These excursions were not stiff, formal outings. When Elizabeth states 'in the meadows as much as possible with the children', one senses that she was playing games with them, as she did as they grew older when she joined them for cricket, archery or battledore. She helped them make an Aunt Sally, a game which was very popular; she went fishing for eels with them; she encouraged 'their romps'. She suited the occupations to the ages of the children; the little ones were taken to see the lambs, the boys to watch the steam thrashing machine.

One of the most surprising aspects of the family life revealed in the diary was the number of outings in which the children were involved. From quite a young age Elizabeth and Herbert took them for drives. Sometimes these were purely pleasure outings like the 'drive around

Lady Harland's grounds' at nearby Wherstead Lodge, and at other times they all accompanied Herbert when he had a business call to make. While they were quite young, too, Elizabeth would walk with them the three miles to Ipswich to call upon a friend, or to meet another child returning from school. At the age of five and six, Allan and Bertie were joining their parents at the theatre. Their other big treat for that year was to see what Elizabeth called The Wild Beast Show, the advertisement for which ran:

Edmonds' (late Wombwell's) Royal Menagerie.
[Ipswich Sat. Mon. & Tues.]
On Saturday (weather permitting) headed by the Band of the Establishment, drawn by the largest Elephant in England.

Obviously the weather did not permit for Elizabeth writes: '*December 1854*. Took the children to Ipswich on Saturday to see Wild Beast Show, but it was not opened.' The children, however, were not to be disappointed. Although unable to leave home herself on the Monday: 'Mrs Marskall took the children to the Wild Beasts Show on Monday and afterwards went with Alice to school'. Did Mrs Shalders not object to Alice's late return? If she had, one doubts if it would have worried Elizabeth.

By growing up in the country the children had the best of both worlds. They had the freedom of a very large garden backed up by the fields and meadows of the farm itself and the neighbouring woods in which they could play and explore. They had the opportunity to fish in the ponds and streams, and a donkey and later ponies to ride to take them further afield. They had other children of similar background within walking or riding distance with whom they could play and furthermore they had parents who were able and willing to provide them with additional advantages for recreation.

'*September 1863*. Monday. Began making croquet ground before the house. Tuesday. Worked on croquet ground.' Elizabeth was quick to follow fashion. Croquet had been introduced into England from France in the early 1850s, the first sets going on sale in London in 1854. The game proved immensely popular among those families who had sufficient space in their gardens to accommodate a ground. The Cotton family were playing the sport five years before the establishment of the All-England Croquet Club at Wimbledon.

Elizabeth's relationship with her children was a close, caring one. She was involved in all their activities, sometimes directing, at other times simply participating in a way which will seem very familiar. Yet it was not a claustrophobic relationship; she was neither the doting mother who wished to retain total control of her child and its affections nor the clinging parasitic vine who uses her offspring as a means of succouring her own life. She had sufficient interests of her own to fill her leisure, but unlike Mrs Jellaby in *Bleak House*, she does not allow them to take over her life to the detriment of her children's welfare. She seems to have achieved a satisfactory and satisfying balance. She displays a mind open to all new challenges and ideas; she moves with her children rather than imposing her will upon them.

Close knit though the family unit was – and the sibling-bonding remained strong throughout their lives – Elizabeth actively encouraged the children to be outgoing by providing them with the opportunities to extend their range of experiences and friendships. Being gregarious by nature, Elizabeth took the young children on afternoon visits to her friends in Ipswich, and Amor Hall offered a welcome to many. There are numerous references to mothers and children coming to spend the day, with fathers calling for them in the evening and joining them all for supper. Some came by invitation, others just 'dropped in', but all, we feel, were made welcome. As early as 1854 the young Alice was bringing home her 'best friend' from school to stay for the weekend; a pattern that was to be repeated when the boys started day school in Ipswich, when they would bring home with them on Saturday afternoon four or even more of their classmates. During the summer holidays there was a succession of young visitors to the farm at Washbrook.

13 August 1861. Tuesday. Edwin Edwards, H. Miller, E. Bates, E. West and Walton Turner came to stay with our boys. *14th* With the boys. Saw them play cricket. Archery and fishing each day and sometimes had to prevent their quarrelling and played cards with them in the evening. They stayed the rest of the week.

There must have been times when it was difficult to remember who was in the house.

29 July 1862. Tuesday. To Grammar School to hear Speeches. Took our boys home with E. Rowland, E. Edwards and Walton Turner . . . Wednesday. The boys hunted eels in our pond and had great fun and sport. Little girls went with me to see the boys and helped to catch the fish. E. Rowland left in the evening. Thursday. Edward and Byatt Foster came in the morning. Edwin Edwards and Walton left in the evening. *1 August* Friday. With children seeing pond emptied. We have taken a great many eels from it. Saturday. Took Edward and Byatt Foster home. Sunday. To church. Mrs Foster and children called. Walked part of way home with them. Monday. Morning took boys to Mrs Foster's and walked to meet them when they came home in the evening.

Of course Elizabeth did have a small domestic staff who bore the strain of having to cope with the increase in bedmaking and laundry, not to mention the cooking of the vast quantities of extra food needed to satisfy the appetites of growing schoolboys, but she certainly did her part in helping to amuse all the children as well as transporting the visitors to and fro. I doubt if many of us could behave with as much generosity as she did following a friend's confinement: '5 *September 1863*. Saturday. Seven of Mrs Walton Turner's children spent the day with us.'

BIRTH AND DEATH

In May of 1854 Elizabeth had conceived her fifth child. She gives no indication of her condition and carries on her usual routine, but during the very early stages she has to contend with the unspecified illness of Alice that has already been noted. The usual round of summer activities followed with just one mention that she had called on Dr Durrant at the end of August. This might have been to confirm her pregnancy or to discuss her father's state of health which, although it had not been mentioned before, was now giving cause for concern.

3 September 1854. A letter from Susanna on Monday morning to say my father was much worse. Went to him and remained all day. Tuesday morning took Alice to school and remained with my father who died at eighteen minutes past five in the afternoon. He has been insensible since I have been sent for and Susanna says he became so early on the Monday morning.

Although James Haxell was in his eightieth year, he had been quite hale prior to the onset of his final illness. Possibly both he and Alice had suffered from the same lingering infection prevalent that year. The *Suffolk Chronicle* which records Haxell's death also has:

a considerable increase within the last few days of the sickness prevailing in the town and neighbouring villages. . . . Diarrhoea of an aggravated type is still very general and to this it is our melancholy province to add that the cholera is also broken out in the town. . . . Pure air, cleanliness, wholesome diet and the avoiding of mental excitement and undue fatigue are indispensable. Should proper treatment be delayed and the attack be allowed to pass into the second stage, in which collapse and spasm present themselves, it is then that the recovery of the patient becomes doubtful.

We can only guess at the emotional distress Elizabeth suffered on the death of her father for she records only the practicalities which took place:

September 1854. Arthur came to Brook Street this morning and Margaret in the afternoon. Wednesday to Ipswich with Herbert. Purchased mourning. Called at Brook Street and at Mrs Shalders' and took Alice home with us. Arthur and Margaret came to Washbrook on Thursday and on Saturday Herbert went to Ipswich to attend Father's funeral.

The immediate conclusion to draw from this last statement is that Victorian women did not attend funerals, but this is not borne out later when Elizabeth records: '*February 1858*. Miss Leath's funeral. Herbert and I walked to Washbrook Church and met the funeral there.'

We are faced here with one of those sweeping generalisations about the Victorian age which conveniently forgets that the reign encompassed sixty years during which span attitudes and customs must have changed, yet many of us have the notion that the Victorians loved funereal pomp. With such a large family we would have expected them all to be there at Haxell's funeral, yet three daughters and one son were absent. Do we take this as evidence of a feud between father and some of his children or simply that at that period the gathering of the family for the interment was not considered important? The possibility of a major rift in the family seems unlikely, unless very recent, since in his will made two years before his death, Haxell had left his estate to be divided equally among his ten children.

With the death of her father came the ending of Elizabeth's family ties in Ipswich, for within two weeks of the event, her sister Susanna left for London. By the end of September the last link with the family home was severed when its contents were offered at public auction. Presumably none of the family felt the need to add to their own homes any of the 'neat mahogany dining and keeping room furniture, oil paintings of horses, books or the cabinet pianoforte.' Haxell's effects, for probate purposes, were declared to be valued at under £1,500, but the real estate must have raised a considerable sum. Haxell owned the property in one of the town's major business and residential thoroughfares. The Rate Book for 1853 shows that the gross rateable value for his house, yard and outbuildings was £56 per annum, at least £10 more than the rest of his neighbours and in addition there was a further assessment of £25 on his stables. Then there was the farm, which he may have owned, and if he did not then there was at least the remainder of his lease and the stock and crops on it. All in all, he must have been quite wealthy.

The task of winding up the estate fell to Arthur, and Elizabeth records that he visited her regularly during the late autumn and throughout that period. At the beginning of November she had another upset:

2 November 1854. Thursday. Herbert went to Orford. Arthur with me this and two following days and on Saturday night when he was driven to Ipswich, our groom after leaving the White Horse where Arthur was staying, drove in the town to see some friends of his own. The horse fell down, injured itself and the luggage cart and fractured the man's collar bone. Arthur was sent for and after seeing the groom attended to came back with him to our house, at about two o'clock in the morning. I was waiting for the man's return, not choosing to leave doors open at night time.

The groom, or yardman, lived in; hence Elizabeth's concern for his late return. Her remark about not leaving doors unlocked at night may surprise those who believe that in the 'good old days' such security was unknown, particularly in country districts. In truth, the newspapers of the 1850s are full of reports of burglaries and attacks upon property as well as street robberies and assaults. Businessmen and local residents had their own equivalent to the contemporary neighbourhood watch schemes.

January 1855 found Elizabeth, busy as ever, helping Alice prepare her books for her return to school, and going with Herbert to choose the secondhand cab which was to be used to take Bertie and Allan daily to school in Ipswich. Her confinement was expected towards the end of January for on the 25th of the month comes the cryptic comment: 'Mrs Porley came to stay in the house.' This was not her usual mode of description for a visitor. A chance encounter with this lady's name in another household on the 1851 census revealed that her profession was that of 'monthly nurse'.

Although her midwifery and child-nursing skills were not required immediately, she had in fact arrived at an opportune moment, for within the week, on 30 January, Elizabeth was taken ill with influenza. She records that Mr Hammond, the doctor, called to see her on 1 February and continued to do so. That she was really ill is borne out by her making no further entry in her diary until:

On Wednesday 14 February, our third little daughter was born at 11 o'clock at night. Mr Leath stayed a few days with Herbert from the 24 February, and on Thursday 1st March I went downstairs. Poor baby appears very delicate.

Elizabeth followed the pattern of a two-week lying-in period which continued well into the twentieth century. When she does 'come downstairs' she allows herself a month before again taking up an active social life. Both she and the child had been affected by those two weeks of influenza prior to the birth. The child's health continued to give concern: '22 *May 1855*. Mr Hammond vaxinated our little baby Ethel, who has not until now, been strong enough to bear it.'

Vaccination against smallpox as late as fourteen weeks after birth must have been unusual since Elizabeth remarks upon it. In a thriving infant it was probably performed at two to three weeks if we may take Charles Dickens as our authority:

> 'Baby yours?'
> 'Girl?'
> 'Bo-o-oy!' roared John.
> 'Also very young, eh?'
> Mrs Peerybingle instantly struck in. 'Two months and three da-ays! Vaccinated just six weeks ago-o! Took very fine-ly!'
> (The Cricket on the Hearth, Chirp the First.)

However, Elizabeth must have felt confident enough that all was well with Ethel when in early June she and Herbert left home for their annual holiday tour. Returning a fortnight later she found: 'The dear children quite well, but Baby had been sadly a day or two.' By the end of that week the baby had caught cold and worried her mother enough to send for the doctor, but plans were now under way for the baby's christening, a rather grand family affair which took place on the afternoon of Saturday 21 July:

> Friday. A party of our friends came from London to stay with us. On Saturday our dear little baby was christened Ethel Constance. Mr de Grey who christened Baby afterwards dined with us with Mrs Lazenby who came from London with Rea and Henry Page, Arthur and Anne. Mr Leath and Mr Martin dined also with us. Rea, Anne and Henry were sponsors.

The visitors stayed for several days and enjoyed various excursions. An air of festivity hung over Washbrook until the onset of a childhood complaint: '12 *August 1855*. On Friday with Herbert and our three eldest children to Felixstow. Took a hamper of provisions with us. The children were delighted with the beach and played on it all day. Our children have the Hooping Cough and we thought the sea air would do them good.'

That Eva and the baby were not taken, may point to the fact that either they were considered too young for such an outing or that they had not shown any signs of the infection. However, one week later:

> 19 *August 1855*. On Friday morning, Mrs Marskall, our housekeeper called us to say Baby was in a convulsion fit. Herbert dressed as quickly as possible and went for medical assistance but he returned to us, nearly two hours before Mr Charles Hammond came to the child. Our little darling never recovered consciousness, and after repeated

convulsion fits died on Sunday night, the 26 August. My sister Anne came from London on the Tuesday following.

What agony of mind must Herbert have suffered as he dressed, ordered the horse to be saddled or put in the shafts of the phaeton and then galloped the three or four miles into Ipswich through the early morning traffic to call at Mr Hammond's house in the centre of the town. What anguish when he discovered the doctor was not readily available and he had to return alone to Elizabeth who, with her nursery staff, was no doubt applying the accepted treatment for infant convulsions to no avail. In an age which has come to rely on telephonic communication and a responsive emergency service, it is hard to comprehend what it must have been like waiting, interminably it seemed, for the doctor to arrive. And when he did come, there was nothing he could do.

We are led to believe that the Victorians accepted their children's death with pious resignation, but Elizabeth betrays here a very natural maternal emotion expressed in anger. An anger which had to be directed at someone, in this case, Mr Hammond. One can almost hear the venom in her pen as she calls him Mr Charles Hammond. Never before or after, does she use his Christian name, just this once, as if, in her own private court of law, she identifies him as the one guilty of the death of her beloved child.

There are a number of conditions which can result in infantile convulsions, including damage caused by a difficult birth and the vitamin deficiency which results in rickets and meningitis. In baby Ethel's case, it is likely that, prone as she was to colds, she contracted whooping cough more severely than the other children and that during a paroxysm of coughing she went into the convulsive state from which her frail body was unable to escape. Thirty days after that happy occasion when Ethel Constance had been received into the Church of England through baptism her tiny coffin was buried in the churchyard.

Elizabeth allowed herself a few days of private grief, too private even to put down in her journal beyond: 'I have no record of a few days following, for they were of great sorrow.'

But not for her the luxury of self-pity, the languishing on a sofa in a darkened room; she had the rest of her family to consider, so: 'thinking it best to take the children from home for a short time, we went to Felixstow on Thursday, 6th September and engaged rooms at the Hotel there for our family.' Here is another example of marital togetherness. Herbert could easily have written to the hotel to book rooms, but the impression is formed that they had discussed the project fully, and that he had thought that the drive to the resort would do her good getting her out again to face the world. He was at the busiest time of the farming year with the harvest, but his wife and family took precedence.

We took the children there on Monday. Herbert returned home after dinner and I, with our children, Alice and Evelyn and the boys, my sister Anne and our nursemaid Jane Farrer remaining at Felixstow. Walked and sat about on the beach Monday and Tuesday. Wednesday walked with Anne to Landguard Fort, the children going with us on donkeys.

For just over two weeks they remained at the seaside, taking long and tiring walks. Herbert joined them at the weekends. In recording the events surrounding Ethel's death, Elizabeth's handwriting never falters, yet her notes for the activities at Felixstowe contain several errors. The numbness of mind which initially accompanied the bereavement has begun to wear off. However hard she tries, the dull ache of her inner pain colours her response to what was happening around her: 'Some wild fowl and sea birds were about the harbour bar, so tired they scarcely moved away from us.'

But life had to go on, and soon her diary was recording the usual daily happenings, though now she was even more concerned for everyone's health. Her anger with Mr Hammond abated and she continued to call him whenever one of the children needed attention. By December Elizabeth would have been certain that she was again pregnant. It is clear that again she took the pregnancy in her stride though she was by now thirty-six years of age. There is no mention of visits to or from the doctor and the only clue to her condition comes in late May when, following a holiday on the south coast, they returned to London for a few days:

21 May, 1856. Wednesday. Walked on the pier [at Brighton] and afterwards to London by railway. Stayed at the York. After dinner to the Olympic Theatre. The performances were 'Retribution', a drama, and 'Stay At Home', but we only saw one act of the first piece as I was obliged to leave the theatre from faintness and Herbert returned with me. Thursday. Herbert went to the Exhibition of French Pictures, but I did not go with him being afraid to remain in a heated room.

The fact that she had to forego the pleasure of seeing the paintings did not mean that she repined in her hotel room, for she adds: 'Went to a statuary shop and purchased a small statuette of Dorothea and an agate vase.'

Sensible precautions led to her staying away from the crowded exhibition, but she had no intention of giving in to coddling herself just because she was in a perfectly natural condition. In June, now in her eighth month, she was still socially active, entertaining and visiting, coping with a change in staff when one nursemaid left and another came, and working in her beloved garden. '*8 June 1856*. Herbert went to Bury market and I went to Ipswich for some flowers and planted them when I returned home. Thursday and Friday in garden and with children.'

Most days she walked with the children, now on school holidays, one day going with them to visit the lambs, perhaps using that occasion to prepare them for the coming event. Visitors still called including, on Friday, 4 July, the local vicar, Revd the Hon. Frederick de Grey, younger brother of Lord Walsingham, who brought with him another brother, the Hon. Brownlow de Grey, and his new wife and two other friends, who were all staying at the rectory. In her own unperturbed way she managed this rather formal visit despite the fact that:

> Our little girl Blanche was born at half past ten o'clock on Tuesday, evening, 8th July. I sat up to tea in my room on the 16th. On the 17th. Herbert went to the Agricultural Show at Chelmsford. Mrs Henry Miller called to see me. Herbert came home the following night. Mrs Allen called on the 19th.

This confinement had gone well. Within eight days Elizabeth was strong enough to take her tea, that early evening ritual which followed the late afternoon dinner, probably sitting out of bed on a sofa. Furthermore, her post-natal condition was such that Herbert felt he could leave her while he stayed away for the night attending the markets in the next county, and Elizabeth was up to receiving visits from her female friends while she was still confined to her room. This birth, unlike the previous one, was probably more like the norm for the time.

It is difficult to assess from the diary how much involvement Elizabeth had with the baby during its early months for she makes no mention of Blanche. There is no record of the first smile or tooth, but then, this is the sixth child and such events would no longer be a novelty. Had she required it when she first embarked upon motherhood, Elizabeth would have found assistance on the management of babies in Mrs Hemans's *Young Women's Companion*. First published in 1832, it was constantly reprinted, giving advice on important items like clothing: ' . . . a thin, light cap, slightly fastened with a bit of tape. . . . a fine flannel round the navel, a linen or cotton shirt, flannel petticoat, and a linen or cotton robe, are soon put on; and where fastenings are requisite, they should consist of tape, without any dangerous pins.' Mrs Hemans further decreed that as far as the mattress of the baby's cot was concerned, feathers were unhealthy, horsehair was better, but bran was best of all as it was more absorbent.

How far Elizabeth agreed with the author on the subject of bathing, we do not know, but the modern reader blenches at the statement:

It would be extremely hazardous to dip the tender body of a newborn babe in cold water and keep it there during the necessary operations of washing; but the use of the cold-bath may be safely brought about by degrees in five or six months after birth, and will be found not only one of the best means of promoting health and strength, but of preventing also many of the most distressing complaints to which children are subject.

If poor baby Ethel was subjected to this, one could say it was no wonder she did not last long. Conversely, if the rest of the Cotton children did endure this regime then its efficacy has to be recommended, since they all survived to a ripe old age, Blanche for example, being eighty-eight at her death. We can be sure, however, that Elizabeth and Herbert both ignored Mrs Hemans's admonition that children should be seen and not heard.

Elizabeth does not impart such an intimate detail as whether or not she breast-fed her children. With the sickly Ethel it is unlikely but the indications are that Blanche was suckled for at least four months, for although Elizabeth continued to go out and about, her movements were more restricted and she never once stayed away over night during that period. However, for the week beginning 16 November 1856 we read: 'Monday, began weaning baby.'

It is also difficult to tell if the family had a formal nursery to which the younger children were relegated with the nursemaids, several of whom over the years seem to have been called Jane. This was pure coincidence, and not an example of the practice of Victorian mistresses who insisted for the sake of convenience that their domestic staff assume a common name. When Amor Hall was sold in 1919 the house was described as having the following accommodation:

Square hall, Drawing room (19'×15') leading to a small conservatory, Dining room (15×15), garden hall, breakfast room, kitchen, back kitchen, 2 staircases to first floor, five bedrooms, bathroom and WC. Two attics over.

Allowing for at least one bedroom reserved for guests (and at times there were more than two couples staying), the rest of the family had to be fitted into the remaining rooms. Did Mrs Marskall enjoy the privacy of her own room? I suspect not since she was obviously on call to the children at night, and on one occasion Elizabeth accuses Mrs Marskall of filling Eva's head with frightening stories, so perhaps she slept in the same room as the younger children. If she did have her own room it must have adjoined that of the children. If we allocate a room to Elizabeth and Herbert, one to the boys, another to Alice and a fourth to the younger girls, it is difficult to see where there might have been a nursery as such, unless it was in one of the large attic rooms. One of these would have accommodated all the living-in staff. We can only speculate on the family's arrangements of the space available to them and it may be that the children had as their own one of the rooms on the ground floor.

HEALTH

The diary brings constant reminders of some of the health problems which plagued the nineteenth century, in particular those associated with poor sanitation and good water supplies. In 1856 there was an outbreak of a related problem in the village: '*12 October*. The children had a holiday on Monday. I walked with them and hearing from Mrs Daldry that her daughter Mrs Grimes's family were ill with fever sent them 2/6.'

Alfred Grimes was by trade what was known locally as a 'higgler', that is he bought dairy produce which he resold in the neighbourhood – a forerunner of the modern milk roundsman. He probably bought his stock from Herbert's dairy and so would have been well known to the family, as were his in-laws, Mr Daldry being one of the workers on the farm. Alfred and Mary Grimes had at least twelve children following their marriage in 1837. There are two ways of looking at this extract. It can be read as a picture of a middle-class Lady Bountiful dispensing charity to the deserving poor, or of the concerned woman, who stops for a chat with a villager and on hearing of another's misfortune wants to help in the best way she can. I prefer the latter interpretation. The mention of the actual amount is surely explained by the housewifely need to account for her expenditure. Two shillings and sixpence would have purchased quite a number of extras for the family, and by giving money, which to us may seem an easy option, Elizabeth was, in fact, allowing the recipients to decide for themselves what their needs were. She could quite easily have sent soup or some other commodity later from her kitchen, but the donation suggests a spontaneous act of generosity. It is possible that the local 'fever' may have spread closer to home, for during the following week Elizabeth 'sent our nurse Jane home to rest for a time as she is not well.'

Over the years, they all suffered from occasional sore throats and colds, probably induced by the resurgence of the typhoidal and choleraic epidemics. Once one member of the family had it, then the others followed and we also have reports of friends and acquaintances being described as ill or 'sadly' – the latter indicating a less severe state. On 6 October 1860 all the children were revaccinated by Dr Bartlet who had now become the family physician. In this Elizabeth was ahead of the precautions which the authorities were to take. The *Ipswich Journal* for the 27 October stated: 'In consequence of the great prevalence of Small pox in the town, a resolution passed at the Board of Guardians on Saturday last, "That the Clerk draw the attention of the Vaccinators to the necessity of extending the practice of vaccination . . ." '

Fortunately the family escaped the smallpox and the more serious of the childhood illnesses which affected those of her relations. *'10 April 1859*. Letter from Kate to say her children are ill from Scarlatina.' *'29 May 1859*. Letters from Rea, Margot and Kate this week. Rea's children have been removed to another school, that of Miss Saxton's having been broken up from the sudden death of one of the children there from Diphtheria.'

However, Elizabeth did have to contend with a childhood nervous complaint. Most mothers have had a child who at some time has developed stomach pains or headaches which when investigated reveal that they coincide with certain dreaded lessons at school or are related to a specific problem with which the child is unable to cope. Allan was eleven when Elizabeth, having noted that he had not been well just before term ended, writes:

> *31 March 1860*. Saturday. Dr Bartlet came to see Allan. He says the poor little fellow must be kept very quite. . . . *3, April*. Tuesday. To Ipswich . . . purchased some toys for Allan, as Dr Bartlet says he must not be allowed books at present. Wednesday. Dr Bartlet called . . . Saturday. Dr Bartlet called to see Allan. The poor little fellow is better. The attack has been upon the nerves, occasioned we fear by rough treatment at school.

Elizabeth refrains from noting if the 'rough treatment' was meted out by the school staff or was bullying from other pupils.

As in most families accidents occurred to all of them at some time. Normally Elizabeth displays a calm attitude, organising and taking practical steps to alleviate the situation (quite unlike my own Victorian grandmother, a farmer's wife with thirteen children, who counted her pulse rate before falling into a dead faint every time one of her children had an accident!) For example, on a visit with her sister Anne to neighbouring Bury St Edmunds:

> *13 May 1855*. On Wednesday, Anne went with Herbert and me to Bury. Anne and I went into St Mary's church when a scaffolding upon which a man was repairing the ceiling of the chancel fell. The man upon it was terribly hurt, one of his arms being broken besides other injuries. We went for surgical and other assistance.

One imagines the two women rendering what help and comfort they could before running off to obtain further help. And run, I am sure she did, if not on that occasion, then she was certainly prepared to do so when eight-year-old Eva was in danger:

27 February 1861. Wednesday. In garden. Evelyn fell into the pond. Before I could run to her she had scrambled out very much frightened and quite covered with mud. I had great difficulty to free her from her clothes. Fortunately she did not take cold.

Elizabeth's fears of what might have been the outcome of this mishap are contained in her next comment: 'Mrs Marskall had again gone home. She is of little use to me.' Yet earlier, in 1859, she had been more than glad to fall back on Mrs Marskall's help when: '*12 June 1858*. Thursday. Bertie was accidentally hurt by his brother in the eye. I was very much frightened at first and sent Mrs Marskall with him to Ipswich to be seen by Mr Bartlet who said the sight was not injured and that the eye would quickly heal.'

This is the one of the few occasions where Elizabeth admits to fear – but how understandable it is. The actual structure of her wording of the incident is interesting. A modern mother might well have written, 'Allan hit Bertie in the eye with . . . a fist, stone, cricket ball . . .' whatever it was that the 10- and 11-year-old boys were engaged in. However, Elizabeth's view seems to be that it is the sufferer who is of the major importance, so only he is named. She is also careful to point out that it was an accident. Was this how it had been explained to her, or how she had to explain it to Papa? There is, however, the hint that she did not feel that Allan was entirely blameless in her rather formal use of 'his brother'. It is difficult to understand why Elizabeth herself did not take Bertie for medical attention. Was she so fearful of the outcome of the visit that she preferred to wait until Mrs Marskall brought back the result or was it that she felt she should remain with the other children and calm them and perhaps at the same time have a very serious talk with Allan about the possible consequences of what had happened? There were other accidents to contend with; in 1863:

25 February. Bertie a little hurt from the pony falling with him.

26 March. In the garden - slipped and sprained my ankle.

3 April. Walton and Alice Turner came to breakfast. E. West came to dinner. The children rode out. Allan was thrown and hurt upon the head. He had to lie down for the remainder of the evening. I stayed with him while the other children had music and dancing.

Elizabeth's early upbringing among horses must have made her very aware of the dangers of concussion. Her concern is shown by the fact that she remained in attendance upon him for the evening. Nonetheless, her balanced outlook on family life is revealed in the fact that she does not deny the rest of the children their pleasures, thus countering the view that in Victorian times when an invalid was lying in a darkened room, the rest of the household were condemned to tiptoe around and engage in quiet pursuits. Not for Allan the consideration given to Esther Summerson in *Bleak House*: 'I could understand the stillness in the house, and the thoughtfulness on the part of all who had always been so good to me.' (Chapter 35) But then, Bleak House was not full of teenagers!

One really begins to doubt Allan's horsemanship for: '*24 April 1863*. The pony fell down when Allan was riding him this morning and cut and injured itself very much. Allan not hurt.'

The early part of 1863 was a long chapter of accidents. Bertie, too had been 'a little hurt from the pony falling with him' in February and Elizabeth had followed her sprained ankle with a heavy fall. '*8 May 1863*. Boys had a half holiday. Went with them, Alice and Blanche into wood after ferns. Had taken rather a severe fall from the bank.' '*10 May* Sunday. Not well. Dr Bartlet came. He says I injured myself when I fell last Friday.'

Her condition must have given cause for concern for the doctor called to see her five times in the next nine days, but she mentions the fact only in the same way she records all other visitors to the house. One possible explanation is that she had again been pregnant and suffered a miscarriage.

A glimpse of mid-Victorian dentistry is given in the diaries. 'Poor Bertie' as his mother often affectionately calls him suffered greatly with dental problems. He was twelve when Elizabeth first records that she met him after school at Mr Leigh's the dentist as 'Bertie suffers from toothache'. We are not told what action was taken on that occasion, but a year later, also in February, she writes: 'Met Bertie suffering from pain in the face from neuralgia'. One wonders if this is a recurrent problem with the teeth or if the first occasion was also induced by cold. However, later that same year: '*10 October 1862*. Friday to Ipswich. Met Bertie coming home ill with toothache. Took him to Mr. Cornell's. He relieved him with chloroform.'

Although in *Victorian England* W.J. Reader says, 'Dentists were hardly respectable, professionally, until the Dentists' Act of 1878, provided for registration after examination', there were a number of practitioners established in Ipswich in the 1850s and 60s residing in the very respectable and fashionable middle-class areas of the town. As with doctors, Elizabeth was likely to change her practitioner, possibly in pursuit of the best treatment. Dentists in the United States had experimented with tooth extractions from patients rendered unconscious by the inhalation of both nitrous oxide gas and vapour of ether. By 1847 London dentists were using ether, but the breakthrough for all came with Sir James Simpson's work with chloroform. This had achieved great respectability and the royal seal of approval when it was used by Queen Victoria to ease her later childbirths. However, its use in Ipswich in dentistry must have been sufficiently novel for Elizabeth to mention it. She might not have been quite so happy had she known that it had led to a number of fatalities, but perhaps Bertie was given one of the newly-invented mechanical inhalers which prevented the administering of too concentrated a dose. It appears that on that particular occasion Bertie was given a palliative dose of chloroform, for a week later: '*18 October 1862*. Went with Bertie to the Dentist's. He had a tooth extracted.'

Most worrying for Elizabeth was Herbert's health. Apart from the times when he is described as being 'sadly', perhaps indicating an excess of food and drink, he was also prone to the vague illnesses which the children had. In 1857 he was obviously suffering from an eye condition: '*8 March 1857*. Uncle George sent Herbert a candle shade to protect his eyes from too much light.'

To those of us whose only encounter with candle power comes when there is a breakdown in electricity supplies, it is difficult to imagine a candle giving 'too much light'. However, if we visualise Herbert working at his farm account books illuminated by a candle we realise that it is a very concentrated source of light. This candleshade gift could either be something decorative similar to that which is nowadays affixed to a wall light, or more likely, the nineteenth-century patent 'Nightshade', a cylindrical metal object about 13 inches high with a diameter of 9 inches which fitted over a shallow candle holder. It had a lid and a small door though which the candle could be lighted or snuffed but, most important, it had large holes punched at intervals all over the surface through which light could be diffused.

Later that same year, Herbert had a fall which might have had disastrous results: '*6 September 1857*. Monday. Herbert had a bad fall while out shooting.' Elizabeth must have been truly thankful that her husband was an experienced shot and that he fell when his gun was unloaded. Just how dangerous the effects of a mishap while shooting could be was to be brought home to her two months later when her niece, Fanny Page, wrote to tell her that her brother-in-law Henry had 'greatly injured his hand while shooting'. '*8 November 1857*. Wrote to Rea. After this frequent letters about Henry whose life was at one time feared for.'

The injury healed in time and by January 1858 Henry was joining in the family festivities and was presumably back at his place of business. It is therefore a shock when we learn that the wound must have become reinfected: '*7 February 1858*. Friday. A letter from Margaret to say that Henry's hand was again much worse.' It is possible that Henry's accident was similar to one reported in the *Ipswich Journal*: 'On Thursday as Fell of the Lion and Lamb Inn, St. Clements, was shooting . . . the barrel of the gun burst and injured his left hand.' Apart from the possibility of smashed or splintered bones, there would have been severe powder burns and the greatest danger of all would be from gangrene.

Early in 1860, in the same month that we first hear of Bertie's teeth problems, Herbert was in need of medical attention: '*19 February 1860*. Dr Bartlet came to see Herbert who has not been well this week. . . . *26 February*. Herbert was examined by Dr Bartlet, who said he must not travel in an open carriage during the cold weather.' His condition must have worried Elizabeth for, as on other occasions, she gave up a social activity to remain with the invalid, as the rest of the entry for that week shows: 'Friday. A Charade Party at Miss Shalders'. Alice acted several characters. I declined going, not liking to leave Herbert.'

There is a tussle of conscience here between her duty to her husband and to her child. Duty is perhaps the wrong word. As for most loving wives and mothers, the decision would have been clear-cut, her husband was ill and needed her – and as he was now sixty, she might have been just a little fearful, particularly as it is likely his illness was some form of lung infection – while there would be other opportunities to see her daughter act at school. By the following week Herbert's health, so she tells us, had improved, but illnesses had been widespread: '*4 March 1860*. A letter from Margaret on Friday to tell me she wished to visit us, as her health required change of air.'

Apart from colds and the bout of influenza prior to Ethel's birth, Elizabeth herself seems remarkably fit, that is until the end of January 1862. Following a dinner party on the 13 January for five guests, one of whom stayed overnight, she writes: '*14 January 1862*. Tuesday. Miss Colbrant left. Letters from Alice, Arabella and Mrs. Turner. Not very well. Dr Bartlet called.' The doctor called again on Wednesday and Thursday, and on Saturday when she made her usual visit to Ipswich she was: 'Not well. Obliged to return home.'

Whatever was wrong was either lingering or likely to flare up at intervals, for the doctor called again three times during the next fifteen days and Elizabeth severely curtailed her social activities, going to Ipswich only to take Eva to school on Monday and bring her home again on Saturday. In all, this bout of ill-health lasted well over a month. However, she had to rally her spirits for she was about to embark on a series of domestic crises, starting with Eva's unhappiness at school.

RELATIONSHIPS

The diary offers interesting side lights on Elizabeth's relationship with her family as a whole and with each of them individually, and from her comments we are able to form some idea of their personalities. Although Herbert and Elizabeth were strong advocates for the idea of the close family unit and enjoyed taking their children out and about with them, I think we can safely assume that the Cotton children were not brought up on the Pardiggle principle. One can imagine the whole family recoiling in horror at this extract from Dickens's *Bleak House* which describes a visit made by Mrs Pardiggle and her five sons aged 12, 10½, 9, 7 and 5:

They attend Matins with me (very prettily done), at half past six o'clock in the morning all the year round, including the depth of winter . . . and they are with me during the revolving duties of the day. I am a School lady, I am a visiting lady, I am a Reading lady, I am a distributing lady; I am on the local Linen Box Committee, and many general Committees; and my canvassing alone is very extensive – perhaps no one's more so. But they are my companions everywhere; and by these means they acquire that knowledge of the poor, and that capacity of doing charitable business in general – in short, that taste for the sort of thing – which will render them in after life service to their neighbours, and a satisfaction to themselves. My young family are not frivolous; they expend the entire amount of their allowance in subscriptions, under my direction; and they have attended as many public meetings, and listened to as many lectures, orations, and discussions, as generally fall to the lot of few grown people.

Poor little Pardiggles. What would they have made of life at Amor Hall? Not for them the outdoor games, the riding and fishing and the running after rabbits. Were they ever allowed fireworks in August – just for their amusement? Not for them 'romps' in the meadows with aunts and uncles. Did they have a Twelfth Night cake sent them every January, and have 'Snapdragon' in December or 'try the All Hallows ceremonies for the next year'? Were they let off school to go to the races, or go to watch the troops reviewed or witness the wonders of a conjuring show? Did their mother take them for walks by moonlight or let them take off their shoes to paddle in the stream on a Sunday? How many friends did they have, to invite to stay or to go to visit? No juvenile parties and dances and outings to the theatre for them. Poor 'unfrivolous' young family. What would they have done with parents who bought them presents of jewellery, Scottish daggers or other trifles? And what would they have thought if their allowances, instead of being directed into charitable subscriptions, had been taken by their mother and placed in the Savings Bank so that when they had need, they could make their own purchases as Bertie did when he wanted a watch.

It is almost too dreadful to contemplate into what sort of adults these children of Dickens's imagination would have grown. Naturally, in the same way that the author shows us only the side of them he wishes to emphasise, so do we see Elizabeth's children through her eyes. In Alice, the eldest of the family, we see the child maturing to a young woman. In many respects during the first journal she is a somewhat shadowy figure since she is away at school for most of the time. We do sense, however, that there is a close relationship between her and her mother, borne out by the number of letters they exchange during her absences. She also obviously felt a close affinity with her younger brothers and sisters, and in spite of the age gap often joined them in their activities. There is a rather sad little entry in the first year of the diary: '*8 March*. Wednesday Eva's birthday. Alice sent her a toy dog, but the present rather frightened Baby.' One can picture the nine-year-old Alice having been given permission by Mrs Shalders to go shopping and her delight in choosing a suitable gift for her sister's first birthday. We can only hope that Elizabeth was less honest to her daughter about the gift's reception than she was when recounting it in her diary.

When Alice had finished her education she occupied the position of close companion to her mother after her return from France, often deputising for Elizabeth on various commissions, and accompanying her to functions. Yet she is not kept confined in any way; she is actively encouraged, as she was from her earliest years, to widen her horizons, to travel to stay with friends and relations and to enjoy an active social life.

Possibly because of their closeness in age, Bertie and Allan tend to be bracketed together in their activities, yet there is just a hint that Bertie, being the elder, is perhaps a trifle more indulged by his mother. However, both boys are encouraged to be 'manly' in their pursuits with an emphasis laid upon sporting activities. In their teens the boys do more with their father, going to the annual Ipswich race meeting in July and joining him for shooting, first rabbits and then game. Yet they still join Elizabeth for walks and visits to concerts and the theatre, and for a time are dependent on her for help with school-work.

Most families contain one child who is 'different' or does not appear to conform with the rest. In the Cotton family this was Evelyn, or Eva, as she was affectionately known in the family. When Alice and the boys were at school, Eva became her mother's companion on walks and visits, and I suspect that a very close relationship developed between them, particularly after the death of Ethel. Until Blanche was old enough to join in these outings, Eva enjoyed her mother's almost undivided attention. It was Eva who went with Elizabeth to meet the boys from school, Eva who accompanied her to the station to greet or see off their visitors. She was also very dear to her father, for after the other children have had their photographs taken:

7 October 1855. . . . Monday. With Anne walked to Ipswich. Called for photographic portraits and returned home by cab. . . . Herbert being very pleased with the pictures of the children wished to have Eva's portrait taken and we took her to Mr. Cade's but the attempt was a failure from her extreme restlessness.

The attempt was not repeated until 1858 when Eva was five. Two years after that both she and Blanche were taken to the photographer and on this occasion Elizabeth gives one of her rare details about the clothing worn:

'3 *September 1860.* Monday. Evelyn and Blanche went with me to Ipswich to have their photographs taken. Evelyn wore a school tunic and knickerbockers.'

This reference may be to what had become the fashion for little girls, but in a way, it is also Elizabeth preparing herself – and Eva too – for the coming change in their lives, for Elizabeth was shortly to lose her little companion when she started school. One senses that it was a wrench for Elizabeth to let Eva go. Was Eva as 'nervous' as Elizabeth declared or was it the over-anxious mother who wrote while the whole family were holidaying the following August with various relations in London:

With Herbert and children to a dinner party at Uncle John's. Wished to take Eva home with me, because she appeared nervous at being left, but Arabella [her brother Edward's wife] persuaded me to leave her. . . . Saturday. A letter from Edward to say Eva is happier. Returned home.

And two weeks later: 'Went to Bentley Station to meet Anne who brought my little Evelyn home with her.'

This holiday having satisfied Elizabeth that Eva could cope with separation from home, she was enrolled as a boarder at school. Alas, all did not go well: '14 *September 1861.* Monday, Little Evelyn went to Mrs Foster's as a boarder.' '16 *September.* Wednesday. Herbert went to Bury. This evening Evelyn frightened us very much by coming home alone. Sent a servant on horseback to tell Mrs Foster the child was with us.'

One can easily imagine Elizabeth's emotions and reaction at the unexpected appearance of her eight-year-old daughter. Like all mothers she would have been racked with thoughts of what might have befallen the child as she walked the three miles of the busy London road, a good part of which was through open countryside. Eva being quite accustomed to walking the route with her mother probably had not been aware of the dangers – her homesickness being the only thing that concerned her at the time.

Fretful and nervous though she may have been on occasions Eva displays a determination of spirit. The initiative she had shown in running away from school may have been excusable in the eyes of her parents, but some of her behaviour may have been described as wilful. Like all the family she had been taught to ride at an early age and the children and their friends rode together regularly. There are frequent references throughout the spring of 1863 to Alice, now nineteen, and the boys sixteen and fifteen, riding round the neighbourhood visiting. At eleven, Eva was in that awful in-between stage. The older ones did not want her tagging along with them and she probably considered the seven-year-old Blanche was too young to join in her activities. During the Easter holidays that year, the house had been filled with cousins from London and local friends. As well as riding, there had been picnics and evenings filled with music and dancing. Is it possible that the pubescent Eva had developed a schoolgirl crush on the teenage son of one of their neighbours while she was sitting on the sidelines watching the older boys and girls enjoying the dancing? Or it could be that since she too had been taking dancing lessons, she had joined in and perhaps been partnered by the object of her dreams? As so often happens, the reader is left to fill in the details which might have accompanied the entries: '6 *April 1863*. Monday. Evelyn called upon the Wests without my knowledge and brought E. West here to breakfast. He spent the day here.'

The Wests who lived in the neighbouring village were old friends. However, Evelyn had clearly flouted not just convention here by calling upon another household so early in the day, she had gone out without permission, she had taken a pony, also without her parents' knowledge and gone off unaccompanied, to return with one extra for breakfast. The last would not have perturbed Elizabeth, but the rest most certainly would. There is no indication of what punishment, if any, was meted out for this misdemeanour. I may be wrong, but I feel that Elizabeth would have greeted her offspring's misbehaviour with sorrow rather than anger; a sending to one's room to ponder on the possible results of the misdeed, or the missing of a treat, being more likely than the corporal punishment which was apparently practised widely at that time: The *English Woman's Domestic Magazine* comments, following a six-month interchange of letters on the subject of flogging in an article in the Saturday Review:

That in this year of 1869, there should be living in England, and in London, a considerable number of women, many apparently in good society, and some of them titled, who are in the regular habit of stripping and flogging with birches, apple twigs or leather straps, their daughters of thirteen years and upwards, must appear to foreigners incredible.

And so too, would it have seemed to Elizabeth Cotton, a loving, well-balanced wife and mother who, in my opinion, proved that she was neither the stereotype 'useless doll' wife nor 'the delicate clinging parasite' mother.

4

Domestic Life

I was terribly afraid . . . of fatiguing antique chairs and dismal stained glass, and musty, frowsy hangings, and all the barbarous lumber which people born without a sense of comfort accumulate about them. . . . It is an inexpressible relief to find that the nineteenth century has invaded this strange and future home of mine and has swept the dirty 'good old times' out of the way of our daily life.

The Woman in White – Wilkie Collins

Coming to Amor Hall as a young bride Elizabeth found that the nineteenth century had not swept away the 'good old times' from her new home, for Herbert had inherited 'all the household goods of furniture, china, linen, plate and plated articles' from his parents and maternal grandparents. Thus Herbert's bachelor home was well provided with items dating back to the second half of the eighteenth century.

The contents of a house in Washbrook of similar proportions offered for sale in 1855 give some idea of what might also have been found in Amor Hall. Brussels and Kidderminster carpets for the drawing-room and dining-room floors; an abundance of tables – Pembroke, pillar and loo in either mahogany or rosewood; hairseated couches and sofas; rosewood chairs with hair cushions; ottomans and handscreens; chiffoniers and a sideboard with drawers; gilt chimney glasses and brass fenders and fire-irons; a fourteen-day French clock in an ebony case; chess and backgammon boards; damask window curtains suspended by brass rings upon brass poles. In the bedrooms mahogany came into its own with the fourposter beds with their drapes and matching chests of drawers, plus those reminders of pre-bathroom days the 'painted washstand and towel horse, basin, ewer and chamber requisites'. It is also possible that among the paintings on the walls at Amor Hall there were, as in that sale and in other Suffolk house sales of the period, those which were described as 'supposed to be by Gainsborough'.

Quite how Elizabeth reacted to the furnishings of her home on her arrival, we have no way of knowing. She had spent her childhood in houses that dated back two hundred years at least and it may be that she yearned for a modern home like those of her friends, many of whom were changing from their sturdy timber-framed houses in the town centre to the elegant and stylish nineteenth-century middle-class version of the Englishman's castle. Constructed in Suffolk whites – a very pale yellow tinged brick, these houses, often situated on rising ground, had not only towers and turrets but dungeon-like basement areas fronted by a dry moat straddled by the impressive drawbridge of steps which led to the front door set high above street level. Such was the style of building that even the semi-detached managed to achieve a grandeur and importance rarely found today. In such a house lived Thomas Leath, and to such a house had moved the widowed Mrs Brooks and her daughter Charlotte from the White Horse. Elizabeth became accustomed to visiting those whose homes were purpose built, where every room had a specific function, a house where the walls were straight with plaster and the floors did not slope, where there were picture rails and skirting boards and well-proportioned windows. All so different to Amor Hall which had evolved over several centuries and been adapted to suit the changing patterns of life during that time. The biggest difference between Elizabeth's home and those of her friends was that theirs was just that – a home – while Amor Hall was still part of the workplace.

Elizabeth was a careful housewife who would not deliberately waste nor set aside objects hitherto serviceable, but by the time we meet her in 1854, her home is being brought into the nineteenth century. She does not tell us exactly what is happening beyond: '*12 March 1854. The Builders began altering our house this week.*' The important word here is 'altering', and what was occurring was major structural alteration in line with the fashion of the times.

During the first half of the nineteenth century many estate owners set about the wholesale remodelling or redevelopment of the houses and cottages on their lands. In some cases this meant moving the inhabitants of a whole village into specially designed new model villages aesthetically pleasing to the landowner, as happened at Milton Abbas in Dorset, and at Chatsworth where Elizabeth caustically comments during her visit there in 1855:

> Went over the Duke of Devonshire's House and grounds. . . . the village of Edensor at the entrance of the park, quite out of character with the people inhabiting, being a cluster of elegant Italian and Swiss villas, and the population not superior to the usual class of agricultural peasantry.

Housing stocks at the end of the eighteenth century had become run down, and the increase in population which occurred during the first part of the nineteenth meant that there was as real a need to provide adequate housing in rural areas as in towns. Many enlightened owners grasped the opportunity either to build or upgrade their existing stocks, not merely from altruism but as a way of declaring their own status. In this they were amply assisted by books of architects' designs for model villages, and while most restrained themselves from copying the Italianate or Swiss style, many favoured the return to the Tudor or Gothic influence. As a consequence, many solidly built brick or stone cottages which should have been roofed with slate, found themselves sporting a magnificent thatch, or if that could not be achieved, then at least an entrance porch was added which could wear a rustic reed roof. Similarly, windows were often constructed to look as if they had been in place for two or three hundred years and gigantic mock Elizabethan chimneys sprouted on quite modest roofs.

When James Hales-Tooke acquired Washbrook and Copdock from the Walsingham family in 1850, he followed the fashion and set about renovating his new property. He probably started with Amor Hall as it was the principal tenancy, and this gave Elizabeth her opportunity to modernise the interior. One of Elizabeth's sketches shows the back of the house as it was in the 1840s. What was to happen in 1854 was the construction of a single-storey extension covering the whole of the rear of the house with a large porch at the front to form an additional entrance hall. The house had been built originally on the medieval hall design with dividing walls added later. One room which underwent structural alteration at this time was the dining room, where James Hales-Tooke-Hales, to give him his full surname, had his initials, his coat of arms and the date of 1854 ornamentally carved into the woodwork of the overmantel. He was probably also responsible for the wooden panelled walls which made an upstairs corridor thus allowing access to a room without going through another.

The house is of timber frame construction, but most of the walls have at some time been boarded and plastered. It is likely that in earlier times at least one of the ground floor reception rooms was wainscoted, but this was removed and the walls plastered, thus giving Elizabeth the opportunity to join in another fashionable trend: '*12 November 1854. At home. During the week helped preparing paper for hanging the rooms.*'

The middle-class fashion for adorning their rooms with papers emulating the rich flock materials which covered the walls in the homes of the wealthy, was part of the move away from the plain classic lines of the eighteenth century which was given incentive by the industrialisation which made wall hangings affordable, especially once the tax was lifted. At least two shops in Ipswich were advertising paper at 4d. or 6d. per piece, or roll, during the 1850s. Elizabeth does not tell us which rooms were being decorated on that occasion, but in the following year she was well into the fashion of her time: '*1855. Bought paper for Drawing room and on Thursday purchased carpets.*'

Elegant eighteenth-century houses had drawing-rooms, smaller ones had parlours and breakfast or morning-rooms. Jane Austen's Emma had

invited her protegée, Harriet Smith, to consider the inferiority of her
suitor's status by comparing the farmer's parlours with the drawing
room at Hartfield. No doubt, in his bachelor days, Herbert had entertained in a parlour. It was in her drawing-room that Elizabeth entertained her guests with music, dancing and cards, and it was for this
room that she purchased her statuette of Dorothea

> and an agate vase. . . . *9 January 1858*. Monday with Rea and children
> to the Crystal Palace. Bought a bronze statuette of the Gladiator . . .
> *17 January*. Rea wrote to me to purchase two small tables for her we
> looked at yesterday. Did so and bought a carved bracket for myself.

The bracket may have been to hold a statuette.

While the drawing-room was assuming more genteel associations, the
Cotton dining-room was used much more than just for meals: '*8 March,
1857*. Ordered Looking glass for dining room . . . *1 February
1858*. Bookshelves put up in the dining room. . . . *5 Dec. 1858*.
Bookcase shelves for sideboard came home.'

It was probably here that the children did their homework and the
family sat in the evenings when they were not entertaining.
Elizabeth's purchases reflect many of the middle-class fashions of the
period:

> *9 December 1855*. Friday with Herbert shopping. Purchased plate at
> Stammer's in the Strand. Dessert service of knives and forks . . . *17
> Aug. 1856*. Mr Allen called on Tuesday with a present from Mrs Allen
> of two embroidered mats . . . *20 Mar. 1859*. Bought a white china
> rose . . . *12 Feb. 1860*. Purchased a pair of carved oak brackets from Mr
> Austin . . . *21 Sept. 1860*. Mrs Allen sent me a present of some
> embroidery in wool for a cushion . . . *7 Oct. 1861*. Bought a very
> beautiful china teapot of the mistress of the hotel . . . *6 Feb. 1862*. A
> man came from Ipswich to regild the picture frames.

All these are luxury items intended to beautify the home. On a more
practical level we learn that in 1857 Elizabeth had a new stove put into
the kitchen. Did she and Mrs Marskall avidly read the advertisements in
the local newspapers which, complete with drawings, extolled the
virtues of the Paragon Prize Kitchen or the Patent American Kitchener
which would 'save half the fuel – cure smoky chimneys – require no
brickwork setting – fully equipped with cooking utensils – clean and
convenient – excellent ironing stoves – will roast, boil, bake, broil and
steam better than any other range – will burn any kind of fuel – yield a
plentiful supply of boiling water and cook for a large family at a cost for

fuel of 1/6 a week'? What more could any housewife ask for? In Elizabeth's case this was not sufficient, for less than ten years later she is again having a new stove installed.

By 1862 Elizabeth is endeavouring to modernise the bedrooms. Out go the heavy mahogany frames to be replaced with the very latest in brass bedsteads for the children, while for her and Herbert the following year there is to be the nineteenth-century counterpart of the modern en suite bathroom: '*17 November 1863*. Had dressing room made.' The later diary reveals that this onslaught on the bedrooms continued. In 1864 she notes that she has had alterations made to both the Blue and the Green bedrooms. Beyond mentioning the addition of a window in one of them, she does not elaborate, but it is possible that dressing rooms were being made for each of them. Some time later she records that she spent time 'arranging the children's rooms'.

While Elizabeth was concerning herself with renovations to the house, Herbert was doing the same with the farm buildings. From about the 1830s onwards, more and more landowners had been persuaded of the necessity of developing their farms into the efficient units needed to produce the food demanded by an increasing population and to reflect the changes in agricultural techniques. The experimental farming methods of the eighteenth-century landowners were beginning to percolate into smaller concerns. Along with the rationalisation of agriculture itself there was an increased interest in producing purpose-built model farms to replace those which had changed little from the medieval plan. Many books were written on the subject containing elaborate plans for farmhouses and outbuildings which bore little resemblance to the old traditional styles which had simply evolved. What happened on individual farms depended very largely on the owner and the resources of the tenant who held the lease. When James Hales-Tooke became the owner of Amor Hall he embarked on a remodernisation programme which involved the farm buildings being totally remodelled, thus leaving the house even more detached from them. How much the tenant was expected to pay towards all this we do not know, but an interesting comment comes in Elizabeth's later diary: '*21 March 1868*.   Mr Wallace spent the day here . . . he said he thought we were spending too much money in labour upon Mr Tooke's land.'

During the period of the renovations, Herbert's farm ledgers show accounts for building materials and the labour costs, but there is no indication of whether or not these were recovered from his landlord. Other information shows the rise in agricultural rents. When George Ranson took Poplar Farm, Sproughton, in 1844 it was on a twelve-year lease with an annual rent of £214. A later note of his shows both the hazards of farming and the rise in land prices:

6 October 1847. Sale at Sproughton Hall, Mr Woodgates. The first four horses averaged £42.10.6. per head. The cows sold dear, they are good stock and very nice ones; the highest with calf by her side made £21. Mr James Walker has hired the farm and at a very dear rent, I think. I know it is 298 acres at £490 or £500; it is not Tithe Free. It is a very uncertain farm, depends a good deal upon the seasons. Mr Woodgates has held it about five years and now obliged to make an assignment for the benefit of creditors.

Between 1858 and 1869 Herbert was paying in the region of £700 a year for his 400 acres. £250 was paid in mid-June with the larger amount in December following harvest and the year-end sales of stock. His bank balance fluctuates between £159–589 in 1858, £40–397 in 1864, and £831–1559 in 1867. In 1869 it fell to £300–400. His income was derived from regular sales of milk and butter, the raising of sheep, pigs and cattle and arable products. The farm ledgers also provide evidence that he fattened individual livestock for others in the neighbourhood.

It is not known if it was at the stage of remodelling the farm or later that the dairy ceased to be incorporated in the house. There are signs still present in the house of the original dairy with its louvred shutters to provide temperature control and the drainage channels for the washing of equipment. Wherever it was situated in Elizabeth's time, the dairy came under her jurisdiction and on more than one occasion was to afford her trouble: '*6 April 1856*. Mary Hubbard left our service and Emily Farthing came as Dairymaid.'

A division could exist between those who were employed in the dairy and those who were part of the actual domestic staff. The former obviously enjoyed a certain autonomy in their own little kingdom, while the latter would be bonded together in a form of kinship with the family. That disputes could arise and cause wide repercussions is shown in the following:

1 November 1859. Friday evening Mrs Marskall detected our Dairymaid, Mary Rumsey robbing in the house to send goods to her friends. Sent for the Police Constable stationed at Washbrook and after examination of the case dismissed both the girl and her father who was bailiff and considered confidential servant, from our employment. On Saturday Mrs Rumsey called with her daughter and tried to bully me into a withdrawal of the charge but the proofs were too clear to admit question.

This account leaves the reader free to imagine the scenes which occurred and ask questions like what was Mary stealing? Was it surplus butter and milk which she regarded as the perks of her job, or had Mrs Marskall caught her redhanded in the pantry helping herself to other 'goods'? Was this the first time it had happened, or was it culmination of other incidents of pilfering? On the face of it, it may seem harsh that her father also received instant dismissal. As bailiff, he held the superior position on the farm. As Elizabeth rightly states, his was one of trust and one that required the respect of those working under him. If his daughter was known to be stealing from her employers, how could they – and the rest of the workers – know that he too was not involved. The evidence must have been strong enough that Elizabeth felt she could not handle it internally and needed the assistance of the local policeman. Although Elizabeth does not state that Herbert was present during the police examination, he surely must have been for something as import-ant as this. I see the case being examined, not in the kitchen, but in the farm office where formality could be maintained and Herbert would have made the decision to dismiss Rumsey who had been called in to hear the charges against his daughter. But there is no doubt that Elizabeth considered herself an equal partner here for she uses the term 'our employment'.

We can picture too the scene in the Rumsey household later that Friday night when father and daughter related events to Mrs Rumsey. The devastating effect on the family of the instant loss of two vital incomes and the tied cottage in which they lived, plus the prospect of court proceedings and the gossip from their neighbours must have been hard for her to bear. No wonder then, that after mulling it over all night, Mrs Rumsey marched her daughter up to Amor Hall to plead with Elizabeth. Had she adopted the right tactics she might have been more successful, but instead of being submissive and attempting to explain extenuating circumstances, she was belligerent. Elizabeth was not the woman to bully; attempts at coercion resulted in an even stronger determination of the rights of the case. Mrs Rumsey, probably as her husband had done, said too much. As far as Elizabeth was concerned the matter was now concluded. But Mrs Rumsey, equally determined, was not prepared to let it rest. She sought a higher authority for assistance.

6 *November 1859*. Wednesday. A letter from Mr de Grey to say the Rumseys had made an accusation to him against the honesty of others in our service. Sent for Mrs Rumsey and her daughter to meet at our house the persons accused – Mrs Marskall, Mrs Parker and Susan Steward our Nurserymaid. The charges made were proved to be false and the Rumseys confessed their accusations were false.

The Rumseys had approached de Grey in his dual capacity as pastoral adviser and local magistrate. Perhaps they genuinely believed that he would be able to succeed where they had failed in getting Elizabeth to drop the charges, but it would appear that in going to him they compounded their crimes by adding perjury and slander. As it happened they caught Elizabeth at a bad time for she had received another letter that day, 'of gross insult from James Nelson'. With that on her mind too, she was in no mood to bear gently with the Rumseys. Besides which, she now had to find a replacement dairymaid. 'Saturday . . . In the evening Jane Warner came as Dairy Maid.'

DOMESTIC STAFF

During his bachelorhood, Herbert had had a housekeeper to attend to the domestic arrangements and she was probably still there when he brought his new wife to Amor Hall in 1843. It is likely that changes took place once the young family started arriving and Elizabeth felt she required someone more suitable to the changing needs of the household. The widowed Mrs Marskall – another Elizabeth – was introduced to the domestic scene some time before 1851. In the census of that year her age is given as thirty-four, but we cannot be certain this is correct for by the 1861 census she has only attained forty! We know little about her beyond the fact that she was born in Hadleigh in Suffolk and had married into a family well rooted in that locality. We know too, that she had at least one child, a daughter, who occasionally came to spend the day with her mother.

By 1854, when we are first introduced to her, Mrs Marskall is very much a trusted and valued member of the household. Her role as housekeeper was varied: she appears to have been responsible for the cooking, assisted by the kitchen-maid, she supervised the domestic staff, acted as occasional mother-substitute to the children and was left totally in charge of the household during the absence of Elizabeth and Herbert. In the same way that her duties were unspecified, so too, were hours of work. She must have had some regular time off during the week, but Elizabeth only records that she was actually away from the house for any length of time when she 'went home' three times a year, usually from Monday to Thursday, although there is one reference to her taking a long weekend from Friday to Monday. Her break normally came immediately after the Cottons had returned from one of their holidays.

It is not possible to gauge from the diary what type of relationship existed between mistress and housekeeper. Based on generalities, we can assume that Mrs Marskall would have been classed as 'a superior type of servant'. She may have been the daughter of a small tradesman with a sufficient education to be able to deal with household management, or it is possible that she came from a background similar to Elizabeth's own and had she not been widowed early might have found herself in a like position. Since she and Elizabeth worked closely together, there must have been some rapport between them for several years at least. The children spent much time with her and when Elizabeth was unable to escort them, Mrs Marskall was her substitute:

> *20 August 1854.* Thursday. Sent children with Mrs Marskall to see Alice . . . *10 December.* Mrs Marskall took the children to the Wild Beasts Show on Monday afterwards went with Alice to school . . . *26 October 1856.* Mrs Marskall went to Ipswich for the children. . . . . *4 September 1859.* Saturday. Sent Mrs Marskall with Eva to Ipswich to meet the boys and go with them to a Panorama.

We remember too, that when baby Ethel was taken ill it was to Mrs Marskall that the nurserymaid first reported, leaving her to break the news to the parents.

At the beginning of 1861 it seems Mrs Marskall had problems of her own. On the fourth of February she went home for her customary break, but for some unexplained reason she had gone home again at the end of the month. On the 27th Evelyn fell into the pond. Elizabeth in recounting the episode for the diary remarked: 'Mrs Marskall had again gone home. She is of very little use to me.' This comment marks a deterioration in relationship with the housekeeper, for the next time Elizabeth mentions her it is again in a derogatory fashion. In October of that year, after Elizabeth had questioned Eva about her running away from school she wrote: 'We think the poor child has had bad advice from Mrs Marskall our housekeeper.'

This hints at the bond which existed between Mrs Marskall and the children. Eva may have misinterpreted what Mrs Marskall had said, but no doubt the housekeeper was reprimanded for her interference. Possibly Elizabeth now resented Mrs Marskall's influence upon the children, and that familiarity was beginning to turn stale. Alternatively, Mrs Marskall's own home situation may have been worrying her, but whatever the cause, matters came to a head in February of the following year. Elizabeth, who had been ill on and off throughout the month, was concerned about Eva's school problems too, when: '*22 February 1862.* Saturday. Mrs Marskall gave me notice she wished to leave.' So now, having just undertaken a series of visits to find a suitable school for Eva, Elizabeth had the task of seeking a replacement for Mrs Marskall. The housekeeper stayed on until 5 April, either working out a statutory period of notice – though six weeks seems an odd period – or simply waiting until Elizabeth was suited. Her going was recorded with the simple words 'Mrs Marskall left today', no hint of any sad farewells or tributes for all she had done for the family. However, her departure marks a change in domestic arrangements, for thereafter no one was to occupy the position in the way she had done.

Elizabeth would have made use of one of the several domestic agencies in Ipswich to find her new member of staff. Having specified her requirements the agency would arrange the interviews for her: '25 *March 1862*. Tuesday. Dined with Mrs Foster. Saw some persons who wished to take housekeeper's place.' From this set of interviews, Elizabeth selected a likely candidate, one about whom she wished to know more. '27 *March 1862*. Thursday. With Herbert to Tattingstone to hear character of Miss Cooper from Mrs E Clarke.'

The Clarkes held the principal farm in that village and would have been known to Herbert. Presumably Mrs Clarke gave Miss Cooper a glowing reference, for she was offered the position at Washbrook. Did Mrs Clarke reveal, however, that Miss Cooper was in fact a relation of her husband and that 'the character' she gave might have been somewhat biased? Miss Cooper duly took up her duties on 7 March and that is the last we hear of her. Elizabeth does not mention she had dispensed with her services, but an entry that has never before appeared in the diary now occurs within three weeks of Miss Cooper's appointment: '26 *March 1862*. In the kitchen.'

References to being in the kitchen continue throughout May. Between 5 and 13 May there are no entries of any kind beyond the day being written, suggesting that Elizabeth has no time for any other activity. Either Miss Cooper was given instant dismissal or her cooking was of such a poor standard that Elizabeth had to supervise her. It is hardly necessary to point out that middle-class 'lady' though she might be, Elizabeth was perfectly able to turn her hand to running the kitchen. She may have thought her troubles were at an end when she hired Miss Beard as housekeeper at the end of May. This lady should have been admirably suited to the post: she was the sister of another local farmer and at the time in her fifties. She lasted a mite longer than Miss Cooper, but: '25 *July 1862*. Gave Miss Beard notice to leave.'

When her month's notice expired, Elizabeth had changed her requirements: 'Miss Beard left. Mrs Harwood came as cook.'

Quite apart from the everyday needs of the household, a good cook was essential as the Cottons entertained frequently and often on an impromptu basis. Without doubt, the cook or housekeeper in question would have needed to be of an equable temperament and with the ingenuity to cope with the demands made upon her. Mrs Harwood appears to have been a good choice and remained at Amor Hall until August 1865. During her three years the domestic arrangements ran smoothly with only the odd upset: '9 *March 1863*. Monday. Gave the kitchen-maid notice to leave, but she begged me to let her stay.'

Although unnoted, Mrs Harwood and Elizabeth parted company and Elizabeth went again on 14 August 1865 'To Ipswich to engage a person as cook . . . *16 August*. To Ipswich to see servants . . . *17 August*. To Ipswich to see servants . . . *19 August*. To Ipswich. Engaged Sarah Dent as cook.' Mrs Harwood, meanwhile, was seeking a new post for herself: '*4th October 1865*. Mrs Lacon called for character of Mrs Harwood.'

This practice of calling upon a former employer to gain a character reference for a prospective servant must have been interesting for the ladies concerned. Sometimes they would be approaching those already known to them as Elizabeth did when in 1854 she called upon Mrs Waspe at Belstead Hall in the neighbouring village. On other occasions it would be to strangers: '*26 February 1868*. With Bertie and Alice to Harkstead. Called upon Mrs Rudson to enquire about a servant.' Quite apart from satisfying the natural curiosity about the interior of other people's houses, it gave the prospective employer an opportunity to see what type of establishment the servant had been used to. Although the ladies' interview was probably conducted with a degree of formality, we may assume that on occasions it allowed for a certain amount of social chit-chat. However, if Mrs Rudson was responsible for giving H.Amos a good character, then her standards were obviously not those of Elizabeth: '*29 February 1868* Hired H.Amos as cook at £14 a year.' . . . '*5 March*. H.Amos came as cook.' . . . '*7 March*. Sent cook away for intoxication.' This is the only time Elizabeth ever mentions how much she paid any of her servants. It is difficult, without going into statistics to say whether or not £14 was a reasonable wage, though two examples show that it was well under what could have been expected five years earlier. The *Ipswich Journal* for 1863 gives the following:

> Good Plain Cook to act as Housekeeper in Clergyman's family. Five children and six servants. Assistance given to kitchen. Wages £20 with Tea, sugar and washing.

Alternatively, for those wishing to make their fortune, there were opportunities to be had further afield:

> To Good Domestic Servants and Married Agricultural Labourers. Free passages to Australian Colonies; Cooks and Laundresses £30–£35; Housemaid £25–30; General Servants £25–30; Nursemaids £20–25. Skilled and tried servants much higher.

Perhaps low pay was one of the reasons why Elizabeth suffered so many staff changes, but certainly after the departure of Mrs Marskall, the domestic tenor of the house was never entirely satisfactory.

26 February 1866. Our parlourmaid and housemaid gave notice to leave. . . . *8 March*. Several servants called about our vacant place . . . *20 March*. Engaged Mary Taylor as parlourmaid. . . . *28 March*. Letter from a servant I expected here today, to say she had taken a better situation. Went to Register Office. . . . *9 April*. Alice had some trouble with two of the servants quarrelling. Gave them notice to leave. . . . *11 April*. Mrs Cattermole came to speak about her daughter . . . *17 April*. Engaged two servants to take the places of kitchenmaid and housemaid. . . . *10 October 1867*. Hired Ellen Taylor as housemaid. . . . *26 June 1868*. Sent Elizabeth Woods the housemaid away for dishonesty. Her mother came to speak to me . . . *3 August*. Mary Giles gave notice to leave. . . . *25 June 1869*. Jemima Barnes came as Parlourmaid . . . *18 October*. Gave Parlourmaid notice.

Several of the girls involved would have been quite young, and most of them came from local families, which explains why on some occasions the mothers came to talk about Elizabeth's decision to sack their daughters. It is not clear if Mrs Cattermole came to speak about her daughter because she was one of the quarrelsome ones who had been dismissed or if she had heard that there was a likely vacancy and she was seeking the post for the girl. This lady occupied a position in the village of Washbrook in her own right as a dressmaker and by virtue of her husband's role as a policeman.

Of all the servants at Amor Hall, the ones who were most highly thought of and the most loyal to the family, apart from Mrs Marskall, were the nursery staff. In 1855 Jane Farrer was the nursemaid and it was she who accompanied the family to Felixstowe following the death of the baby. She left in June, 1856 and was replaced by Jane Steward. The reason for the first Jane's departure may well be explained by a later reference which shows Elizabeth's concern for the girl: '*18 January 1857*. Thursday called upon Mrs Allen and to see Jane Farrer who is very ill at her Aunt's house at Hintlesham'. The second Jane may not have been very strong either for in the October following her appointment, Elizabeth notes: 'Sent our Nurse Jane home to rest for a time as she is not well.'

By 1861, Blanche was the only child at home all day, and the nursemaid of the time, according to the census, was an eighteen-year-old called Maria Bishop. As the dairymaid was listed as an Eliza Bishop, we can assume that one sister secured a position for the other. As neither rates a mention in the diary we must suppose they were satisfactory although not particularly highly regarded. On the other hand, one feels there was genuinely pleasure all round when on '*23 September 1863*. Wednesday. Children came home to dinner. Our old nurse Jane Osborn called.' This was probably one of the two Janes, now a married woman.

The fact that she felt free to call upon the family suggests a mutual regard and affection.

One of the few disappointing aspects of the diaries is Elizabeth's failure to mention food. Doubtless, alongside her carefully kept account books which she mentions occasionally, she and the cook kept a record of what food was generally purchased and consumed and what menus were prepared, especially those for her dinner parties. This information is not available, beyond a list of the quantities of meat purchased during the first few months of 1863 which appears in one of Herbert's ledgers. For the month of February there were two necks of veal, each about 5lb. in weight, a breast of veal, boiling beef and suet, 32lb. of beef for roasting and a forequarter of lamb. However, for those who, like myself, gain a vicarious pleasure from reading of the quantities of food consumed in Parson Woodforde's household during the eighteenth century, this is a decided disadvantage in forming a rounded picture of what life was like. So, although Elizabeth frequently mentions taking meals, we are rarely ever told of what these consisted. The only times she does mention the constituents of a meal is when on a holiday tour she is presented with something strange to her or that is not up to standard. For example, while in the Lake District: '25 May 1857. Had carp and oatmeal bread for dinner', and after visiting Flamborough Head: '4 June 1857. Dined at the Star Inn, a sort of house call for the boatmen. The landlady tipsy, but the little girl waiting upon us clean and neat. The bread and meat good, the pastry suspicious looking.' In Scotland in June 1860 'Lunched at a small inn where they could give us nothing but oatcake, milk and whiskey'.

Occasionally Elizabeth mentions food which has been sent as a present. Every year without fail, her sister Anne in London sent the children a 'Twelfth Cake' for 6 January. This apparently rich fruit cake seems to have been replaced by the Christmas cake which we now regard as traditional, with similarities to the Christmas puddings of the past, in as far as the Twelfth Cake contained little silver trinkets with symbolic significance, like a ring for impending marriage. I have been unable to discover if the Twelfth cake tradition was one in general practice which died out when the Christmas festivities increased later in the century, or if this was something the Haxell family maintained long after its general demise. Something similar exists in Ireland with a token-filled cake forming part of the Hallowe'en celebrations.

Having made a passing reference to Christmas, perhaps here is a suitable place to mention what we are told of the festivities in the Cotton household during the 1850s and 60s. It is refreshing to know that preparations for Christmas did not start so early in past years, neither did the festivities themselves linger on for days and even weeks. Unlike the exciting picture of Christmas at Dingley Dell portrayed by Dickens, it would appear that Christmas Day at Amor Hall was spent as a quiet family day. However, Elizabeth, never lagging behind the fashion, announces that they have adopted one of the Prince Consort's innovations:

24 December 1854. Sunday. At home. Monday Christmas Day. Had a Christmas Tree for the children.

10 December 1855. [In London] Monday shopping and to Bazaar for presents for children . . . Christmas Day. Mr Leath stayed. Mr Martin spent the evening here.

20 December 1857. Tuesday. To Ipswich. Bought Christmas Tree. Mr Leath came on Thursday. Christmas Day Friday. Mr Martin spent the evening here. Saturday. My birthday. The children had the Christmas Tree in the evening.

By 1859, the festivities were starting to be increased, and on Christmas Eve:

The two eldest daughters and son of Mrs Marshall spent the afternoon and evening with us and Mr Leath came. A romp with the children who had crackers, a snapdragon etc. and music.

That year too, Alice's friend Emily Betts spent the holiday at Amor Hall, and it was on this occasion that we have an indication of the growing middle-class obsession with the nineteenth-century equivalent of television. '26 December 1859. Monday. My birthday. Gave the children presents. Edward sent some stereoscopic slides as a present.'

Eighteen-sixty was an interesting year in that Christmas Day fell on a Tuesday. This caused some official concern, leading the town council of Ipswich to issue a decree to the effect that in view of the holiday, the traditional Tuesday market would be held instead on Wednesday. Elizabeth did not even record the 25th as being Christmas Day. She merely wrote against the date, 'At home with children.' There were two absentees that year: Alice, who was spending her first Christmas away from home, and Mr Leath, who had been present every year since the diary began and possibly for long before. On 11 September Elizabeth wrote, 'Heard bad news of Mr Leath.' No further comment is made about him. We can only assume that he had died, though there is no record of this having taken place in Ipswich. Since he had been very much part of the family Christmas, his absence, like Alice's would have been keenly felt. There is no mention either of Elizabeth's birthday that year.

During the 1860s we learn that it has become the fashion to decorate the house with holly and evergreens, though these are not put up until a day or two before Christmas Day. If Elizabeth does not provide us with pictures of blazing plum puddings and roasted geese and turkeys, she does tell us of two items which graced her table around Christmas time: '*16 December 1861*. Rea sent us a present of a Stilton cheese . . . *24 December*. A present from Arthur of a barrel of oysters.' Both these commodities were regular gifts sent down from London. In return Elizabeth and Herbert sent the relations who lived in the city gifts of game during the season – 'Herbert shot five brace of game before breakfast. Sent three brace to Uncle John.'

The family itself would have been self-sufficient for beef, mutton and pork – 'Sent hams to Kate and Mary' – as well as rabbits and game. They would have had a plentiful supply of dairy products, their own flour for bread and a kitchen garden to provide all their vegetables, and there was a poultry flock, which was increased by a novel gift: '*22 February 1857*. Mrs Allen sent me a pair of guinea fowls.'

Furthermore, Elizabeth utilised the free gifts supplied by nature, regularly organising excursions with the children to gather mushrooms from the farm fields. These were no doubt used not just at the time, but preserved in various forms as soups, ketchups and pickles. Similarly, she gave the boys and their friends the task of 'walnut tree brushing' to harvest the crop from the trees, one of which still stands today in the garden. It is characteristic of Elizabeth that she should turn a chore into a game, and we may be sure that the teenage boys gained great satisfaction whacking the nuts from the branches. Again, those walnuts which were not kept for later eating would be preserved and join all the other jars and pots containing jams, fruit and vegetables which were stored away in the large pantries. '*3 March 1869*. In kitchen looking to preserved meats etc.'

Although Elizabeth made many shopping trips she rarely mentions the mundane purchase of food except in relation to those items which were either gifts for invalids or luxury items for the family: '*9 March 1858*. Tuesday called to see Miss Leath who is very ill. Ordered jelly and fish in the town for her.' Presumably the jelly was of the calves' foot variety which was considered so beneficial to invalids. It was, however, too late for Miss Leath who died two days later.

26 September 1865. With Alice called upon Mrs Burrell. Took her some grapes. . . . *10 February 1868*. Called upon Miss Harmer who is very ill. Took her some champaigne.

Whether she actually purchased the champagne or took it from the large cellar at Amor Hall, where traces of the old wine storage racks still remain, we do not know. Elizabeth certainly was not a supporter of the temperance movement, for she herself drank moderately: '*19 Nov. 1868. Alice's birthday. Herbert and I drank her health.*' There was an occasion too, when she sent a cheque to her brother-in-law to pay for the wine he had sent. She also believed in the efficacy of wine as a restorative:

> *26 July 1869.* With Alice and Allan to see Stephen Sparks who has gone home from working in the fields ill. *27 July.* Evening called upon Stephen Sparks and took him some wine etc.

However, she did not approve of drunkenness:

> *12 October 1867.* Returning home saw Mr G.Allen's labourers in great danger from being intoxicated. Sent a policeman home in charge of them.

One cannot help admiring yet again the strength of character Elizabeth shows; her innate ability to take command of a situation and deal with it summarily. The woman who could 'send a policeman home' with inebriated labourers was the same woman who wrote letters to people in high places and stood up for herself in arguments. But she was also a woman who knew when and how to use her feminine charm to effect, as she did when she returned from France after having settled Bertie at the French college:

> *20 April 1864.* The Custom House Officers very civil and allowed our luggage to pass without examination. I said we had Bon Bons etc and they replied they would not disappoint my children by stopping their presents. Some gentlemen near us very indignant because the goods they were endeavouring to hide were seized.

CLOTHING

Apart from food shopping, and making purchases for the home either of the utilitarian variety such as carpets and wallpaper, or to adorn the rooms like vases and statues, Elizabeth gives the occasional glimpses of clothes-buying. The evidence does not suggest that she was particularly clothes-conscious; we have no elaborate detail of the gowns she wore, though we do know that she was wearing the crinoline, a fashion which held many hazards. In the early 1860s the *Ipswich Journal* reported the statistics that in London in the course of three years, 2500 women had suffered serious, even fatal accidents through these dresses catching fire. Equally horrifying was this report, dated 1863, with the headline 'Serious Accident from a Crinoline':

> At an archery meeting near Hitchin, Mrs Chesshyre, wife of an Essex clergyman, dressed in the prevailing style of fashion, suddenly sat down on the grass and in so doing snapped one of the steel hoops which supported her dress. Unfortunately, the sharp end penetrated her body and inflicted a severe internal wound. Medical assistance was fortunately at hand but the haemorrhage was stopped with great difficulty.

Elizabeth herself ran into problems by wearing the fashion while on holiday in Scotland: '*11 June 1860*. Posted to Ballachulish. The mistress of the Inn at Conset Ferry mended my dress, and lectured me upon the impropriety of wearing a crinoline.' It is unclear if it was the fashion itself to which the Scotswoman objected or if she regarded the billowing dress as unsuitable wear for the type of holiday tour Elizabeth was enjoying. If it was the latter she was proved correct the following day: 'When getting into the boat the wind caught my dress and I should have been thrown into the water, had not a man caught hold of me.'

From the few random items she gives us, we can sketch in a little about the materials used in clothes, the increase in ready-made garments and some fashion trends. The more graphic details occur in the later diary when her daughters are becoming fashion-conscious:

> *1 June 1858*. Thursday. Posted to Lands End . . . while here caught in a storm. I went into a hut on the heath to dry my dress by the peat fire and the material being mixed with worsted shrank most absurdly. When we returned to Penzance, our landlady, after telling me no ready made dresses could be had at Penzance, and no dressmaker would work during Fair time, managed to have my dress again made wearable.

The practice of having clothes tailored was adhered to for the boys. Perhaps this was in the long run an economic move; one can almost hear Elizabeth instructing the tailor to leave hems and seams sufficient to allow for growth:

> *28 October 1855*. Friday. With children to Ipswich. Ordered great coat for Bertie . . . *1857*: Had the boys measured for clothes . . . *1859*: Took Allan to be measured for clothes . . . *1863*: Ordered a suit for Bertie.

Of Herbert's clothes we hear nothing beyond: '*3 January 1867*. Mr Hales Tooke sent Herbert a German wool waistcoat', which refers not so much to the origin of the material as to the method of embroidery employed upon it. However, we may assume that Herbert, like the rest of the family, had new clothing at those unexpected moments when the family suffered a bereavement.

3 September 1854. Wednesday to Ipswich with Herbert. Purchased mourning . . . *1867:* Letter to say Uncle George died yesterday. To Ipswich with Herbert and children to order mourning . . . *1868:* Letter from Anne to say my poor Uncle John died at 6 o'clock yesterday morning. To Ipswich to purchase mourning.

Going into mourning clothes for a member of the family was one thing, but to the modern reader it is hard to understand the motive which impelled such wear for a public figure, yet immediately following the news of the death of the Prince Consort: '*17 December 1861.* Tuesday to Ipswich. Purchased mourning. The boys with me.' It is possible that for Elizabeth this was merely the purchase of token mourning in the form of black ribbons or veiling, but it may have entailed more for the boys who were members of a school which had had close association with Prince Albert.

There were, of course, happier occasions to buy clothes for. In the course of the later diary we accompany Elizabeth to London to attend the weddings of her nieces: '*15 September 1864.* To Ipswich with Alice. Shopping. Ordered things for Emily Page's wedding.' Elizabeth does not tell us what the 'things' were, though she is slightly more expansive when it comes to Fanny's wedding, at which Alice and Evelyn were to be bridesmaids. The invitation had come six weeks before the actual ceremony, giving ample time for the girls' dresses to be made. We are told nothing of the garments, but we do get a hint of pre-wedding preparations: '*25 March 1867.* Wednesday to London with Alice, Bertie and Evelyn. Evening to shops and arranged with Hairdresser.' This short entry is a reminder of the very long working day which was the norm in mid-Victorian times.

There is only one other reference to hairdressing and that is in relation to the younger girls. In May 1866: 'Called for Eva and Blanche [from school]. Had their hair cut and dresses fitted.' We know too that they had other items bought for them which may reflect what the smart young mid-Victorian girl was wearing: '*7 December 1864.* Called for girls and bought velvet caps for them . . . *1865:* Bought plaid dresses for little girls.'

But it is Alice's wardrobe that is shown in some detail:

24 November 1858. Monday afternoon called at Miss Shalders for Alice and bought her a hat . . . *25 December 1859.* . . . Thursday to Ipswich with Alice. Purchased a cloak for her . . . *13 May 1860.* To Ipswich. Alice with me. Purchased a cloak for her . . . *3 December 1863.* Ordered riding dress for Alice . . . *14 June 1864.* Margot made Alice a bonnet . . . *7 October 1864.* To Ipswich with Alice. Bought her a blue silk dress . . . *10 October 1864.* Bought Alice a jacket . . . *28 April 1866.* Alice was fitted for a new Riding Habit.

It is possible that Alice's needs were included when in May 1867 Elizabeth went to 'Ipswich with Alice. Purchased black satin dress and print dresses.'

We see that Elizabeth's own wardrobe is changing with the introduction of ready-to-wear silks and satins as well as the cheaper print ones. The black satin was probably for evening wear as would have been the brown silk which she bought later. Elizabeth has the infuriating habit of giving us just a hint of current fashion: '*26 December 1861* Mr & Mrs H. Miller called during our absence and left a lace collar as a present for me. . . . *27 December.* Called at Mr Miller's [a draper] and purchased of him sleeves to match the collar given to me yesterday.'

The fashion for detachable collars and cuffs is one that has waxed and waned during the present century, but we have not re-introduced that of oversleeves. Elizabeth was quite accustomed to wearing these, and once beguiled a period of enforced waiting by making herself a pair: '*11 June 1860.* Crossed Loch Creran at Sheen Ferry. Waited in carriage for return of ferry boat and made myself a pair of sleeves of some warm plaid I had purchased at Oban.' Obviously, the middle-class Victorian lady who travelled without a lady's maid to care for such things made sure that her sewing equipment accompanied her.

If Elizabeth was not particularly interested in clothes she certainly did like jewellery, and again we learn a little of the current fashions:

2 July 1854. Friday. Herbert bought me a gold and coral brooch . . . *1855.* Bought myself a Diamond Cross at Cass's in Regent Street . . . *1856:* Purchased a garnet cross for Alice . . . *1857:* Rea sent Alice a very handsome brooch which she has brought home for her from Geneva . . . *1858:* To Barnstaple by rail. On our journey found a cross, apparently of rubies dropped by some ladies who got out upon the road. Gave it to the station master.' [Dare we think that conscience wrestled with temptation here?] . . . *1859:* Took a lock of Blanche's hair to Mr Cole to be made into a ring . . . *1859:* With Herbert to a Musical Entertainment at the Corn Exchange. Lost a hair bracelet in the confusion of leaving . . . *1860:* Rea gave Alice a locket set with pearls . . . *1864:* Gave Margot a ring with a diamond cross upon it . . . Bought a gold chain . . . Bought a gold cross . . . Sent Margaret a locket with a piece of Blanche's hair and my own . . . [At Emily Page's

wedding] Mr Welsh gave Emily and Fanny each a diamond ring . . .
1865: bought a watch and chain for Alice . . . *1867*. Herbert bought a
coral bracelet for me at Lamberts . . . *1868*: Sent Alice a gold neck
chain.

Herbert seems to have been especially partial to coral since both the
items he bought for Elizabeth contained it. Was Elizabeth indulging in a
personal longing when she purchased the diamond cross in London? As
this happened in 1855, I conclude that she had received her share of her
father's estate and felt justified in spending at least some of it upon
herself. However, she was also generous, probably using her own
reserves to buy the ring set with diamonds for her younger sister,
Margaret. This item, plus the locket which contained locks of hair, were
very special parting gifts for Margaret who was leaving to go to Australia. Blanche's hair was included in preference to any of the other
children's because Margaret was the child's godmother. This latter gift
must have had especial poignancy for both sisters. They had always
been close despite the age gap and Elizabeth must have felt she was
sending a tiny part of herself to accompany her sister into her new life,
probably realising too that she was unlikely to see her again for many
years, if ever.

IN THE GARDEN

Elizabeth may have been on only the fringe of fashion in clothes, but
where gardening was concerned, she was very much a part of the
current trends. The diaries abound with references to being in the
garden, making visits to nurserymen and bedding out the plants she has
purchased. She is both knowledgeable and experimental in what she
does, and there is every reason to believe that she did most of the work
herself, employing the services of a man to do the heavy digging and to
look after the lawns, or greens as she calls them, for by this time
Ransome's had produced its popular grass-mowing machines. But it
was in her passion for ferns that Elizabeth showed she was united with
thousands of other middle-class women up and down the country.
    David Elliston Allen, in his most readable *The Victorian Fern Craze*,
writes 'At the height of the fern craze in the middle fifties, we have an
excellent example of a society in the grip of a powerful emotion, "a
collective projection" rooted in some deeply buried psychological layer.'
Chauvinistically, the author Charles Kingsley commented on the 'prevailing Pteridomania' that had descended on womenfolk all over Britain.
'The abomination of Fancywork – that standing cloak for dreamy idle-
ness – has all but vanished since the Lady-ferns and Venus's Hair

appeared.' He had cause to know better than most the powerful emotion evoked by fern mania, for his daughter Charlotte's *Ferny Coombes: A Ramble after Ferns in the Glens and Valleys of Devonshire*, was published in 1856.

Ferns, which grow wild throughout the British Isles, had failed to provoke any special attention in the past. They were brought into fashion by a combination of events. In the 1790s, Captain Bligh returned from his second voyage to the West Indies with thirty-seven species of fern still surviving from their voyage, and John Lindsay, a surgeon in Jamaica, reported his success in raising ferns from spores. Although there was a limited botanical interest, it took industrialisation to give the impetus needed to make fern-growing popular. The introduction of gas into towns for shop and street lighting and into some homes led to problems of pollution with which we have become all too familiar. Indoor plants which had flourished in drawing rooms and conservatories tended to suffer. However, the invention of the Ward case, a glass tank or portable conservatory in which plants could flourish without supplies of fresh air or water was particularly suited to ferns. Unfortunately, the very high tax on glass at the time meant that only the wealthy could enjoy the cases which allowed 'a study peculiarly suited to ladies . . . the subjects so bright and clean, so ornamental to the boudoir' (D.Elliston Allen). However, with the development of greatly improved sheet glass which culminated in the glories of the Crystal Palace, and the early repeal of the tax, Ward cases and conservatories became well within the reach of the middle classes, and it was not long before, as Elliston Allen quotes from E.Newman's *History of British Ferns*, 'The cultivation of Ferns is becoming a fashionable pursuit . . . almost everyone possessing good taste has made, more or less successfully, an attempt to rear this tribe of plants'.

Elliston Allen also concludes that 'ferns were uncannily in time with the spirit of the age. They matched the new mood of sombreness – the craze opened as men's clothes quite suddenly, turned black'. In addition there was a growing interest in the different varieties for their intricate artistic value, and fern tracery began to appear in pictures, on decorative glass, curtain materials and wallpapers as well as on buildings. There are still small terrace houses in Ipswich built in the 1850s and 60s which carry intricate fern tracery on the stonework above the front door. It may be that Elizabeth was caught up as much in the artistic appreciation of ferns as she was in their actual cultivation, for her pocket sketch-book contains several examples which she had observed. In the same way that the present gardening enthusiast has a wealth of expertise to draw upon so too had the mid-nineteenth-century addict. Thomas Moore's *A Handbook of British Ferns* had appeared in 1848, but Elizabeth may already have been familiar with most of its contents since the work had been previously serialised in the *Gardener's and Farmer's Journal*. She may even have possessed the miniature pocket-size volume, described by the *Phytologist* as 'small enough to be carried in a lady's reticule' and was armed with this when in 1857 she visited the Lake District, where for the first time she mentions gathering ferns. Moore's second book came complete with colour plates and a manual for identification and specific locations, as did many others on the subject. The scramble among ladies, and gentlemen too, to secure the rare and the unusual was on, and the bemused labouring classes were quick to latch on to this eccentricity. By 1849, the guides at the summit of Snowdon were happily touting fern roots at 6d. a time, while the rural poor scoured their neighbourhoods to produce the 'weeds' for which good money would be paid. In less than twenty years the native ferns had become scarce since great quantities were taken annually for sale in the London markets causing Miss Nona Bellairs, a collector, to write, 'The poor Ferns, like the wolves in olden times, have a price set upon their heads . . . We must have 'Fern Laws' and preserve them like game.' (*Hardy Ferns: How I Collected and Cultivated Them*).

The excitement generated by fern collecting is revealed in the account the young Norfolk woman, Ann Gurdon, gives of part of her holiday tour in 1855. Like Elizabeth later, she found the Lake District the ideal place for finding specimens: 'Walked about a little, picking up a few roots of fern before we came in. NB found a new fern which was a great thing. We took it up by the roots, if we can only keep it alive till we get home.'

Elizabeth seems to have been bitten by the craze following the holiday in 1857. Thereafter we read regular accounts of the forays she made locally to increase her collection: '24 July 1859. Tuesday. Collecting Ferns with children. Wednesday in the garden. Thursday Fern collecting with Mrs Allen.' '30 April 1860. Began making Fernery in the garden and worked at planting and arranging it all the week.'

In making her fernery, Elizabeth pre-empted by nine years *The Fern Garden*, a book so popular that it went into eight editions within a decade. The author, Shirley Hibbard, had strong views on those who made fern gardens. Would Elizabeth have been pleased to know that she ranked amongst those who were of 'a pure and simple taste which finds pleasure in the culture of plants which have no gaudy blossoms to attract vulgar attention . . . no claim beyond chaste simple outlines, rare shades of green and brown . . . growth neither noticed nor cared for by minds unschooled to simple elegance and exquisite delicacy of form'? But long before these pronouncements, Elizabeth and her friends were all indulging in pteridomania:

6 September 1860. Mrs W.Turner and Mrs H.Miller spent the day here. Walked and collected Ferns . . . In the morning with children collecting Ferns . . . Walked with Evelyn on Hintlesham road. Collected Ferns. *12 April 1861*. The boys spent the day in Bentley Wood and brought home some Ferns.

By 1862 Elizabeth had become an expert and learnt too, some of the dangers involved in the pursuit of the hobby:

12 September. Friday. To Chattisham with children collecting Ferns. Found *Adiantum Nigrum* and *Trichomanes*. *4 March 1863*. Afternoon ferning. Collected a large quantity . . . *8 May*. Boys had a half holiday. Went with them, Alice and Blanche into wood after Ferns. Evelyn came to meet us in the chaise. Had taken rather a severe fall from a bank.

The creation of her fern garden was only a minor part of Elizabeth's plans for a garden to reflect her taste. Like thousands of modern gardeners, one of her favourite pastimes was to drive with Herbert and the children round the grounds of the local gentry where she made careful note of what she liked and thought would look well at Amor Hall. The garden still bears traces of Elizabeth's handiwork and it is believed that the giant sequoia which stands proudly in the front of the house may well have been planted in 1850s. Can we picture Elizabeth standing in the nursery gardens selecting the strong young specimen just imported from America? The magnificent cedars of Lebanon also appealed to her greatly, judging by the number of times she drew these in her sketchbooks.

On those days she was not engaged elsewhere, the words 'in the garden' appear with regularity. Occasionally she tells us the specific work she is doing or what flowers she is planting:

1854: Thursday a drive with Herbert to Bramford . . . Purchased some flowers and planted them out next day . . . *1855*: Worked a great deal in the garden this week. . . . *1856*: Wednesday I went to Mr Rea at Ipswich for some flowers and planted them out when I returned home . . . *1857*: Thursday planted seeds in the garden . . . Ordered Pinks at Mr Rea's . . . *1858*: Thursday Planted out shrubs . . . To Rea the gardeners for flowers . . . *1858*: Planted out flowers . . . Took up tender plants in the garden this week.

And so it continues. In between all her gardening activity she had even more chance to review the results of others – and pick up tips and ideas – at the many horticultural shows she attended with Herbert. When she needed to know more about a subject, she went off to find out how others did it: '29 *August 1859*. Wednesday . . . called with Herbert upon Mr & Mrs George Ranson, to see their manner of preserving plants during the winter.' She must have been impressed by what she saw for she wasted no time in joining this fashion: 'Monday In the garden. A Pit for Preserving Flowers began to be made in our garden.'

By 1860 she is arranging to have trellis-work placed on the green, and later she makes a garden upon the green, in other words the lawn is being enclosed and she is making island beds. As time passes the garden becomes an extension of the house, a place to entertain: '29 *August 1864*. We were all sitting upon the grass in the garden this afternoon when Mr Burrell called.' There are references too, to taking tea or coffee with guests on the lawn.

The garden was a perpetual challenge, specially to her design skills. First there was a covered walk to be made in the garden and, '7 *December 1864*. Began making arbour on green to hide the dairy and kitchen windows.' Next she turned her attention to the pond and stream that ran through the lower garden at Amor Hall. These were not to be allowed to run wild; cultivation took place around them and thanks to Bertie she was able to introduce flora into the water: '9 *June 1865*. Bertie brought home some waterlilies he had taken from the river.' . . . '13 *February 1866* Made alterations in the garden, arranging flowerbeds in the grass plots . . . 2 *May*. In the garden all day making a rockwork fernery from the ruins of Washbrook Church . . . 4 *May*. To Mr Gilbert's gardens . . . Afternoon in garden planting on rockwork . . . 5 May Afternoon with Evelyn and Blanche collecting Ferns.'

Like all gardeners she had to face disappointment: '15 *May 1866*. Planted out flowers . . . 16 *May*. Found all the flowers I planted yesterday apparently killed by the frost.'

Eighteen-sixty-seven found her making an arch to support a Pinsapo tree and planting beds of Nemophila, but the grand project for that year was the re-laying of the croquet ground which had served the family so well for some years. The foundations for this were dug deep and in so doing, one of the labourers found an antique silver coin, which must have caused great excitement. The croquet ground was to have a screen of trees and Elizabeth records that she has ordered them. Still the work was not finished: '31 *Jan.1868*. Began making rose garden . . . 1 *February*. Finished laying down grass in rose garden . . . 7 *February*. Attended to trellis-work being placed round the rose garden.' Here as in other work which involved structural alterations or heavy lifting, Elizabeth's contribution was of a purely supervisory nature.

Elizabeth expended a great deal of both effort and money upon the garden, from which she derived great pleasure, but a reminder that the farmhouse and the garden did not belong to them must have come home to her when she conceived a plan to put trellis-work on the house walls to carry her prized climbers. She needed permission from her landlord for such a venture: '*6 April 1868. Mr Tooke came and made plans for trellis work upon the house.*' Perhaps it was seeing all the care and expense involved in the garden which prompted Father Wallace to make his comment on the amount that the Cottons were spending on the place. Little did Elizabeth realise when she designed the rustic fencing to skirt the drive and separate the garden from the lane, the other side of which were the farm buildings, that soon her beloved garden would be no longer hers to enjoy, and that she would have to start all over again somewhere else.

5

Education

*Teach these boys and girls nothing but Facts. Facts alone are wanted in life.
Plant nothing else, and root out everything else.*
                                    Hard Times – Charles Dickens

*The course of instruction consists of reading, writing, arithmetic, etymology,
geography, grammar and history; vocal music is also beneficially introduced.*
        *The Moral, Social and Religious Condition of Ipswich
            in the Middle of the 19th.Century* – John Glyde

When it came to choosing schools for their children, Elizabeth and
Herbert were to find that mid-nineteenth century Ipswich offered them
a wide variety. Their contemporary, John Glyde, who was much given
to the use of statistics, records that in 1850, twenty years before the
introduction of compulsory education, 618 males and 470 females were
contained within the forty-four first and second class boarding and day
schools operating in Ipswich. There were a further thirty-three private
infant schools, thirty of which he describes as dame schools, which
catered for 960 children of both sexes. For the mass of the child population, some 1932 children, there were twenty-seven charity schools, set
up and maintained by religious bodies and parochial school boards. Like
all good reformers, Glyde uses his statistics to the best advantage, just as
he chooses carefully what material he should present for his case. On
the subject of infants' schools he writes:

> The great majority of them are kept by persons not merely wanting
> the ability efficiently to instruct the young, but in many points totally
> unfitted, and we are sorry to say, in more than one instance, morally
> as well as intellectually, for so important an undertaking. Widows,
> who through misfortune feel themselves unable to obtain a livelihood
> by any other means, open a 'dame school' as a last resort, and by
> means of a large cane and other injudicious modes, succeed in
> frightening the poor little things into keeping their tongues and limbs
> still for hours daily.

Glyde's chief concern was for the education of the children of the
masses; consequently, although he gives the numbers involved, he does
not interest himself in those establishments which he terms 'first and

second class day and boarding schools' with which the Cottons would have had dealings, and whose advertisements appeared in the *Ipswich Journal* and the *Suffolk Chronicle* usually in advance of a new term:

> Miss Foster begs to announce that the present Vacation
> will terminate on Monday, 30 January 1854.

Most of these schools, especially for girls and small boys, were run in private houses by widows and their daughters, or by unmarried ladies. Most of them too, were very small establishments. Mrs and Miss Jennings advertised that they took 'six boarders to instruct in English, French and Music', adding that they provided a 'Happy home for Orphans'. Miss Johnson took six boarders and four daily pupils, while in 1851 Mrs and Miss Shalders had seven boarders ranging in age from 12 to 15.

The competition which existed between the various establishments is shown by the 'extras' which they had to offer. In 1854 Mrs Shalders, announcing her removal from the old part of the town to Bolton Hill, where new building had taken place, adds that 'A French Protestant Lady has been engaged to teach her language and drawing'. Not to be outdone, at the Establishment for Young Ladies in Lower Brook Street, Miss Foster was offering 'German and French by a resident governess'. That it was necessary to compete in the market for pupils by pandering to the demands of the customer is shown in the delightful advertisement placed by Miss C. Smith who provided 'Preparatory Instruction for Little Boys'. She 'hopes to reassemble her little boys on the 24th.January, and finding that the airy and desirable walk from town is made an objection by her friends [i.e. the parents] on account of taking up the time of Domestics, [the maids, no doubt, were somewhat tardy in returning to their household chores after delivering the young master to school] she will provide an attendant to call for those little pupils whose parents may consider them too young to walk alone.'

For those boys too old for either Miss Smith's, or Mrs Stedman's which catered for those up to twelve or so, and who did not enter the Queen Elizabeth Grammar School, there were, just down the road, the private Grammar School run by the Revd C. Paglar, H. Buxton's Academy and Dr Christian's School which specialised in Modern and Ancient Languages. All of these had the advantage of being in one of the large, early nineteenth-century houses which had been developed in the roads overlooking the beautifully landscaped parklands which surrounded the Elizabethan mansion built on the dissolved abbey of Christchurch. Other schoolmasters aware of the needs of a changing society were providing not just the traditional classical education of a gentleman but also a sound commercial training.

So why, with all the choice before her, did Elizabeth select the schools she did for her children? In the case of Mrs Shalders, acquaintance, if not friendship, may have been the reason. Bearing in mind the relatively small population of the town and the fact that those engaged in commerce were confined to an area covering approximately a quarter of a mile in any direction from the central Cornhill, it is likely that most families were known to each other. Mrs Shalders's husband had been a bookseller in the town, supplementing his trade with the customary circulating library and ticket agency for concerts, lectures and other social functions as well as receiving advertisements to be placed in the local newspaper and holding the replies for collection. It is quite likely that the Haxells met the Shalders when they first settled in Ipswich for the names of Elizabeth and two of her sisters appear within a page or two in the same baptismal register as some of the Shalders children. It is even possible that the girls all attended the same school. We do know that Elizabeth seemed to have enjoyed an informal relationship with Mrs Shalders once Alice had joined her school. It is hard to resist the temptation to parallel the situation with Jane Austen's *Emma*. In the same way that Mrs Goddard was on evening visiting terms with Mr Woodhouse as a useful addition to a card party, so perhaps was Mrs Shalders to James Haxell. Certainly it was to him that she imparted the news of Alice's mystery illness in 1854, leaving him to pass it on to Elizabeth.

We also glean from the diary that Elizabeth felt free to visit Mrs Shalders whenever she was in Ipswich so that she could maintain regular contact with Alice, and that the relationship was more than merely a professional one is borne out by the fact that Elizabeth continued both to write to and visit Mrs Shalders long after Alice had left the school. Of the education provided by the school we are given no clues, except that Elizabeth was sufficiently pleased with the music instruction to reward it: '*7 June 1857*. Bought a silver soup ladle to give Miss Ellen Shalders as an acknowledgement of her attention to Alice's music.' It is worth pausing here to say that when Elizabeth says the ladle is silver, she means just that. Later entries concerning her own domestic purchases are quite specific about silver and silver plate.

The traditional picture of girls' schools of the period comes at the very beginning of the diary. Elizabeth has taken the six-year-old Bertie with her to visit his grandfather in Ipswich and while they are in the town: '*26 February 1854* Met Alice walking with the school.' Balanced against this formality comes a remark such as: '*12 December 1858* Alice stays the night with Miss Shalders to enjoy breaking-up frolic.'

Although we do not have access to any of the school books belonging to Alice or her schoolfellows, three exercise books of Mary Anna Furness who attended Radcliffe House School in 1855 give some indication as to the type of instruction being given to girls at that time. Unfortunately,

Miss Furness or someone in her family did not prize her school books as much as a later researcher and during the 1870s and 80s some of the pages in the exercise books have been used as a scrap book for newspaper cuttings. Interesting though these items may be, they are available in the newspaper archives, while many of the beautifully handwritten exercises are now lost. However, from what remains it is possible to see that most of the girls' work was in the form of copying and presumably learning by heart what had been copied, including poetry. Geography took the form of a series of notes about the geological structure, climate, flora and fauna and so forth of a country, starting in this case with Persia. History was centred around a monarch and the events of a whole reign compressed into one page of careful handwriting. Presumably French and German were extras and perhaps involved more oral work, for neither language is found within the pages of Mary Anna's exercise books, but Latin is. Admittedly it takes the form of a list of Latin proverbs and phrases, but if the young lady was expected to learn these lists by heart, there is no doubt that at the end of her school days she would have had a working knowledge of the language – sufficient that is to help her own children much later with their homework. Also worked on the list theory was spelling. Each list consisted of seventeen words beginning with the same initial. However, the words were not just learned purely as an exercise in spelling, each was defined, so that in effect the pupil was building up a large vocabulary as well. The final subject was Grammar, and Miss Furness spent most of 1855 'parsing' such sentences as 'In your youthful amusement let no unfairness be found.'

One exercise book is devoted to arithmetic – that year's programme dealing with the Rule of Three. For those who have complained bitterly that our arithmetical instruction seemed to bear no relation to reality for few of us would be called upon to supervise the digging of gigantic holes or the filling of baths which unaccountably leaked, the sums tackled by the 1850s young woman seem to have much more in common with modern maths teaching. She would be much more likely to respond to the problem of whether she should buy 185¾ yards of foreign black lace at 13/5d. per yard or 213¼ yards of British white lace at 17/9d. per yard. Even if she did not marry, the young Lady was likely at some stage of her life to have to take over the management or at least supervision of the household accounts and therefore it was entirely relevant that her early arithmetical training should consist of working out the price of a nine-pound leg of pork at 1/1½d. per pound, or the relative prices of a loin of veal at 1/4d. per pound or a fillet at 1/1½d. Similarly, other computations revolved around the purchase of everyday groceries through to such items as silver-plate ware and linen. But the mathemat-

The Old Coach Office. Front (left) and rear (right).

(left) Nos 40, 38, and 36.

(below) Carved weather-boarding on Nos 40 and 38, 1875.

1. Brook Street, Ipswich.

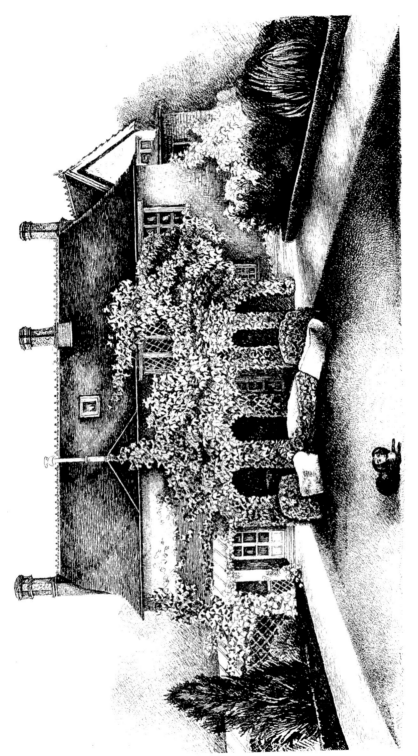

2. Amor Hall, Washbrook, September 1870.

3. Amor Hall farm before renovation in the 1850s.

4.   St Mary's Church, Washbrook, from the vicarage field.

5. Washbrook Church,
7 March 1866.

6.   Evelyn and Blanche in the garden.

7.   Alice and Bertie Cotton on horseback, 1870.

8. The Cotton family some time in the 1870s. Bertie standing; left to right: Blanche, Mrs Cotton, Alice, Allan and Evelyn.

ical problems were not confined purely to the domestic; even the 'delicate minds' of young ladies were thought strong enough to deal with simple interest – and couched in such terms as those that follow, many of us would have found the problem worth considering:

My respected uncle Dixon left me a legacy of 500 gns. eight years ago. Not then having any particular need for the money, I agreed to let it remain in his executor's hands on condition that he allowed me interest at the rate of 3½% per annum. What is the amount now due to me?

For argument's sake, let us assume that this is the type of teaching which Alice received during her years at Mrs Shalders's school. When the diary opens in 1854 Alice, who is nine, is a full boarder, returning home only for the holidays. The school terms ran from late January through to just before Easter when a break of about ten days was given. The second term lasted from April until the end of June when the summer holiday took place with the third term starting at the beginning of August. A week's break was usually given for Michaelmas at the end of September, the term then continuing until mid-December.

As time went on, Alice came home for the occasional weekend, often bringing with her another boarder, but in May 1859, her mother wrote to request that Alice should become a weekly boarder, so that she might, as Elizabeth has it, 'take Saturday as a holiday at home'. When Mrs Shalders retired the running of the school was taken over by her daughter. That this was not a change for the better is revealed in the comment: '*1 November 1857*. This week correspondence with Miss Shalders upon her neglect of Alice. She promises more attention shall be given if we consent to her remaining at the school.' The schoolmistress must have kept her promise, for Alice remained at the school until Elizabeth had made plans for her further education: '*18 March 1860*. Wrote to Miss Shalders to say Alice would leave the school at Michaelmas.'

An indication of the fluctuating fortunes of private educational establishments comes the following week with the rather sad entry: '*25 March 1860*. Called upon Miss Shalders. She said she should try to part with her school as her best pupils were leaving.'

Alice actually left the school at the end of June. It may be that Elizabeth's notice to Miss Shalders was meant to indicate that Alice would not return for the Michaelmas term, or very possibly Elizabeth's plans came to fruition earlier than she had anticipated. The decision on what was to happen next to the almost 16-year-old Alice may have come from the girl herself or be another example of Elizabeth's following the fashionable trends set by her acquaintances in Ipswich. Among her

many visitors during July, Elizabeth notes that Mrs F. Ransome has
called with a Mlle Colbrant, and three days later, Elizabeth returns the
call on Mademoiselle at Mrs Ransome's house in Ipswich:

> *6 August 1860.* Monday. Preparing for Alice's going to school . . .
> Packing up all day . . . Wednesday. To London with Herbert. Alice
> with us . . . Called upon Mlle Colbrant. Had a dinner party in the
> evening. Most of our relations came . . . Friday. With Alice to Lon-
> don Bridge Station. Met Mlle Colbrant there with her other pupils. We
> placed Alice under her care . . . returned home.

Elizabeth gives no clue to the emotion she must have felt in parting with
her daughter who was to study at Mme Colbrant's school in Fontainbleau. No more weekends at home; no opportunities to call and see
Alice whenever the fancy took her. Ten months were to elapse before
Elizabeth and Herbert next saw their daughter, and then they would
travel to France to combine a holiday with bringing her home for six
weeks before she returned in August 1861 for the second year of her
continental studies. We may assume that it was a very polished young
woman of seventeen and a half who came home the following year:

> *20 June 1862.* Went with Herbert to London Bridge Wharf to meet
> Alice on her return from France with Augusta Colbrant. Alice recog-
> nized us before the boat stopped.

Alice has now emerged from childhood and its restrictions and is ready
to take her place as her mother's companion and occasional delegate.
During her absence from home contact was maintained by frequent
exchanges of letters. We marvel once again at the postal service of the
1850s that when Alice left London on Friday, 10 August, her parents
received confirmation of her safe arrival at Fontainbleau from both her
and Mademoiselle by early the following Monday. The post also
brought birthday and Christmas presents for those at home and took
gifts to Alice. Elizabeth allows herself the merest touch of emotion when
she notes that it is Alice's birthday but it is being kept in France that
year.

Mlle Colbrant shows a glimpse of the role played by middle-class
'working women' in the mid-nineteenth century, acting as a recruiting
agent for her mother's establishment in France. Since we know that
several of the schools for young ladies in Ipswich had French women on
their staff to teach their language while at the same time perfecting their
command of English, it is possible that she had served her apprenticeship in this way and thus built up her contacts. She certainly spent a
great deal of her time travelling for she was again in Ipswich at the end

of 1860 when she spent 26–28 December as the Cottons' guest at Washbrook. Possibly the young Frenchwoman visited other provincial towns searching for pupils, but she certainly had a London connection, at Dr Ancram's Academy in Kensington Gardens, where Elizabeth found her in the days leading up to a departure for France with her English pupils old and new. One might be forgiven for thinking that Mademoiselle was a lady of mature years, late forties perhaps, since she held such a responsible post in chaperoning the young English girls on their journeys. The evidence of the ages of her parents and brothers and sisters suggests that she was in fact much younger. In Augusta Colbrant we have another flaw in the stereotype picture of mid-Victorian life; we do not expect young middle-class ladies to be travelling unaccompanied in pursuit of commerce. Yet socially acceptable she must have been for she continued to visit Ipswich and stay at the home of Mrs Ransome and while there she received all the courtesies normally accorded a guest. Elizabeth even appears to assist her in touting for custom: '*13 January 1862. Monday. Mr and Mrs Foster, Rose and Minna and Miss Colbrant came to dinner. Miss Colbrant stayed the night. ' . . .' 10 February. Minna Foster left home to go to Fontainbleau.' At least when she arrived Minna would have the consolation of a welcome from Alice for the Cottons and the Fosters had known each other for some time.

Like the Haxells, the Fosters resided in Brook Street where Robert Foster carried on trade in piano and harmonium sales as a supplement to his work as a professional musician. He not only taught music, he arranged many of the musical events in the town, for example we noted earlier that George Ranson took his bride-to-be to a concert given by Mr Foster. While Robert Foster was building his profession, his sister had for some years run a private school for girls on the premises, assisted by Robert's wife when she was not engaged in bringing up her family. However, in 1859, Louisa Foster retired as an advertisement in the *Ipswich Journal* reveals:

> Miss Foster, On relinquishing her school, begs to return her sincere thanks to her Friends and the Public for their kind support during so many years. The establishment will be continued by Mrs Foster. Peculiar advantages in music offered. Resident French Governess Mlle Bournoville.

The Fosters provide a good example of the interlinking of families, for Louisa is to be found later on the 1861 census at The Grove, a large house at Hintlesham where she is listed as the sister-in-law of the owner, Byatt West. The children of this family as well as the Ipswich Fosters were schoolfellows and playmates of the Cotton children. One of the Foster boys also bore the first name of Byatt; possibly his uncle was his godfather.

It was to Mrs Foster that Elizabeth turned when seeking a school for her second daughter, Evelyn. It is likely that the child would have followed Alice to Miss Shalders's school had it not declined, for Elizabeth notes: '6 *February 1859.* Eva went to stay with Miss Shalders on Wednesday.' This was just before Evelyn's sixth birthday, but since it was another eighteen months before she started school, we can only deduce that the experiment was not a success and that the mother decided to postpone sending the child for full-time education. Thus it was in September 1860 that Eva started school at Mrs Foster's as a day-girl, a situation which suited the rather nervous child that she was reputed to be. However, just over a year later she was enrolled as a boarder. She started school on Monday, 14 October, but by the Wednesday evening, the child's homesickness was such that she left the school, possibly slipping out at the end of the afternoon with the day-girls. We have already looked at the consternation which her unexpected arrival home must have caused. Elizabeth returned Eva to school the following day and thereafter continued to do as she had with Alice, visiting on Tuesdays and taking the child to have dinner with her and Herbert at the White Horse and calling on Saturdays either to take her shopping or to bring her home for the weekend. However, the long Christmas holiday must have unsettled the girl even more, for within three weeks of the start of the spring term there was further upset: '20 *February 1861.* Thursday. A letter from Mrs Foster to say Evelyn fretted very much for home. Called to see her and finding the poor child appeared lonely and unhappy took her home with me.'

This episode represents, I feel, the care and concern of both parent and school for the well-being of the child. One senses that Elizabeth is torn between her maternal instinct to have the child return to be with her all the time and her practical understanding that the child must be educated and learn to be independent. She was also faced with finding a school which would suit Eva. Two possible establishments presented themselves. Elizabeth interviewed the first on the following Monday and the second on the Tuesday. Of the latter she wrote: '25 *February 1861.* To Ipswich. Called upon Miss Appleby. Found she had no scholars and declined placing Eva with her, fearing she would not be happy.' On the 27th, Elizabeth called on Mrs Foster for advice; a decision was made, and the following day, Friday, Evelyn began attending Miss Clarke's School as a day boarder.

This arrangement obviously pleased Evelyn, for we hear no more of her school problems and, as the later diary reveals, she completed her education at this school as did her sister Blanche who joined her there in September 1863. Evelyn's unwillingness to submit to a way of life that caused her so much unhappiness resulted in a break in the tradition established by Alice and her London cousins of the girls becoming boarders. Happily both Elizabeth and Mrs Foster were able to cope with Evelyn's problems, for it in no way impaired their personal relationship; the two women continued as close friends, visiting each other and sharing social engagements. Neither did Evelyn appear to hold Mrs Foster responsible for her unhappiness at school for she was content to spend the odd day at Mrs Foster's, with Blanche to keep her company, when Elizabeth needed to have the children out of the way.

While acquaintance or close friendship may have guided Elizabeth's choice of schools for her daughters, much deeper consideration would have underlain the selection of suitable schools for Bertie and Allan. On the first page of the journal for 1854 Elizabeth notes that Alice is about to return to school, but no mention is made of educational arrangements for the boys until a year later when they start at Mrs Stedman's school in January 1855, by which time they are eight and seven respectively. This raises the question of what teaching the boys were given before then and by whom was it given? There is no reference to a governess being part of the household, neither does Elizabeth indicate that she taught the children herself on any formal basis. On the other hand, it may be that she would not feel the necessity to impart this information to her journal and that her references to being with the children are the times when she undertook their education. There is surely enough evidence from the literature of the period for us to assume that all the Cotton children learned to read and write at their mother's knee:

8 January 1854. Sunday at home. The rest of the week with children walking, drawing and reading . . . *5 February*. In the garden on Monday. Walking, reading and drawing Tuesday and Wednesday . . . *12 February*. . . . Drawing and walking with Bertie and Allan in fields and on roads.

To some this may seem like a very dull and dreary regime, to others the epitome of education in its very widest sense. The daily walks undertaken primarily in pursuit of the Victorian ideal of a healthy body gave the mother and children an opportunity to talk with each other, and the children to observe their surroundings and to learn through experience. Watching her draw and paint would have heightened their awareness of objects they had previously taken for granted. Assisting their mother in the collection of mushrooms they would have learned from experience about fungi, and in the woods as Elizabeth looked for ferns the children would have absorbed far more information than they could from a textbook. The fact too, that both boys accompanied their parents (as their younger sisters were to do later) on drives around the locality meant that they were given the opportunity to extend their range of experience and meet new people but perhaps most important they had the chance to enjoy the company and conversation of their parents, in particular their father. One tends to assume that the male parent left the early upbringing of his children to their mother and that his interest in them was only wakened when they reached their teens. This was certainly not so in the Cotton household. Unless Herbert was a totally henpecked husband who was made to take his wife and children with him on drives for the sake of a quiet life – which seems most unlikely – then we can assume that he actually enjoyed having his young family around him.

Could this be one of the reasons why, when the boys did start their formal education, they went as day pupils rather than boarders as Alice had. The arrangement involved the parents in a number of problems which would not have arisen if they had merely opted to send the boys away to school. First, as happens under similar circumstances today, it was necessary to have additional transport available for the 'school run'. In their case, the Cottons purchased a secondhand cab for the children, though this meant that a horse and a groom were tied up for certain periods of each day. However, none of this seems to have worried the Cottons, and in due course Bertie and Allan joined Mrs Stedman's school in Ipswich. At the time of the 1861 census Lucy Stedman was in her forties, her husband William was an accountant and they had two sons aged fifteen and ten. Perhaps it was having boys of her own that led Mrs Stedman to choose to teach boys rather than girls as was more usual for a lady teacher. It was acceptable for a woman to teach small boys, but surely rare for a woman to be coping with boys up to twelve as she did. There is no record of the number of day-boys she took, but certainly Allan and Bertie could have boarded with her, as the census reveals that she had ten boarding pupils ranging in age from six to eleven. We can only hazard a guess at the actual size of the school from the fact that apart from herself there were two female teachers in their twenties and a sixteen-year-old apprentice teacher. Three living-in servants attended to the needs of the household. It is possible that William Stedman acted as a father figure to the whole establishment, and given his profession, he may well have acted as mathematics teacher.

Of their time at this school, we are told very little apart from: '1 September 1856. To Ipswich Horticultural Show on Thursday. Alice went with us and the boys who went with Mrs Stedman's School, joined us there.' And each year in November for the four years of the boys' stay at the school there is an item which reads: 'The boys stayed at Mrs Stedman's all night as she invited them to see Fireworks exhibited.'

The boys' pleasant, cosy school life was to change rapidly in 1859. Amid the entry relating all the pleasant social functions an ominous note is sounded:

16 January 1859. Wednesday, Alice, Bertie and Allan went to a dinner party and dance at Mr George Ranson's. Thursday with Herbert to Ipswich. Boys with us. Called upon Mr Holden and entered the boys' names as day boarders at the Grammar School.

Although there was a wide choice of academies for young gentlemen available, among the gentlemen farmers of the neighbourhood and the better-off tradesmen of the town, there was really only one school which was considered worthy of turning out the true scholar and gentleman, and that was the ancient foundation then known as the Queen Elizabeth Grammar School. 'By the middle of Victoria's reign,' writes W.J. Reader, 'many Grammar schools had dwindled to grubby squalor in unfashionable districts. Their buildings, almost certainly old, would probably be tumbledown and their masters, quite possible, likewise.' This had been somewhat the case with the old Ipswich Grammar school, but in 1851 the Prince Consort had laid the foundation stone of the new buildings which were situated in the healthy and fashionable higher ground above the town. As the name of the school implies, the curriculum offered had been a limited Classical one. During the 1830s the changing pressures of the nineteenth century led to the school prospectus noting that particular attention was given 'to a complete preparation for either of the English Universities with regular instruction in Latin, Greek, and a general English education including writing, arithmetic and mathematics. The Hebrew language was taught to those pupils who could with profit enter upon its study and French could also be learned as an optional subject.' The type of education was likely to produce 'a strong muster of the gentry, clergy and yeomanry of the county.'

In sending the boys to the Grammar School Elizabeth was following the fashion set by many of her friends. Just as today, parents often extend their own social circles as a result of the friends their children make at school, so had Elizabeth widened her circle which now included the draper and his wife, Mr and Mrs Henry Miller, whose two sons were to remain close friends of Bertie and Allan and were to follow them to the Grammar School. Similarly their country neighbours were also enrolling their sons. Many, no doubt, were impressed by the new buildings, and since Mrs Stedman's school was just down the road, it is likely that there was a link between the establishments. At the time the boys entered, Mr Holden had just been appointed Headmaster and was endeavouring to make his mark; among his innovations was the introduction of German and geography, but science was still not included in the curriculum.

Whether or not it was a reflection on the standard of Mrs Stedman's teaching, life seems to have altered radically for the boys once they started their new school, and Elizabeth adapted her routine to accommodate the change.

> *30 January 1859*. Monday. The Boys went to the Grammar School. . . .
> *6 February*. Monday. Arranged mineralogical specimens. Evening helped boys with their lessons . . . Other days fitted up Cabinet for Minerals . . . and evenings helped boys. . . . Sunday. At home. Helped boys with Scripture lessons . . . *27 February*. Sunday. At home. Helped boys. Monday walked to Ipswich to speak to Mr Holden about our boys.

One wonders what prompted the last action. Was it that Elizabeth felt that the boys had too much homework to do? On two Sundays they had foregone church in order to tackle their work and Elizabeth had remained with them. Was this the caring mother who sat with them to soothe and assist, or the harsh taskmaster who stood over them to ensure the completion of the exercise? I incline to the former proposition, and imagine that on the Monday it is an irate mother who resolutely marches into Ipswich to beard the headmaster in his study. I fear, however, that she found Mr Holden less tractable than either Miss Shalders or Mrs Stedman. Having expended both physical and nervous energy on this encounter, she records that she 'took a cab part of the way home' – and if she was like most of us, she probably held imaginary conversations with Holden all the way home in which she gained the upper hand. Whatever may have been discussed with the Headmaster, Elizabeth continued to record for most of the following Sundays 'Helped boys.' The pattern was set: '*27 March 1859*. . . . Alice at home on Saturday. In the garden and helped with boys' lessons. . . . Other days in the garden and helping boys with lessons. . . . Helped boys with Maps and lessons.'

With what relief must they all have greeted the ten days given for the Easter holidays, but in May she again records that 'Evenings attending to boys' lessons' are still going on. Elizabeth's own educational skills are shown: '*7 November 1858*. Translated from German. . . . *11 September 1859*. Wednesday afternoon with boys studying Latin.'

Alice had a Michaelmas holiday in October but 'None given at the Grammar School'. Perhaps it was Elizabeth's annoyance at this, or merely her desire to bring enjoyment to the lives of her children, which brought about the event that occurred during a visit to Washbrook from her brother Edward and his wife Arabella with her sister Rea. The adults all visited the races and then the theatre on the Wednesday. Late that evening Rea's husband, Henry Page, arrived from London:

> *16 October 1859*. We all went to the Races again on Thursday, taking Alice and our boys with us. We had met Bertie and Allan on their way

home from school the day before and their disappointment at seeing us go to the Races without them had been so great that their Aunts helped me persuade Papa to take them with us next day. The children were all very pleased with the day's amusement and when upon our return home in the evening we joined them all in a romp their enjoyment was extreme.

There were no repercussions to this day's truancy as there were on a later occasion. By 1862 the headmaster, Dr Holden had been at the school long enough to have imposed his own standards, especially where discipline was concerned. We are told in *The History of the Ipswich School 1400–1950* that

Each Saturday morning Holden saw the punishment books kept by the Masters and added his comments. Caning was comparatively rare, though when administered by "the Doctor" it was intended to be a lesson not to be forgotten. Summoned to the Sixth Form Room, the culprit was given a terse review of the situation, and asked for an explanation, which, if not satisfactory, was followed by anything up to twelve strokes given with "vigour and precision".

We must again use our imagination to flesh out the events recorded in the diary: '2 *January 1862*. Bertie and Allan went to London to stay with their uncle Edward.'

The boys returned on Monday, 20 January and started the school term on the following day. From other accounts given by Elizabeth, we can be sure that during their stay, the boys had had a hectic round of visits to exhibitions, theatres and family parties, all of which may have been culturally and socially stimulating, but may have left them somewhat less than fresh for the start of the academic term. Not content with a full school day, they then went that evening to 'a party at Mr Walton Turner's' in Ipswich, no doubt arriving home late. Elizabeth had been ill enough that week to warrant the doctor being called to her and that may account for why she allowed the boys to have a holiday on the Wednesday. We can only hope that she was sufficiently recovered to withstand the visit made to her by Mr Holden the next day. Equally, the headmaster must have felt a deep concern about the boys to make the journey to Washbrook: perhaps there were other problems. In June 1863 Herbert took the boys out of school to attend the races with him as he had done in previous years, but this time they did not get off scot free: '27 *June*, Saturday. . . . The boys kept in at school for going to the Races.'

There is no clue as to how Elizabeth and Herbert reacted to this detention on the Saturday half-holiday. Elizabeth probably inwardly raged at the injustice to the boys for what was, after all, a parental decision, while to Herbert, attendance at the races was part of the education of an English country gentleman.

It might be useful to consider here what future the parents had in mind for their sons. When they sent them to the Grammar School were they anticipating an academic career for them, for during Holden's reign at the school standards rose and several boys gained scholarships to Cambridge? On the other hand, bearing in mind the long agricultural tradition of the Cottons, it must surely have been Herbert's hope that at least one of his sons would carry on the farm, and that the other could be found another farm in the area if he wished it. Both boys were encouraged to visit Agricultural Shows with their father, attend farm sales and participate in the leisure pursuits of the countryman of hunting and shooting. Several of their closest friends came from farming backgrounds and they frequently exchanged visits with the Rope family who farmed extensively in the north of the county. There is no indication in the diary that either of the boys disliked the country life, in fact they positively relished the riding and hunting in particular. Yet neither was to become a farmer. Was this another example of the fashionable trend of the mid-Victorian period, that rather than have her sons being merely tenants of land that could never be theirs, Elizabeth encouraged them to become members of a profession which would make them their own masters? Was Elizabeth influenced here by her brothers and brothers-in-law, who owned their businesses and their own property? Did she sometimes stop and look at the money Herbert put into the house and buildings at Amor Hall only to realise that their tenure could, on the whim of the landlord, cease? Maybe she and Herbert could read the signs of the coming depression in agriculture and thought it best the boys should look elsewhere.

It must have been more than just the boys being given a detention which led to their leaving the Grammar School, but strangely, no reference is made to this decision. When the diary for 1863 closes there is no indication that the boys, now 15 and 16, will not be returning to school in the new year. Yet that is precisely what happened. Perhaps neither was doing as well academically as he should, or it may be that having decided on a future career, the Grammar School was not providing the necessary foundations. In the event, Allan became 'a private pupil' of Mr Burrell, the clergyman of St Mary Elms church in Ipswich, and Bertie, after a crash course in French, went in April 1864 to study for a term at M. Fournial's College in Melun, just south of Paris. Bertie had either not taken French as an extra at the Grammar school or he had not made the progress his mother had hoped. Elizabeth attached great importance to her children being fluent in that language. The idea that young ladies should be sent to school in France in order to perfect their conversational prowess and achieve that little extra 'polish' was accepted, but it is not often we hear of young men doing the same.

In the autumn of that year Bertie joined Allan for private coaching with Mr Burrell. Quite how long this lasted is not made clear in Elizabeth's later diary. Bertie appears to have enjoyed a considerable period of time off at home, during which he accompanied his father on business trips, rode to hounds, took part in boat races on the Orwell, joined a choral society with Alice, and acted as driver and escort to his mother – the generally accepted leisurely life of a young country gentleman. In contrast, Allan, having completed his studies with Burrell, went in 1865 to study in Norwood where, as Elizabeth proudly reports, he passed his preliminary law examination in March 1866. He was admitted to the Law Society in 1872 and practised, on and off, as a solicitor until his death in 1917.

From the diaries of Elizabeth Cotton it is possible to see that of all her children, Bertie is the one she holds most dear. She parts with him with much greater reluctance than she had with Alice under similar circumstances, actually allowing herself to show emotion in: '*19 April 1864. Parted with my dear Bertie.*' During his absence she remarks on several occasions that when she has visited the priest, Father Kemp, they have talked about 'dear Bertie'. Although she shows concern for Allan, one senses that here is not quite the same closeness between mother and son. If it was his own choice to take up the law through a desire to help people, a strong sense of justice and fair play and the determination to fight for what was right, whatever the cost, then in this it was he, perhaps, who most resembled his mother. Throughout the diaries there is no clue whatsoever as to what Bertie's final career choice would be. With his sporting interests, musical talent and strong inclination towards the religious life, he could have been a perfect example of the stereotype country parson. But that life was rapidly passing into history, and the Cottons did not have the contacts to procure him a comfortable rural living. So instead of the cure of souls, Bertie opted for the cure of the body: '*13 October 1869. Bertie went to Norwood to study for the Hospital.*' He eventually joined the Army Medical Service and on his retirement came back to end his days with his sisters. None of the family married.

We have perhaps wandered far from the early education of the Cotton children, but the remark that none of them married is in a way significant, for had we examined the family as it might have appeared in say the first decade of this present century, we might have been forgiven for thinking that here was a family which had been brought up in a narrow, confined social atmosphere where opportunities to meet and make relationships were severely limited – almost like characters in one of the novels of Ivy Compton Burnett – but in fact this was not the case. Apart from their school lessons, each of the children was given the opportunity to take instruction in subjects that would enable them to take their place with ease in social activities.

The three girls all had private music lessons, and Alice showed some skill. As a young woman she went on to play the organ and in the later diary, Elizabeth records that on one occasion when Alice was trying the instrument at a church, she pumped the organ for her daughter, an activity which will revive older readers' memories of the bellows action and mystify those who are accustomed only to electrically powered church organs.

For further tuition in singing, Elizabeth sought the best teacher to be found in Ipswich: '1 August 1858. . . . Tuesday with Herbert and Margaret to Ipswich . . . called upon Mr Nunn to speak to him about Alice taking singing lessons . . .'

Thanks to the Bianchi family, the musical life of Ipswich was of a high standard for a provincial market town at this period. At the beginning of the century, the musically-gifted Italian couple Gaettano and Maria Bianchi had settled in the town and became a major influence on the development of standards both through performance and teaching. Their children were to continue the tradition; the daughters offered instruction on the harp and the pianoforte as well as in singing and dancing, while their brother combined his talent as a music teacher with that of an optician. Bearing in mind the relatively small population of the town, would it surprise the reader to learn that George Bianchi was married to a Miss Shalders – no doubt also a competent musician like her sister Emily? To have been taught by Bianchi carried kudos and was considered almost as a qualification, as the following advertisement in the *Ipswich Journal* shows: 'Miss Taylor (pupil of late Bianchi) Begs to announce that she is willing to attend the piano at the homes of her pupils.'

Robert Foster, whom we have already met, was by the 1850s renowned for his arrangements of public concerts which featured celebrities, but he was also probably the leading instrumental teacher in Ipswich. It was with him that Alice took her advanced training: '9 Dec. 1862. Tuesday. Mr Foster gave an amateur concert at which his pupils performed. Alice played upon pianoforte. I went with Bertie and Allan to hear her.' From this one might assume Elizabeth is talking of a simple end-of-term concert, but the *Ipswich Journal* adds the details for us:

Mr Foster's Pianoforte Class Concert.

A very interesting and pleasing amateur concert was given at the Lecture and Music Hall on Tuesday evening by the pianoforte pupils of Mr Robert Foster, on the occasion of breaking up for the Christmas Vacation. Mr Foster has been accustomed to hold these class concerts at his own residence, but finding that a larger number of friends were desirous of attending than he could accommodate, he resolved to hold it in the Lecture and Music Hall on this occasion. . . . This practice of class playing was introduced into the system of musical instruction by Benedict some years ago when Mr Foster was invited to co-operate with him. Its object is to bring advanced pupils into a uniform manner of playing, with corresponding expression and in the strictest time, and it is peculiarly well adapted to give the full benefit of the master's judgement and experience. The overture from *Der Freischutz* was played in a manner which took the audience by surprise, considering that the performers were young girls not more than 15 years of age, and two of them were not more than 11 or 12. *La Harpe Eolienne* was executed in strict harmony and obtained an enthusiastic 'encore'.

The music critic made at least one mistake; Alice was in fact just eighteen. The fact that all the pupils were female points to the fact that as a general rule the development of musical skill was considered to be a necessary feminine accomplishment. There are those who tend to be scathing about the Victorian Miss who idled away her time at the piano. Too often the accomplishment has been dismissed as being just another required asset for becoming a socially acceptable prospective wife. So it might be, but there are other considerations. As those of us who endured piano lessons in our youth and gave up on them know only too well, self-discipline and dedication are needed to play even passably. Are we right then to disparage the young Victorian lady who used her free time not only in practice to achieve a high standard of performance but also in copying out music borrowed from friends, perhaps making her own arrangements and generally developing an appreciation and understanding of musicians and their work. In an age devoid of mechanical entertainment, the competent pianist was able to give pleasure and entertainment to others as well as herself whether it was by playing at formal gatherings of friends, acting as accompanist for a singer, or merely providing background music for the rest of the family in the evening as they attended to their various hobbies. That may sound dull, but a pianist could so often be called upon to give young people the opportunity to turn an evening gathering into an impromptu dance. On the practical level, in an age when a middle-class girl was not expected to undertake employment, one who had been properly educated musically found that, in the event of becoming a middle-aged spinster or widow in straitened circumstances, she was able to supplement her income, in a totally respectable way, as a music teacher. How often too, these musically-adept Victorian women were able to use their gifts to bring pleasure to those outside their own circle. Many, in their work in Ragged Schools, Sunday schools and other charity establishments, gave the children of the poor their first taste of music. Did Elizabeth Cotton give any conscious thought as to why she encouraged her daughter's musical ability? I doubt it. I suggest that she was merely following an established pattern from her own youth. That music continued to be of interest to her and her sisters as they grew older is shown in the two following extracts:

9 July 1859. To a dinner party at James Nelson's. Met Aunt Robert, Mathilda Nelson, Henry Page and Rea, Edward and Arabella and Anne and Margaret. In the evening music and dancing. Mathilda played several pieces from different operas most beautifully. I had not met her since we were young children together.

23 August 1859. We were in Anne's room all the morning hearing my sisters and Aley trying over music.

This conjures up a delightful picture of the four females ranging from the unmarried 45-year-old Anne down to her niece some thirty years her junior united by the common interest in music. (Incidentally, the diminutive 'Aley' had been adopted quite recently, but was not to last as did Rea for Rebecca, Margot for Margaret and Kate for Catherine, possibly to her sisters Elizabeth was known as Lizzie.) We may assume that the 'trying over music' was not limited to playing. Anne or Margaret or both, may have had good voices, and by the summer of 1859 Alice had had a year's specialised tuition from her Ipswich master.

Lindley Nunn, to whom Elizabeth entrusted Alice's vocal development, had succeeded Robert Foster as organist at the civic church of St Mary Le Tower where he was fast building up the fine choral tradition which has persisted. The weekly lessons, suspended while Alice was in Fontainbleau, resumed on her return. Where earlier in the diary Elizabeth had written on Tuesdays that she accompanied Herbert to Ipswich, the entry for that day from September 1862 always includes 'Alice took Music Lesson'. Furthermore, music played more and more part in the family's evening entertainment:

13 October 1862. Monday   Rose Foster, Miss Lockley and Miss Betts came to stay with us. Evening Music. . . . Tuesday. With children and friends to Village School. Mrs Foster came in the evening. Had Music and games. . . . Wednesday. To a Bazaar at Holywells with children and their friends. Evening Music and games.

Alice would not have been the only performer, for we know from earlier entries that Emily Betts, Alice's longtime friend from schooldays, also took music lessons and shared Alice's enthusiasm, and Rose Foster would not have been her father's daughter if she had been unable to play the piano.

All this emphasis on music may lead us to view Alice as the typical, rather 'prissy' Victorian Miss, but this was only one side of her 'rounded' education. Riding was introduced for all the children at an early age. '22 *March 1856*. On Monday went a long walk, the children having two donkeys upon which they alternately rode.' Although there is no reference to its acquisition, a pony was later added for the children's use.

> *24 January 1858*. Tuesday with children a walk. Took the pony with us and the children alternately rode. . . . *28 March*. Saturday. Walked with children who had the pony and donkey and rode by turns . . . *26 September*. . . . Boys' Michaelmas Holidays began on Tuesday. . . . the children riding, fishing etc. . . . *23 January 1859*. Wednesday. Alice and Eva rode. I walked with them. . . . *17 April*. Called upon Mrs Allen, the children went with me, taking the pony with them to ride alternately.

One cannot help wondering how Elizabeth determined who should ride when, and of the quarrels which must have ensued. Neither does it take much stretching of the imagination to visualise what must have been the effect upon the children when they were taken to see the displays of horsemanship. If these equestrian displays were as exciting as the one depicted by Thomas Hardy in *Far From the Madding Crowd*, then we can be sure Bertie and Allan, if not the girls, would have tried to emulate some of the tricks they had seen upon the poor pony.

By 1860 another pony has been added to the stable and a horse is being used as well: '1 *April 1860*. Monday. The children and Margaret rode the grey mare, William [the groom] accompanying them on the black pony, which is too spirited for inexperienced riders.' The donkey, however, has not been pensioned off, still being pressed into service for quite long journeys: 'Alice walked with me to Ipswich, Evelyn and Blanche rode with us on their donkey.'

The two voluminously dressed ladies walking beside the donkey carrying the little girls evokes one of those idyllic rustic paintings so popular at that time. Yet it strikes an incongruous note when considered in relation to the crowded narrow thoroughfares of the town itself. Elizabeth does not relate where in the town they went, but we must hope they left the animal before venturing into the area which occasioned this letter to the *Ipswich Journal*:

> Allow me to call attention to the reckless and furious driving round the New Post Office Corner by butchers and dealers, and the shouts

and whistles from the blue slops (the traditional trade clothing) for pedestrians to get out of their way is, in itself a sufficient nuisance, leaving aside the endangering of person's limbs and lives.

Over the next two years Elizabeth does not draw much attention to riding which was now an accepted part of the family routine. However, it is one thing to pick up the rudiments of horsemanship on the family pony assisted by the groom, but to be proficient one needs expert tuition. It may be coincidental, but within a week of the item which notes that Bertie had fallen with the pony, we read: 'Alice took a riding lesson of Mr Tripp.' This was obviously successful and resulted in: 'Saturday. Alice and the boys went a ride with Mr Tripp the riding master and joined Mr Foster and his children.'

Again it looks as if Elizabeth is following the fashion of her friends. By April the family were all riding here and there in the neighbourhood exchanging visits with 'horsey' friends. Undeterred by a couple of falls, Allan at this time had become an enthusiast, and the pony, possibly the 'spirited' black one mentioned earlier, was such a favourite that he was accorded a special honour: '*20 April 1862*. To Ipswich with the children. Had the pony's photograph taken by Mr Strokes.' Riding as both exercise and pleasure continued to be a major part of the children's lives, certainly until they left Washbrook in 1870. The boys both became keen huntsmen and for Bertie at least, riding was to continue for most of his life. A correspondent recorded in 1989, 'In the early years of this century my wife's mother used to ride with Capt. Cotton'.

Nowadays it would be a brave mother indeed who would take her eight- and nine-year-old sons to a dancing class. But if the Cotton sons were to take their place in the social life of the middle classes, then they must learn to dance. No doubt such instruction helped in developing good deportment as well as providing a more disciplined form of physical exercise than the rough and ready football games they had at school. Furthermore they would learn the polished social graces and manners associated with dancing. '*13 December 1857*. Wednesday. With Herbert, Alice and the boys to Public Dancing Lesson at the Assembly Rooms.'

It is interesting to note that both parents were involved in this event. Perhaps Elizabeth felt that their father's presence as well as her own would curb any mischievous behaviour on the boys' part or it may be that Herbert was genuinely interested in watching his sons join in. The Assembly Rooms offered dancing instruction twice a week. On Tuesdays Miss Stainton held sessions at 11 a.m. and 2 p.m. while on Wednesdays the establishment was given over to Mr Alfred Bowles, another of the town's musical impresarios. Apart from arranging winter concerts, he held classes in dancing and drilling, so perhaps it was the latter activity which was more in evidence when the young Cottons joined his Wednesday afternoon classes. These 'Public Dancing Lessons', as Elizabeth calls them, served another useful purpose in that they allowed the children and their mothers to meet their social equals and extend their range of acquaintanceship. By 1863, the ten-year-old Evelyn had started her dancing lessons, so that in due time she would be able to join her brothers and sister not only at evening parties but also at the small dances which were increasingly being held at private houses.

That the ability to dance was considered an essential part of the education of all young people in the middle classes is revealed in several unpublished diaries. Elizabeth Rope of Fressingfield crams into the small space allowed in her pocket diary details of the dances she attended in both public and private locations in her neighbourhood, while the young bachelor George Ranson relates with gusto:

1 January 1842. Saturday. The New Year commences with a fine day. I rode down to Saxmundham last evening on horseback; arrived there at six o'clock, from Sproughton 23 miles distant. Went to a pleasant Ball at the Bell Inn; the party consisted of about 450 of the principal families of the county and called the East Suffolk Yeomanry Invitation Ball. Dancing was kept up with good spirit till near the dawn of day. I left at 6 o'clock and arrived home in time for breakfast.

Given the opportunity of the 'education' provided by Elizabeth and Herbert, Bertie and Allan would, some years later, have been able to write in a similar fashion.

6

The Social Round

Took tea with Mr and Mrs Moore and accompanied them to concert of Sacred Music. After supper we returned home.

Elizabeth Cotton's Diary

With the ladies of *Cranford* and the rather shadowy older ladies of other nineteenth-century fiction fixed firmly in my mind, I had believed that a social life for married women of the middle classes consisted entirely of tea, cards and the occasional sober entertainment mentioned above. Fiction, too, had indicated that at more frivolous functions like parties and dances the mature woman's role was that of chaperone to daughters and nieces. How often are we presented with a picture of either the solicitous, over-protective, usually widowed, mother valiantly trying to guide a wayward son or daughter or the slightly vulgar nonentity whose efforts to procure an eligible son-in-law cause acute embarrassment. The one resorts to religion for succour, the other finds her comfort in gossip over the tea-tray.

I found it hard to accept that the older woman, restricted as much by her clothing as by social convention, could lead a full and enjoyable social life. Preconceived ideas suggested that beyond visits to friends close by, a woman rarely, if ever, went to gatherings without her husband. Thus the range of activities in which Elizabeth Cotton and her friends engaged confounded my belief that leisure time for females, both young and old, consisted almost entirely of fancy-work, reading and piano-playing. Although these had their place, there was a great deal more to be had, and Elizabeth took advantage of the wealth of entertainment available to the middle class and industrious working classes in mid-Victorian Ipswich and beyond.

In *The Best Circles*, Davidoff makes a distinction between public and private entertainment, showing that as Victoria's reign lengthened there was an increase in private entertaining, that is, more socialising within a closed circle of acquaintances and less participation in large-scale publicly provided entertainments. To some extent, the two diaries of Elizabeth Cotton also show this trend, which came a little later to Ipswich than it did to London.

ART AND THEATRE

If one of the farmers in my home village volunteered the information that he was off to London for the day to attend an exhibition and see one of the long-running musicals at the theatre, this would be accepted as perfectly normal behaviour. But, should he announce he was off to view the Summer Exhibition at the Royal Academy, this would, to say the least, raise many an eyebrow. If he were one of the more wealthy landowners, it might be supposed he was going with an eye to a good investment. The idea that he might be interested in the pictures for their own sake would be hard to comprehend. Perhaps this is because, on the whole, we do not nowadays discuss art for art's sake, conditioned as we have become to looking only at how much a painting 'might make at auction'.

Since there was such a strong emphasis on the art of drawing in the Victorian girl's education, it becomes natural to assume that the female population might show an interest in the exhibition of works of art, but for it to be a popular pastime with men generally seemed unlikely. Thus, when I first read Elizabeth's accounts of her frequent visits to galleries and exhibitions in London and elsewhere, I thought, in my twentieth-century-conditioned way, that Herbert had accompanied her purely as a matter of form. Closer reading revealed that this was not so; far from simply trailing behind her, Herbert actually had his own opinions on the works they saw. Did this mean that Herbert was unique? Not so. The young farmer from Sproughton, George Ranson, who spent much of his leisure in the hunting-field and upon the dance-floor, offers us an additional insight into the tastes of the Victorian man:

15 June 1842. I returned home from London by Orwell Steamer. I spent my time principally sightseeing, one day at the Royal Academy and one day doing the Exhibition of Paintings at the Society of Water Colour Drawings. . . . Went to the Exhibition at the Royal Academy. The Exhibition was very good indeed. . . . Went to view the cartoons at Westminster Hall, designs for the new Houses of Parliament.

During the 1980s we were often exhorted to return to Victorian values. Many in the sphere of the Arts might wish this could be so, especially when one learns that at the beginning of the nineteenth century the British Institution had been formed 'to encourage and reward the talents of the artists of the United Kingdom; so as to improve and extend our manufactures, by that degree of taste and elegance of design, which are to be exclusively derived from the cultivation of the Fine Arts'. This was later endorsed by Sir Thomas Lawrence who as president of the Royal Academy believed that exhibitions of Old Masters could seriously mislead the public. 'If such a public exhibition be at any time thought necessary, it should be at stated and long intervals, and after the public Eye has been left to the undisturbed view of the effects of living Genius . . .'

That there was a general interest in the practice of art as well as in viewing it, is shown by the number of books of instruction which were published – over two hundred in the first sixty years of the century. How to draw and paint landscapes and flowers, make transparencies, cut silhouettes – 'most genres possible to the amateur artist' – were dealt with in these manuals. Probably the most popular writer-instructor was David Cox whose work Elizabeth saw in 1859. Elizabeth spent much of her free time drawing and in line with the fashion of the period, copied the examples given in the books as well as taking inspiration from what she saw around her in daily life. Visiting the exhibitions of other artists' work was vitally important to her and formed part of every visit to London. Following a viewing, she was likely to fill several pages of her diary with a list of the works and the artists, sometimes giving a personal comment on what she liked best. Many of the names have passed into oblivion, some titles revive memories of prints we saw in our grandparents' parlours, and other artists are now enjoying renewed recognition. A few days spent in the capital meant cramming in as much as possible.

3 June 1855. . . . Rest of the week at home until Saturday, when I went with Herbert to London. Called upon Uncle John on our way to the York Hotel and after dinner upon Edward. Went with Herbert to the Haymarket theatre. Saw 'Gnome of the Hartz Mountains'. . . . *10 June,* Sunday. To Hampton Court. Went through the Picture Galleries and walked in the gardens. Monday . . . to Exhibition of Painters in Water Colours, and in the evening Anne went with Herbert and myself to the Princess's theatre. Saw 'Henry VIII' and a farce. The play was beautifully got up. Charles Kean played Wolsey, Mrs Kean Queen Katherine, Mr W. Lacey the King and Miss —— Anne Boleyn. Arthur took breakfast with us on Tuesday morning and afterwards I went with Herbert to the Art Palace at Sydenham. On Wednesday we went to the Exhibition at the Royal Academy. Wednesday evening to Olympic theatre saw 'Perfect Confidence' and 'Still Waters Run Deep'.

The following day the Cottons set off for their tour of the Midlands, but On 8 December they were again in London:

Saturday. To London . . . Evening with Herbert to the Haymarket theatre. Saw 'The Man with Many Friends' and 'The Little Treasure'.

Miss Blanche Fane played very nicely in the last piece. Had supper at Oyster Rooms as we returned from the theatre. . . . Monday . . . to Exhibition of Prints of E. Landseer's Pictures. Evening to hear Albert Smith's Entertainment. . . . Tuesday. With Herbert to the Cattle Show and in the evening to the Princess's theatre – 'Don't Judge by Appearances', 'Everyone Has His Faults' and 'Muleteer of Toledo'. . . . Wednesday with Herbert to see Exhibition of Pictures and Prints of Edwin Landseer. . . . Friday. Evening with Herbert to the Adelphi theatre. Saw 'The Jersey Girl', 'The Camp at Chobham' and 'Valentine and Orson'. Keeley played splendidly in the 'Camp at Chobham'. Saturday. Returned home.

That visiting exhibitions was not, for the Cottons, merely the socially acceptable thing to do is, I believe, reinforced by the second visit made to the Landseer exhibition. However, as these extracts show, the Victorians took pleasure in a diversity of entertainment. *The Rail Road Book of England, 1851*, which is a mine of information about London and the variety of entertainment in the capital, lists twenty-two theatres, among which Her Majesty's and the Princess's in Oxford Street provided 'legitimate' drama of tragedy and comedy; the Haymarket, the Lyceum, the Strand and the Olympic specialised in comedy, farce and melodrama, while the Adelphi apparently had 'nondescript pieces peculiar to itself but of singular attraction and popularity'.

Albert Smith's *Entertainments* were of a very specialised nature, being of dioramas and panoramas. In 1857 he was presenting *The Illustrated Ascent of Mont Blanc* and *A Tour of the Rhine*, and in 1858 was honoured with an invitation to perform before the Royal Family. *The Southwold Diary of James Maggs* has a reference to Barron's Oyster Rooms in London, a popular place for theatregoers to enjoy a supper of oysters and dry champagne. Elizabeth rarely mentions eating in public while in London, so I cannot help wondering if on the occasion noted earlier it was to Barron's she went. Her brother Arthur later married a Miss Mary Barron in London, so this might account for the visit.

The pattern of twice-yearly visits to London continued for some years and on every occasion visits to art exhibitions occupied almost as much time as those to the theatre.

10 May 1856. Saturday to London. . . . Went with Herbert in the evening to the Princess's theatre. Saw 'The Winter's Tale'. The play was beautifully put upon the stage, especially a Bacchanalial (*sic*) scene introduced in it. . . . Monday. To Exhibition of Royal Academy. Stansfield has one picture, 'The Abandoned', far superior to anything I ever saw before of his. Besides this I liked 'The Death of Chatterton' by Wallis (*sic*), and by the same painter, 'Andrew Marvell Returning the Bribe'. We went to the Adelphi in the evening and saw 'Like and Unlike' in which Madame Celeste played the heroines. 'The Urgent Private Affair' and 'My Precious Betsey' written entirely for Mr Wright. Tuesday to Exhibition of Old and New Paintings in Water Colours. Corbauld has several pictures and one of them, 'Nobody Axed You Sir She Said', the best I have seen of his. Haaghe, Prout and Mrs Harrison exhibited some nice pictures. In the evening to the Haymarket theatre. Saw three pieces, but the only one worth seeing was 'The Evil Genius', in which Backstone as the evil genius and Compton as an old postman acted capitally. On Wednesday to Tunbridge Wells by Rail. . . . *21 May*. . . . afterwards to London by Railway (from Brighton). Stayed at the York. After dinner with Herbert to the Olympic theatre. The performances were 'Retribution', a drama, and 'Stay At Home' . . . Thursday. Herbert went to the Exhibition of French Pictures.

10 December 1856. Wednesday. With Herbert to London. In the evening went to Albert Smith's Entertainment. . . . Thursday. Herbert went to the Cattle Show and I called on Arthur, Edward and Uncle John. Returned to the York to dine with Herbert and went with him to the Olympic theatre. Saw 'Wives as They Were and Wives as They Are' in which Mrs Stirling played the principal character and 'Jones the Avenger', a farce written for Mr Robson and in which he acts very well. Friday . . . went to Princess's theatre. Saw 'The Midsummer Night's Dream'. Mr Kean has revived this play very beautifully, but the acting was not so effective as I had expected. 'The Rose of Amiens' was the second piece. The King of Oude and his suite were in the theatre this evening and attracted a great deal of attention. The jewels worn by the King were of enormous size and lustre. . . . Saturday with Herbert to Dulwich. Stayed with Rea and Henry. We went to the Dulwich Gallery of Paintings. . . . Monday. Shopping and to the National Gallery of Paintings. Dined with Uncle John. Returned home.

Their return to London in the following month set a new pattern. Previously most of their entertainment had been provided in public places and they had stayed in a hotel:

31 January 1857. Saturday. With Herbert to London. Stayed at my brother Edward's house in the Strand. We were invited to see some Private Theatricals performed by himself and friends. They played 'Little Toddikins', 'A Pretty Piece of Business' and 'Urgent Private Affairs'. Edward, his wife, Margaret, Anne and Arthur were amongst the actors with some gentlemen I did not know. After the play Edward gave a supper.

This is a good example of the trend among the middle classes to develop their own private entertainment on a fairly large scale. Reading Elizabeth's account, the impression is formed that the plays performed had been well rehearsed, that these were not just the impromptu charades which featured in Victorian family life. Neither was it a case of a group of very young men and women coming together using play-acting as an excuse, for Elizabeth's relations would have been in their thirties and in Anne's case forties. The episode evokes memories of a similar venture in Jane Austen's *Mansfield Park*, where the young Bertrams and their friends make preparations for a theatrical performance. The difference is that there we are looking at early nineteenth-century country house society – the Bertrams' father was a knight – while here we are talking about members of the solid Victorian middle classes.

From the pleasures of private theatricals on this visit, Elizabeth and Herbert went to Dulwich to spend Sunday and Monday with Rea and Henry Page. On the morning of Monday the Cottons, accompanied by Rea and her two daughters, went to the Crystal Palace, which had been re-erected at Sydenham following the Great Exhibition of 1851. In the evening of 2 February 1857 their party, extended by a few close friends of the Pages, went: '. . . to the Surrey Music Hall to hear Mr Thackeray lecture upon George III. The Hall was crowded and the audience, chiefly men, gave great applause. After some trouble procured a cab to take us home, but the horse was too tired to work upon the slippery road, and we left the cab when about two miles from Dulwich and walked home.'

Elizabeth was indeed fortunate to attend this lecture. Thackeray had recently returned from a successful tour of the United States where he had lectured on 'The Four Georges', but there were not to be many more such opportunities to hear him for he was dead within that year.

In May, they were again in London where they:

Went to the Olympic theatre. Saw 'Daddy Hardacre' in which Mr Robson and Miss —— played reasonably well, and 'Young and Handsome' . . . *18 May 1857*. Monday. To Exhibition of Royal Academy. In the evening with Herbert to a Musical and Dramatic Entertainment by Mr and Mrs Gorman Reed at the Gallery of Illustration. . . . Tuesday. To Exhibition of Watercolours – of which I have mislaid the catalogue I marked. Afterwards to the Zoological Gardens, Regents Park.

It is hard for us with our access to the excellent natural history films made all over the world, to appreciate what must have been the impact upon the Victorians at seeing the strange animals on display. The big attraction at the Zoo in 1857 was a wombat. Elizabeth made no comment on what she saw, neither did she record, as other diarists of the time did, that the weather on Sunday, 17 May was 'melting' (see F. Watson: *The Year of the Wombat*).

The day after the visit to the Zoological Gardens, Elizabeth and Herbert set off upon their annual holiday tour. Their first destination was Manchester, which might have seemed an unlikely place for a vacation, but they were going for a specific purpose. In April a large exhibition of art treasures had been mounted there, a grand affair which was officially opened in May by Prince Albert who had at last been given officially the title of Prince Consort.

> Thursday. Spent the day at the Exhibition of Art Treasures. The collection of Murillo Paintings most beautiful. . . . Friday. Again to the Art Exhibition. The name of Art Treasures well expresses the genius of Arts gathered here. If we had the time to spare, two weeks instead of two days might well be spent in studying the different schools of painting and other works of interest. One statue, 'Eve Startled at the First Sight of Death', very much pleased me. The paintings by Etty do not look so well as some of his I have seen in the Royal Academy. Hunt's 'Awakened Conscience' and Wallace's 'Death of Chatterton' appeared remarkably admired, but we heard most extraordinary and ludicrous criticism upon many of the very beautiful works of Arts. The Refreshment department badly attended to.

Can we find early evidence of the north/south divide in that penultimate sentence?

The Exhibition of the New Society of Water Colours in May 1858, aroused Elizabeth to comment:

> Many pictures of Welsh scenery and nearly all good. Two rather clever by E. Morin of 'Feeling the Pulse' in real and imaginary illness. Some good architectural pieces by Prout and well painted Figures by Carl Haaghe. Only one of H. Warren's Eastern Landscapes but a large picture by him of the 'Song of the Georgian Maiden' from G. Moore's poem of 'Lalla Rookh'.

The focus of public interest that year was the centre-piece of the Royal Academy show: 'Tuesday. To the Royal Academy of Painters. The picture attracting most notice was the 'Derby Day' by Frith. A railing round the painting and several policemen protected it from the crowd.' She then lists those pictures she particularly liked, among which were several with a Spanish theme by Phillips and 'many beautiful but miniature pictures of Eastern Life by Lewis.'

'Evening to Princess's theatre. Saw 'Faust and Marguerite', 'The Green Business' and 'Samuel in Search of Himself'. The Mephistopheles

Mr Charles Kean, Marguerite Miss Lequerk.' *Faust and Marguerite* enjoyed a certain reputation. The Princess Royal, writing to her Mamma from Prussia confessed that though she had read it, she had never had the courage to see it. The Queen, who had, promptly recommended the play to her.

The Cottons continued their visits to art galleries:

Wednesday. To Exhibition of French paintings. A beautiful picture of a dog, 'Barbara', by Rosa Bonheur. 'The Zingari' by Decamps. A most clever picture by T.L. Gerome called 'The Dutch after a Bal Masque'. Many charming genre paintings by Frere and others and two pictures of Faust and Marguerite by Amy Scheffer.

On their return from an extensive tour of the south west of England, they arrived back in London to spend more time on art: 'Friday to Exhibition of Water Colours. Best pictures by Branwhite, Cox, Margaret Gillies, Taylor and Hunt. Evening to Lyceum theatre. Saw 'Going to the Bad'. Mr Robson and Miss Wyndham the chief performers and 'A Cabinet Question'. Saturday to the Exhibition of the Royal Academy and returned home.'

The following year found the Cottons changing their pattern slightly. There was no January visit to London and it was July before they could see the exhibitions.

7 July 1859. Thursday. With Herbert to the Royal Academy. Some very nice pictures in the collection but no one in particular I found better than the others. . . . Friday. To Exhibition in Water Colours. One architectural painting I liked very much. It illustrated a quotation from Longfellow's poem of Nurenburgh, 'In the Church of Sainted Lawrence stands a pix of sculpture rare,/Like the foamy sheath of fountains rising through the painted air.' The other pictures I liked were 'A Father and Daughter', 'The Young Mother', and 'Effie Deans', by Margaret Gillies, many small pictures by W. Hunt of small Fruits, Flowers, Birds' Nests and Shells, all capitally painted, and some beautiful landscapes by Richardson, Branwhite and Evans. After seeing these pictures we went to the Rooms of the Society of British Artists, mistaking it for the British Institute. However, having time to see the others before leaving London, we remained an hour here, and Herbert said he liked some of the landscapes by Boddington better than any he had previously seen this season. . . . *11 July*, Monday. To the British Institution. All the paintings here are Gems of Art. Many are by the old Masters, but I think I admired the Gainsboroughs of whose pictures there was a larger collection than I had ever before seen. Of these the full length portrait of Mr and Mrs

Hallett in one picture was my greatest favourite and I returned to it again and again. One of Etty's pictures of the Magdalene was beautiful and many by Sir Joshua Reynolds fine, though several are sadly faded. Companion portraits of a Lady and Gentleman by Franz Hals, not beautiful, but strangely life-like and interesting. . . . Afterwards to the Exhibition of French Pictures . . . Rosa Bonheur exhibited two studies of Blossoms . . . 'Huntsman Taking the Hounds to Cover' – Thomas Couture, a voluptuous picture of the decadence of Rome. Several good pictures by Charles Fortin and many by Edward Frere.

From 1860 onwards, Elizabeth seems to have less time to comment on what she has seen. She and Herbert still visit the various exhibitions on each visit to London, and on occasions, space is left on the diary page as if she fully intended to write up the details later. London was not the only place where Elizabeth might see paintings. There were several practising artists living in Ipswich as well as sculptors, engravers and wood carvers whose work was patronised by the local community. Exhibitions of major artists were also mounted in the town for the benefit of those unable to travel to London.

11 October 1857. Monday. To Ipswich with Alice to see some pictures shown at Mr Hunt's. They were 'Saved', by Landseer and a small picture by him of the Queen and her children in Scotland, and 'Home and the Homeless' by Faed. . . . *25 October*. Tuesday to Ipswich. Lunched with Herbert at White Horse and went with him to see Mr E. Smith's Exhibition of Paintings. . . . *25 April 1858*, Tuesday afternoon met Herbert at Ipswich and went with him to see some pictures at Assembly Rooms.

It is, I think, clear that Herbert enjoyed looking at paintings almost as much as Elizabeth did. On two of the three occasions quoted above, he would have spent the earlier part of the day doing business in the cattle and corn markets. We might expect him to spend the rest of the day in conviviality with his colleagues. It also appears that Elizabeth did not need to be accompanied by her husband as a matter of propriety, since on the first occasion she and Alice went to the Show on their own.

Ipswich supplied them too with a range of theatrical experience. The Theatre Royal, where the young David Garrick was reputed to have made his stage debut in the 1740s, had undergone a facelift in 1803 when a Norwich journalist had described the splendours of 'yellow, heightend with gold' and a 'ceiling painted to represent a light sky'. By the 1850s these splendours had worn thin and Elizabeth comments in 1855 on how cold and uncomfortable the theatre was, a view echoed by the *Ipswich Journal* in 1862 in its report that: 'The boxes were miserably cramped, with wooden planks for seats, uncushioned and bitterly cold. Every other part was equally inconvenient and uncomfortable and the theatre cold throughout.'

The plays seen at Ipswich were performed by touring repertory companies and occasionally by groups of amateurs like the officers from the regiments quartered in Colchester and Ipswich. Elizabeth and Herbert enjoyed the theatre hugely and introduced their children into the audience at quite a young age, for example, Bertie and Allan were only six and five when they were taken to see *Jack Shepherd* and *Box and Cox*.

6 January 1856. On Monday evening we took Alice and the boys to Ipswich Theatre. Saw 'Faint Heart Never Won Fair Lady', 'Deaf as a Post' and 'The Wandering Minstrel'. . . . *15 January.* Tuesday evening to Ipswich Theatre with Herbert, Alice, Bertie and Allan with us. Saw 'The Mandarin's Daughter', 'The Spoiled Child' and 'Mrs White'. . . . *17 February.* Friday evening we took Alice, Bertie and Allan to the Theatre. The performances, which were for the benefit of the manager, Mr Gill, were 'All is Not Gold That Glitters' and 'The Virtuous Stranger'. The house was well attended.

In between these family visits, Elizabeth and Herbert had attended three other performances, one of which was 'patronized by Members of the Borough'. '*21 March 1858.* Wednesday. To Ipswich Theatre with Herbert. Saw "Masks and Faces" and "Delicate Ground". Very good acting. Mrs Seymour and a company from London performed . . . Saturday with Alice and the boys. Saw "Belphegar and Crinoline".'

A contemporary advertisement in the *Ipswich Journal* gives an example of a weeks's repertoire at the theatre:

Monday: Surrey Drama – *The Masked Mother; Laughing Hyena.*
Tuesday: Juvenile Night – Panto – *Don Caesar de Bazen.*
Wednesday: *The Secret Agent.*
Thursday: Variety.
Friday: Benefit for Mr Morellini – clown.
Saturday: *Hamlet.*
With every evening the comic pantomine *Sleeping Beauty in the Wood.*
Centre Upper boxes 3/-, Side 2/-, Lower 1/6, Pit 1/-, Gallery 6d.
Doors open 6.30. Performance 7pm. Half price at nine o'clock.

Ipswich could also offer such highlights as, on *21 October 1855,* 'Wednesday evening to hear Fanny Kemble read 'As You Like It' and on Thursday evening to hear her read 'Macbeth'. Liked her reading best in the tragedy. . . . *30 November 1863.* Monday evening with Herbert to hear Fanny Kemble read 'Othello'. Alice, Bertie and Allan with us.'

These events took place not in the theatre but at the newly-built Corn Exchange where the price of tickets (6/- and 3/6) reflected the type of audience expected. There was however, a sensible reduction for family tickets, so for the five Cottons the evening's entertainment would have cost either 15/- or 28/-.

By 1861 tastes were changing. Between 17 and 28 September of that year they attended performances of *The Bohemian Girl*, *Il Trovatore*, *Satonella* and one evening 'took our children and Walton Turner to the theatre. Saw "Der Frieschutz" and "The Beggars Opera".'

An evening at the opera could both stimulate and amuse and visits to Covent Garden were frequent, with *Don Giovanni* and *Lucia de Lammermuir* recorded in 1862, and in June 1868 two visits within a week:

> . . . to the opera at Covent Garden. Saw the Comic Opera of 'Martha'. Patti, Grossi, Sagliagico and Grazioni took the principal parts. Herbert very charmed by Patti singing 'The Last Rose of Summer' in English when encored. . . . 6 June. Evening to the Opera. Saw 'Roberto Il Diavolo'. The concerted music was well done and the acting and scenery marvellously grand but the solo singing not so good. The incantation scene nearly occasioned a real tragedy, a tall column falling upon one of the nuns as she clung to it. She appeared senseless when carried out.

Early 1863 provided a great deal of public entertainment. By this time their parties to the theatre in Ipswich contained not only their own family but friends as well: '8 *January*. . . . We took our own children [Bertie, Allan, Evelyn and Blanche] to the theatre and with them E. Rowland, George and Henry Rope and Edward and Byatt Foster. Hired an omnibus to take us there and back. Saw "Lady of the Camelias", "Family Jars" and "Harvest Home".' Obviously neither Elizabeth nor Herbert were worried about the effect the *Lady of the Camellias* might have on the young people, though this play had caused a great deal of comment earlier in some circles.

Apart from the theatre, there were other public entertainments available. Those which Elizabeth and Herbert attended reflected both their tastes and particular interests and often their suitability for young people. We know that the children were taken regularly to see the annual display of horsemanship and to the circus. In the later diary Elizabeth also notes that on two consecutive days she sent the servants to see The Wild Beasts Show.

We have already seen that music flourished in the town and Elizabeth was frequent in her attendance at concerts. During 1854 for example, she and Herbert heard both *The Creation* and *The Messiah* as well as such musical entertainments as that advertised as *Music of Various Nations* given by Mr Phillips, a member of the English Glee and Madrigal Union.

Saturday evening a concert at Ipswich Theatre. Vocal and instrumental. Performers Clara Novello, Herr Reichart, Sutori on the violin, Piatti on cello and Arthur Napoleon on the piano. Great complaints were made by the audience of the coldness and uncomfortableness of the reserved seats which were in the pit of the theatre.

But no comment whatsoever on the performance of Arthur Napoleon, 'the interesting young Portuguese pianist', as he was described in the advertisement for the concert.

'*9 March 1856*. Friday evening with Herbert to a concert of sacred music at Ipswich. Mr and Mrs Weiss and Mr Mason sang. . . . *11 January 1857*. Monday evening with Herbert to a concert in the Corn Exchange. Miss Dolby sang.' Four years later this lady has adopted a more professional mode of address: '*28 October 1861*. With Herbert to a concert given by Madame Dolby and Mr Stainton.'

There were other musical occasions, possibly on less serious level. '*21 July 1857*. Monday with Herbert to an entertainment given at Ipswich by Mr Mayhew. . . . *5 February 1860* Thursday evening with Herbert to a concert given by Miss Poole and Mr Ramsden upon the old ballad music of England. Took Alice with us.' The renowned Christy Minstrels also paid several visits to the town. Elizabeth and Herbert went to hear them in 1860, and the boys and the younger girls were to attend later concerts given by them. There were too, many opportunities for light-hearted amusement:

25 October 1857. Tuesday. Evening with Alice and the boys to see Conjuring Tricks at the Mechanics Institute. . . . *9 May 1858*. Friday evening Alice and the boys went with their father and myself to Woodin's Entertainment of Oddities at the Lecture Hall. . . . *5 August 1862*. Tea with Mrs Foster and to an amateur concert in the evening – the entertainment very absurd. . . . *12 December 1862*. With Alice and boys to a performance of Charles Matthews at Home at the Corn Exchange. Very clever indeed. . . . *11 February 1863* To tea with Mrs Foster and went with her and our children to Mr Blitz's performance. He professed to perform conjuring tricks, but these were only excuses for a raffle at which people won gold and silver watches and some plate goods. Mrs Foster had previously won a plated claret jug, but none of our party was successful this evening.

Signor Blitz enjoyed a very successful run of five weeks at the Lecture and Music Hall where seats could be had for as little as 3d. He advertised that fifteen gold and silver watches would be given away each week, as well as all the other presents which were 'larger than ever'. Elizabeth's perceptive remark that his purported conjuring was an excuse for a raffle was borne out by a small piece which appeared some weeks later in the *Ipswich Journal* to the effect that 'the Wolverhampton Magistrates committed a person known as Signor Blitz, for seven days, for carrying on an illegal lottery in the Corn Exchange Wolverhampton'.

Amid all the entertainments, serious or light-hearted, culturally stimulating or soporific, including 'A Ghost Entertainment' to which the younger girls were taken by their parents, one wonders how Elizabeth came to deny her family such delights as 'M. Desarias and his Parisian Troupe of Histrionic Dogs and Monkeys and Mr George Hodson, the Irish comedian and vocalist'. Or an evening at the Mechanics Institute where they could go on 'A Tour through the mountains of Switzerland with Capt. D'Orilli with vocal illustrations by Mlle de Moa and Brilliantly Illuminated moving scenery'. With all the foreign names that crop up in the advertisements and references to performers one wonders how many were in fact like Signor Brunoni in *Cranford*, the bearers of very English-sounding surnames.

In the 1850s, apart from the large family dinner parties they attended in London, most of the entertaining the Cottons received outside the home was on a small scale except for that offered by their friends the Rowlands, whom we first meet very early in the diary: '*5 April 1854*. Friday Went to a dinner party at Mr Rowland's of Akenham.' The Rowlands helped to extend the Cottons' range of acquaintances and on one occasion their choice of guests provoked Elizabeth to an interesting piece of social comment: '*1 October 1856*. With Herbert to a dinner party at Mr Rowland's of Akenham. Amongst the guests were two ladies Miss Edwards and Miss Gale whose dresses were more masculine than feminine. Their conversation agreed with their appearance and assisted to make some amusement.'

Invitations were, of course, repaid and the Rowlands were included in the parties Elizabeth gave for visiting members of her London family. The informality and gaiety of these is conveyed vividly when Edward and Arabella Haxell and Rea and Henry Page are guests at Amor Hall:

> *16 October 1859*. Friday. Called upon Mrs Allen and persuaded her to join us this evening. Mr and Mrs Rowland, Mr and Mrs Allen and Mrs H. Miller dined with us. In the evening Music and dancing. . . .
> Saturday. After dinner to Mr Rowland's at Akenham Hall. Had a most delightful evening and I fear romped.

The supposed stuffiness and observed decorum of the middle-class Victorian is absent here. One can almost hear the Rowlands saying as they were leaving on Friday evening – or possibly in the early hours of

Saturday morning – 'You must come over to us tomorrow night'. There is a spontaneity about the occasion which causes Elizabeth to respond with an equally spontaneous emotion even though she fails to elaborate for our benefit exactly what form the 'romping' took. There are, throughout both diaries, frequent references to dinner parties either at home or at the houses of others. Elizabeth needed very little excuse to give one, and she appears to have enjoyed being part of a large group. Most of the meals were followed by music of some sort, and dancing if there were sufficient numbers to warrant it. When the boys were not yet in their teens, they and Alice were receiving invitations to dinners and dances: '16 January 1859. Wednesday. Alice, Bertie and Allan went to a dinner party and dance at Mr George Ranson's.'

The reference quoted above is useful in showing that the children were not bound to the same social circles as their parents. Although the Ransons were neighbours, Elizabeth's socialising with them was restricted to the occasional afternoon call usually in relation to an exchange of children's visits: '4 July 1858. . . . I called upon Mrs G. Ranson, Eva and Allan with me. . . . Thursday. George and Charles Ranson spent the day here. Had fireworks in the evening – Blanche's birthday.' The children continued to attend parties at the Ransons' home and one occasion offers an insight into the dramas of another family's life: '21 December 1866. Our children dressed to attend an evening party at Mr Ranson's when two of Mrs Ranson's little boys called to say their Mamma had fallen down in a fit and remained too ill to receive friends.' The following day: 'Bertie and Allan called upon Mr Ranson and found Mrs Ranson rather better'. What interpretation can be placed on the latter remark? Elizabeth would have felt a natural concern for Mrs Ranson's well-being, yet she herself did not go to enquire after her. Was it that the relationship between the adults did not allow for a call at such an intimate moment or quite simply that as the boys were the ones who had been invited to the party, it was socially correct that they should make the enquiry?

However, there were times when the whole family were involved: '15 January 1860. Tuesday. Evening to a dance at Mr H. Miller's. Alice and the boys with us. Enjoyed the evening very much. It was called a juvenile party, but there were as many of the children's parents dancing through the evening as the young people.'

How did they cope with the numbers at these functions? These people are not the very wealthy living in large country houses with ballrooms and huge dining-rooms and a small army of domestic staff. Elizabeth tells us of an evening party at the Rowlands for forty guests in 1862, yet the census taken the year before shows them having only two living-in maids. Similarly when Elizabeth gave a dinner party for forty-five, she had at most three domestics to call upon. Were women from the village recruited just for the occasion, or did the mistress of the house enlist the services of outside caterers, like Cocks, the pastrycook in Ipswich who specialised in events like balls, routs, and evening parties? I suspect that many middle-class hostesses did as some of the ladies in the fictional Cranford, rolled up their sleeves, donned an apron and worked hard behind the scenes, before putting on their evening dresses and party front. As for the size of rooms for these parties, it is worth noting that many Victorian houses built for the middle class had rooms which were conveniently provided with large interconnecting doors which could be folded back to form one very large reception area. But even so, how, with all those enormously wide skirts, did they all fit in? And who provided the music for the dancing? Elizabeth provides an answer to that on one occasion:

> *6 August 1867.* Tuesday. Evening arranged with Miss Bransby to play Quadrilles on Thursday evening. Wednesday, Fanny Page came to stay. . . . Thursday. A croquet party at home – Miss Meadows, her sister Margaret, Miss Bryan and her sister, Ada Moore, Mr Kemp, Mr Wallace, Capt. Walsh, Dr Rowland, Mr E. Rowland, Mr H. Jackaman, Mr Allen and Mr Dawson. Dancing [i.e. quadrilles], after croquet. . . . *10 August.* Dinner party at home. Mr and Mrs Meadows, Dr and Mrs Moore, Mr Kemp, Capt. Walsh, Miss Belle Meadows, Miss Bryan and Ada Moore to meet Mr Draper. He arrived by the seven o'clock train and stayed.

From the many references in the diary, it is clear that it was common practice among Elizabeth's acquaintance to provide entertainment for house guests by introducing them into the host's circle of friends. In this extract we see the special arrangements made to honour the fact that her niece Fanny Page has recently become engaged. The young people invited to the croquet party included those who had met Fanny during the visits she had made since childhood. This was, however, a formal occasion, hence the provision of a professional musician to play for the dancing rather than relying on one of the company to oblige. The more formal dinner party which followed two evenings later was much more for 'the grown-ups' – and was held especially to welcome Fanny's fiancé Mr Draper. And just in case, while we are reading these accounts, we should think we are living in a world of the idle rich, we are reminded that Mr Draper has not been able to arrive before the 7 o'clock train on Saturday because he is a working man and businesses do not close on Saturdays. If we are of a romantic inclination we might ponder on the fact that Captain Walsh was present on both occasions. Was he there for Alice or was he betrothed to one of the other young ladies?

When considering weddings during the period, the diaries lead us to the conclusion that these became a much more social event as the century progressed. George Ranson's account of his brother's wedding in the 1840s suggests that only a few very close members of the family attended the ceremony. When Elizabeth's sister Kate marries James Nelson in London in August 1855 Elizabeth makes no mention of it, not even to note that she has received an invitation to the marriage, as she does when her brother Arthur is to be married to Mary Barron in 1859. The fact that she declined that invitation when she was obviously close to Arthur, suggests, I believe, not that she was antagonistic in any way, particularly as she had gone out of her way to entertain Mary as Arthur's fiancée, but that attendance at weddings was not considered to be as important as it has since become. However, by the mid-1860s things had changed and middle-class weddings were becoming much larger affairs. Elizabeth and Herbert attended the weddings in London of both her nieces:

22 September 1864. Emily's Wedding. Took Alice to Henry's house to be bridesmaid. Then drove on to Camberwell Church and met the bridal party. Emily looked remarkably well. There were about forty at the wedding, nearly all of whom were relations. Henry appeared very unhappy the whole time, and Rea was often much affected. After Breakfast Emily and Tom left and the company went into the garden and afterwards danced and cards. Emily had some good presents made her. Mr Welsh gave her and Fanny each a diamond ring. We gave a set of silver salts with spoons in a case, and many other articles of plate were also given.

Unfortunately we do not know who the generous Mr Welsh was, or why Henry Page was so unhappy. His new son-in-law, Tom Lazenby, was certainly well known to him, for the Lazenbys crop up regularly in the pages of the diaries. It may be that they were close business associates or even relations of the Pages. Perhaps this is an example of a fond Victorian papa being overcome at the prospect of losing his beloved daughter.

When her turn came Fanny received a silver salver as a wedding gift from the Cottons. Bertie and Evelyn were also included in the wedding party, Evelyn joining Alice as a bridesmaid. The details of Fanny's wedding are sparse but illuminating: '*26 March 1868*. Fanny married to Mr Draper at St. John's Church, Camberwell. Large party at Henry Page's to Breakfast, and dance in the evening.'

Here we see the formalising of the occasion. Dancing had taken place at Emily's wedding, probably of an impromptu nature, but for Fanny's there was not just the traditional wedding breakfast but also a full-scale arranged dance for the evening. Rea and Henry Page were leading a much grander social life in Dulwich than Elizabeth did in Suffolk. Rea had established a routine from 1860 onwards of giving each January what Elizabeth on one occasion designates as a ball. Elizabeth and Herbert declined invitations to these, but in 1863 Alice goes to London on her own for the week to attend it, and thereafter it becomes part of her social calendar.

From 1864 when the second diary starts, Elizabeth and Herbert spend more time at parties where music and cards form the after-dinner entertainment, while the dances and balls are attended by the younger people. When she is in London, we may assume that Alice is chaperoned by her aunts or married cousins, but at home in Suffolk, Elizabeth seems quite content that her daughter should attend parties accompanied only by her brothers. Most of the dances were held in private at the homes of friends, but we also read that Alice, Bertie and Allan attended the Mayor's Ball at the Town Hall in Ipswich.

EXCURSIONS AND OUTDOOR ACTIVITIES

There were, too, a great many outdoor functions to attend, and again we see the development of activities which embraced not just the family, but were extended to include close friends. When we have house guests, we take them out and show them the sights of the locality, and so too did the Cottons:

> *22 July 1855.* On Monday to Felixstow. Herbert drove Henry, Rea and Anne, and I went in the cab with Mrs Lazenby, Mr Leath and Arthur. Our horse knocked up at Trimley and so we had started by an omnibus passing, when Herbert came back in the phaeton for us. Some of our party went upon the water. Tuesday. Rea, Henry and Arthur left. Wednesday I drove Mrs Lazenby, Anne and Mr Leath round Hintlesham.

In June 1859, Elizabeth and Herbert visited Helmingham Hall, the beautiful Suffolk home of the Lord Tollemache. Elizabeth was so en-amoured by all she saw there, that it was to become a favourite place to take guests:

> *4 June 1859.* Saturday. With Herbert to Helmingham. Went over the Hall, the seat of the Tollemaches. The place is kept up in its ancient state, the drawbridges over the moat being drawn up every night, and all the furniture of the house being antique and generally richly carved. A few suits of armour hang in the hall and family portraits and books all over the different lower rooms. In the Library is shewn the

first book printed in England and a manuscript written by King Alfred.

23 October 1859. [The Pages and Haxells are visiting Washbrook.] Monday. To Helmingham. At first fearful we should not see the Hall as Mr Tollemache's family was at home. Fortunately we met the steward Mr Beckett, and Herbert knowing him, he very politely walked with us over the greater part of the house, the grounds and the stables. Caught in the rain about four miles from home, but no one suffered from it. After dinner our friends left us.

Highly popular too as a pastime was either 'going on the water' or watching the events at regattas. From Ipswich it was possible to travel down the Orwell by steamboat to the port of Harwich and the adjoining town of Dovercourt: '9 *June 1854.* Saturday with Herbert to Harwich Regatta. We drove to Shotley, then by ferry boat to Harwich. Dined at the Cups Hotel, had tea at Shotley when we returned there in the evening and then drove home.' And, two years later: '14 *September*, With Herbert on Wednesday to Harwich by Steam Boat. Walked to Dovercourt and dined at the hotel there. Found the advertised accommodation a deception at this place. Home in the evening by Steam Boat.'

The advertisement of which Elizabeth disapproves is to be found in the *Ipswich Journal*:

Francis Claxton Begs respectfully to announce that the Queen's Head Inn, Dovercourt New Town, opposite the railway station and a few minutes walk from the celebrated Spa is now ready for the reception of visitors. Luncheons, Dinners, etc. supplied at the shortest notice. Private rooms for families and parties. Well aired beds always ready. Wines, spirits, Ales and Stout of the first quality. Good stabling and lock-up Coach houses.

Since the Cottons had arrived by water and were only there for the day, it was presumably not in either the field of well-aired beds or stabling that the hotel fell short. Perhaps Mr Claxton had failed to produce luncheon or dinner at short notice, and the diarist, it must be remembered, was the granddaughter and niece of those in the trade who had set high standards.

The joint interest Elizabeth and Herbert shared in watching the racing yachts became much more intense as the boys grew older and both Bertie and Allan became keen oarsmen:

7 July 1865. To Ipswich Regatta with Herbert, Allan and little girls. We took a boat on the river and remained until the sports were nearly concluded although it rained heavily nearly all the time. . . . *26 June*

1866. To Harwich Regatta. Lunched at Great Eastern Hotel. Bertie went with Mr Kemp to lunch upon the *Pembroke* Man of War. . . . *30 June.* In the evening Bertie went upon the river and Rose and Allan. They were all caught in a terrible storm and came home thoroughly drenched. . . . Afternoon with boys, Blanche and Eva on the Ipswich river to see the championship of the Orwell contested. It was won by the Nautilus Club. Bertie and Allan stayed to Club Dinner. . . . To Ipswich Regatta with Mr Kemp who had tickets for the Corporation Barge. . . . *30 May 1868.* To Boat Races with the children. Our boys won.

The modern female boating enthusiast suitably clad in slacks, sweaters and canvas shoes and equipped with a life jacket may spare a thought for her Victorian counterpart who, undeterred by her restrictive garments, clambered in and out of rowing boats. A development from the day on the river was what Elizabeth called a 'Pic Nic'. This combined the earlier excursion to visit the gardens of some large house with time spent on the river, plus the eating of an alfresco meal rather than being dependent on a local inn to provide food. '*19 April 1865.* With Herbert, our children, Ellen and Walton Turner and Mr Coppinger to Freston Tower. Rowed there and back. Took lunch with us and had it in Woolverstone Park. Went over Mr Berners' gardens and Woolverstone Park.'

The village of Woolverstone lies on the south side of the Orwell. Here, Berners had considerably improved his own house and grounds and built a fine example of a Victorian model village. Freston Tower, a sixteenth-century folly, dominated the landscape as well as affording a navigational aid. It had a varied existence, for example, in 1777 it was occupied by a doctor who advertised short residential stays for the wealthy and their servants while undergoing inoculation against smallpox.

Having enjoyed their excursion, the Cottons decided to repeat it the following year, extending their party to include older friends:

1 August 1866. To Woolverstone Park with Herbert, our children, Mr and Mrs Burrell, M. Carré and M. Nequillant. Saw Freston Tower, the gardens, Hothouses and Ferneries. Lunched in the park and home about 11 o'clock at night. Bertie and M. Carré rowed one boat and Simons the boatman and Allan the other.

What an idyllic picture of a long hot summer day this evokes. One can picture them wandering about looking at all the fine things on show, the leisurely lunch, the young people enjoying games and then the row back to Ipswich in the fading light with the shimmering gas jets of the town lights in the distance to arrive home very late, tired yet exhilarated by such a happy day. Unfortunately all the gaiety was to be marred when Elizabeth went to town on Friday morning and met Mr Burrell:

3 August 1866. Had the great grief to hear from Mr Burrell of the death of his poor little infant Walter. He died in a spasm from disease of the heart about an hour after Mr and Mrs Burrell had returned home from our Pic Nic trip to Woolverstone.

On a less sad note, Allan too had to pay for his rowing activities: '*7 August 1866.* In afternoon to Ipswich with Allan. Allan had his hand – from an abscess upon which he has been suffering – lanced by Dr Bartlet.'

By the following year the picnic party has become very much the fashionable way to entertain one's friends during the summer: '*13 June 1867.* With Alice and Bertie to a Pic Nic Party given by Mr Meadows and his family in Woolverstone Park. Met Major Day, Mr and Mrs Rouse, Mr and Mrs Rhodes, Mr Pytches, Miss Bryant and her sisters, and M. Badlett.' This time some of the party at least travelled by road rather than water, for Elizabeth completes that day's entry by relating that on her way home she stopped in Ipswich to visit her old friend Kitty Cobbold who was very ill.

One of the highlights of the Ipswich social calendar was Race Week. From some of the references in the earlier diary one might think that this was essentially a male occasion. '*9 July 1854.* Herbert went to Ipswich Races on Thursday and Friday.' Similar entries appear for 1855 and 1856 with the additional information that Herbert not only spent the days concerned at the races but he went in the evening to the theatre.

'*August 27 and 28 1857.* Ipswich Races. Herbert went. On Friday I went to Ipswich and bought some fireworks for the children. We let them off in the garden.' This reference to a garden fireworks display in August seemed a trifle mystifying until later references showed that an organised pyrotechnic display was part of the race meeting festivities. Perhaps this is an example of Elizabeth giving her children a share in activities in which they were not yet old enough to join?

16 October 1859. . . . . Tuesday evening my sister Rea, and Edward and his wife came from London to see us. Herbert met them at Ipswich station . . . Wednesday Herbert and I went with our visitors to Ipswich Races. Afterwards dined at the White Horse and went to the theatre in the evening. . . . . Henry Page arrived at our house late at night and we all went to the Races again on Thursday taking Alice and our boys with us. . . . . *4 September 1861.* Arabella and Edward came to see us. . . . . To Ipswich Races and theatre in the evening. Dined at the White Horse. . . . . To Ipswich Races. . . . . *17 July 1862.* Thursday

Herbert took Bertie and Allan to Races. Walked to Ipswich with Alice and little girls and rode home with the boys. Herbert stayed to Race dinner. . . . *25 June 1863.* Herbert took boys to the Races at Ipswich.

The fact that Elizabeth attended only on those occasions when she was entertaining guests, suggests she was not particularly interested in the sport, but this idea is refuted in the later diary:

30 June 1864. Thursday To Ipswich Races. Herbert drove Allan and little girls in the waggonette. Alice went with me in the close carriage. . . . *30 August 1865.* Wednesday   To the Races with Herbert and children. Many friends joined us at luncheon. Boys went to Fireworks in the evening. . . . To Races again. Boys went to Theatre in the evening.

Herbert and the boys continued to attend the Races until 1867, and perhaps some of the entertainment available in the evenings was aimed specifically at a masculine audience. On their way home to Washbrook the Cottons would pass the inn at the edge of the town which boasted that its gardens emulated those of Vauxhall in London:

Vauxhall – Royal William Gardens, London Road.
Mr Stevens begs to inform that he intends opening his beautiful gardens on Race Nights and presenting a variety of entertainments of a novel description in which the following artists are engaged: Madame Geniveve – who will make her terrific ascent of the fiery rope; Miss Lizzy Watson; the renowned Paddy Fannin, the celebrated Irish Comic Singer from the Crystal Palace; Signor Perallo etc. Each evenings entertainment will conclude with a magnificent display of Fireworks.

More to Elizabeth's taste were the steeplechases and the informal races staged by the officers garrisoned at Colchester and Ipswich. Following the hunt became popular too, once the boys became involved. '*8 April 1861.* Monday. To Steeplechase at Bramford with Herbert and the boys. The sport was very good. Enjoyed the day very much. Captain Fitzgerald was thrown and rather hurt.' This particular event excited sufficient interest for the railway company to run special excursion trains from London for it. '*4 April 1866.* Wednesday to Colchester Steeple Races (*sic*) with Herbert, our children and M. Tersynck. The rain fell in torrents all day, but we had a great deal of amusement.'

12 March 1864. Capt. Fitzgerald brought his Harriers to Washbrook. Walked with Herbert and children to see them. Walton and Pearson

Turner with us. My boys rode and the little girls ran with Walton and Pearson and managed to keep very near the hounds. . . . *3 December.* With Herbert and little girls walked to see Mr Nunn's Harriers meet. The Hunt afterwards lunched here. . . . *29 March 1865.* Gave the children a holiday. Walked with them to see the Harriers. Capt. Fitzgerald and the Hunt came to lunch. . . . *5 January 1866.* With Bertie, Alice and the little girls in the wagonette to see the hounds meet at Stratford Hills. Allan hunted. We followed the hounds for some time driving about the roads and lanes. . . . *26 January.* With Bertie, Alice and little girls to see the hounds meet. Met Ellen and Walton Turner with some of their friends. Went into Shrublands Park and left our carriages with Sir G.Broke Middleton's servants while we walked in the park to see the hunt pass us. Allan was with them. . . . *31 January 1866.* Rose rode with Bertie to see the hounds meet.

Elizabeth constantly confounds the picture of a sober middle-class mamma. One would have expected her to adopt a high moral tone on the iniquity of gambling, but perhaps, like all sensible parents, she believed in moderation in all things and that a knowledge of what one's offspring did was preferable to covert activities. Hence the comments: '*8 May 1865.* Officers of Ipswich Garrison Races at Ipswich. . . . *12 May.* The children arranged the wagers they had lost and won.'

The other social functions which Elizabeth attended seem to be much more in keeping with a middle-aged matron of that era: '*16 July 1854.* Thursday. With Herbert to Horticultural Show at Woodbridge. . . . Wednesday. With Herbert and children to Fete at the Rectory. . . . *1 September 1856.* To a Charity Bazaar at the Arboretum. . . . *22 August 1858.* With Herbert to a Musical Fete given at Sir W. Middleton's. . . . *10 October.* Invited by Mr de Grey to see Review of Artillery upon his grounds. Took children with us – the soldiers did not come.'

They were more fortunate in 1863: '*4 September.* Friday. To Shrublands Gardens with Herbert and children. Walton with us. Review of Volunteer Troops. . . . *11 September.* Friday. To Ipswich Race Ground to see Rifle Control with Herbert, children and Walton.'

Throughout the summer months there was a show of some kind almost every week. '*9 June 1862.* Mrs Turner's younger children spent the day with us. Went to Washbrook Fair. . . . *3 July 1863.* Friday. To Agricultural and Flower Shows and in the evening to Fireworks.' In the winter, of course, the highlight of the agricultural calendar was the Smithfield Cattle Show. In June 1862, however, Herbert attended a summer cattle show and he, Elizabeth and Alice spent a day at a Dog Show. Organised events of this nature were in their infancy and this one, held at Agricultural Hall, was the North of England 2nd Exhibition. The Earl Spencer's Clumber Spaniel dog and bitch won first prizes:

'27 *June 1862*. With Herbert and Alice to Dog Show. Very much pleased. Some dogs remarkably handsome. One Clumber Spaniel appeared quite unhappy if persons passed him without shaking his paw.'

As for many families today, a visit to London often follows a similar pattern of sights and places to inspect, so was it for Elizabeth and her family. In 1858, while staying on her own with her London relations, Elizabeth had the conducted tour of the new Houses of Parliament, reminding us that George Ranson had viewed the building plans during his visit in 1844. Later when the children accompanied her and Herbert to the capital, they were duly taken to the Zoo and the Science Museum in Kensington, as well as many other places of historical and educational interest.

We know that Elizabeth also took part in games; she frequently mentions croquet and archery and when the children were young she joined them on fishing trips and she taught them to play battledore. However, she herself did not appear to join them in skating, although she actively encouraged their participation. Whenever the weather was suitable the older children skated on the flooded farm meadows and the little girls were allowed to slide. '1 *January 1867*. First snow this winter. . . . *15 January*. The children and Miss Jane Harmer went upon the ice. . . . *19 January*. Took lunch to the children who were skating on the overflowed meadows. . . . *22 January*. Children skated upon the Chauntry pond.'

The social life of the Cotton children and their wide circle of friends seem enviable. They appear to have had unrestricted freedom to attend parties and dances, theatres and other entertainments, and there seems to have been no curfew limit. Even if mother did wait up for their return, there are a number of references to Alice and the boys returning home at five and six in the morning. While they were all still at school, arrangements were often made for them to stay the night in town so that they would not miss out on such things as Guy Fawkes Night celebrations or end-of-term 'frolics'. They had too, the freedom to invite friends to stay and parents who put themselves out to help entertain the guests. They were taken out on visits and offered every opportunity their parents could afford. Were she living today, Elizabeth would be there with the mothers who take their babies to swimming classes. But, given the limitations of her time, she did her best here too, and actively encouraged the children to bathe in the sea at Felixstowe.

As far as Elizabeth's own social life was concerned, it has been shown, without enumerating every reference to dining out, tea-drinking and casual visiting, that her life was not restricted to the domestic hearth as we have been led to believe it was for the Victorian middle-class woman.

7
Travel

Lynton and Lynmouth greatly destroyed by the 'Got up for Visitors'
improvements.

Elizabeth Cotton's Diary

The discovery that Elizabeth Cotton travelled widely throughout the British Isles during the period 1854–63 was an example of yet another of my preconceptions about the age being proved wrong. History books and the literature of the time had provided information that the wealthy travelled in Europe, and it is well-known that the development of the railways had opened up seaside resorts for the working class day-tripper. It was also understood that friends and relations in one part of the country might make extended visits to others; the town-dweller seeking a change of air in the countryside; the country cousin being given the opportunity to experience the delights of the 'season' in town. But the two-week holiday tour undertaken by a middle-class husband and wife, without servants and their own carriage, came as a surprise. Were the Cottons unique in this? Probably not.

It was when Elizabeth was travelling that she had time to write more fully, giving information about the modes of travel, commenting on the places she visited and the people she met. Since she was more relaxed, she revealed more of herself, her tastes and prejudices, her humour and strength of character. Indirectly we learn about customs in different parts of the country and the problems involved with regional dialects, and details such as the fact that our travellers seem rarely to have bothered to book accommodation in advance, that they expected hotels to provide a bedroom and a private sitting-room, and about the habit of dining 'table d'hôte'. This term encountered nowadays on a hotel menu indicates that a set meal is provided at an inclusive charge, so it would come as a shock to find we were expected, as in Victorian times, to sit down at a large table at a given time to eat our meal with fellow guests.

Many of the holiday tours Elizabeth and Herbert took, usually in June, are familiar to modern tourists, and since many also keep records of their own holidays, I propose that in this section Elizabeth should speak for herself, allowing the reader the opportunity of an uninterrupted account to compare with their experiences. Very occasionally, we shall hear also from the unpublished holiday diaries of two young ladies who made similar tours with their parents.

It was on 14 June 1855 that Herbert and Elizabeth set out on the first of their recorded tours, secure in the knowledge that all would be well at home with Mrs Marskall in charge.

On Thursday morning . . . we started for Rugby by Railway. Waited there an hour, and then went on to Derby. Stayed at Midland Hotel. Friday walked in Derby Arboretum. While walking in the town, when Herbert was at the market, was caught in a storm and took shelter in a cottage, where I met very kind people. Some of their country friends came in while I was there, and addressed each other as Lad and Lass, using thee and thou in conversation. Afterwards by Rail to Chesterfield Ambergate and Matlock. We were detained at the Ambergate Station two hours, from an accident having occurred on the line in which two men were killed. An old lady who travelled with us requested me to change places with her, as she believed the seat in which I was, was more safe than her own. I could not help laughing when doing as she wished. The ride was terribly noisy going through so many tunnels and the old lady very nervous. At Matlock stayed at New Bath Hotel. Herbert was very sadly in the night.

On Saturday we had a carriage to Dove Dale, passing Brassington Moor, Tissington, Thorpe and Ilam Hall. Dined at the Izaak Walton Inn and walked through Dove Dale and back. Made some sketches.

On Sunday walked to Heights of Abraham and to see a water mill. Afterwards went a long way on the Langton road.

On Monday saw Petrifying Wells and purchased a Bird's nest from it. Then to Rowsley by Train – Peacock Hotel. Took a carriage to Haddon Hall and went over the Hall. Very much pleased with it. Our guide – a little girl, told the legends well and evidently was pleased with the notice taken of her. An artist sat in the banqueting room making a water colour drawing of it. I made a sketch of the Terrace. Afterwards went on to Bakewell and having ordered dinner at the Rutland Arms, walked in a storm of rain to the churchyard to see a stone cross there. Saw a shapeless piece of stone, not worth the trouble of finding out. When at the Rutland Arms some gentlemen staying there sent us in a large dish of trout to be looked at, that they had just caught. Went by carriage to Chatsworth. Stayed at the Hotel at Edensor.

Friday. Went over the Duke of Devonshire's House and grounds. All very beautiful and the housekeeper a very agreeable and well-informed person. The Victoria Regia was in bloom, and the well stocked hot houses very tempting. Admired some of the sculpture in the house. Most of the modern pictures we had seen before. The carving in wood in some of the rooms very fine. Walked about the park . . . In the evening went to Buxton. Very unfortunately for us we arrived upon the eve of a grand fete, and found all the best hotels unable to give us lodgings. At last we obtained an attic as sleeping room at the George Hotel and joined a large company living at a table d'hote. This was very comfortless, but we could do no better. The persons we met, were chiefly tradespeople from Sheffield and their expressions and words sounded strangely to us. Their behaviour, especially at meals, was very coarse.

Walked about Buxton. The wells of the place were decorated with flowers and flags. A company of Morris Dancers went round the town, stopping in the best public places and fixing a pole into the ground to which ribbons of different colours were fixed. Young children gaily dressed, danced round this pole, each holding the end of a ribbon in their hand wove patterns of plaids upon the pole – unwound the figure in the same manner and wove another. Received letters from home, all well. Bought presents for the children, and left Buxton, posting to Castleton.

On our way stopped to visit the Blue John Mine. A dirty and rather troublesome undertaking it proved, but we went as far as practicable, each carrying a candle and stooping, climbing or descending as the guide directed. Sometimes we had to advance with the right shoulder forward, and sometimes with the left, always over insecure and painful ground to walk up and generally with our heads about the same height as our knees. It was a great relief when informed we had reached a place allowing us to stand up, but I thought the best sight of all was daylight again. Bought some specimens of the Blue John or Fluor spar and went on to Castleton. Stayed at Nags Head. Many copies of 'Peveril of the Peak' lying in our room. Walked. Saw Shaking Hill and made sketches in the neighbourhood.

Thursday. Walked to Peak Castle. Sketched it. A girl who joined us as self-elected guide showed us Moultrassie Hall and pointed out the path by which Julian Peveril visited Alice Bridgenorth without being seen by her father. She told the story as an undoubted fact, and did not mind my laughing. Went to the Peak Caverns and persuaded by the guide of the place, that it was an agreeable spot to visit, explored another cavern but I think it will be the last. The winding, creeping and crouching of the Blue John Mine was repeated, and as there the return to daylight was most welcome, and here, having the beautiful natural entrance arch of the Peak Cavern to meet as we came from the darkness, the burst of sunlight was grand in the extreme.

Posted to Sheffield, the scenery through which we travelled very fine in a desolate way at first, but becoming flatter as we approached the town and long before we reached Sheffield a dense cloud told us of its direction. Stayed at Royal Hotel. Walked in the evening about the town. A man was haranguing a cluster of persons upon their political rights, we stayed a little to listen to him. Both he and his listeners appeared in earnest.

On Friday walked about the town again, and then by rail to Peterborough. Stayed at Railway Hotel. Had to telegraph for our luggage, which had been sent wrong at March Station. It arrived before we went to bed.

On Saturday walked about Peterborough and went over the Cathedral. Outside very fine and most imposing in appearance, but the interior does not appear to possess so many objects of interest as most cathedrals. Afterwards by Railway to Cambridge. Stayed at White Lion Hotel. Walked about the town, and went over the Colleges. Some of the Halls and Chapels with fine architecture, and the grounds most charming places. Saw Milton's mulberry tree.

Sunday, 24 June. To King's College Chapel. The music, particularly the anthem, beautiful. Afterwards walked about the grounds of the Colleges for hours. Monday. Home.

For today's traveller, there is much in this account which is reminiscent, not least the delay in train services and the misdirection of luggage, particularly familiar to air travellers. Although Elizabeth indicates that they have not booked their accommodation in advance, they obviously had planned their route sufficiently that they knew on which days they would be where so that letters from home could be addressed to the Post Office of that town to await collection. We notice too, that at the beginning of the holiday, Herbert was unable to resist visiting the local market and that Elizabeth was quite happy to wander alone in a strange town and accept hospitality from those unknown to her. Although Elizabeth was in Buxton for the famous well-dressing ceremonies, she makes little comment upon them, her attention having been caught by the children dancing round the Morris Men's pole. From her very detailed description, it seems that she had not witnessed such an event before, which rather dispels the received idea of every village green having its own maypole in the 'good old days'. *Peveril of the Peak* by Sir Walter Scott enjoyed tremendous popularity following its publication in 1822 and we note that the local inhabitants were quick to appreciate the benefits that the book could bring them. Elizabeth seems to have a knowledge of the book, but it was not until the following year that she read it aloud to Herbert. Finally, if we need proof that all Victorian women were not weak, fragile creatures, then her descriptions of the visits to the mines and caves is evidence enough, especially when we recall what she would have been wearing.

The following year the Cottons did not travel quite so far. At the beginning of May 1856 Herbert and Elizabeth spent a long weekend at Orford and Aldeburgh on the Suffolk coast where Herbert shot wild fowl. Returning on Monday, they spent the rest of the week at home before leaving for London on the Saturday, from where:

On Wednesday to Tunbridge Wells by Rail. Stayed at the Kentish Hotel. Went a drive round the neighbourhood in the evening.

Thursday. To Dover by Railway. Stayed at the Lord Warden Hotel. Rode up Dover Castle Hill and walked about the castle grounds. Saw the French packets [steamers] arrive and depart. Most of the passengers who landed looked very ill.

Friday walked with Herbert to Shakespeare's Cliff and afterwards posted to Canterbury. Stayed at Fountain Hotel and went over the Cathedral. Found the monuments and other remains replete with interest. Went to Hastings by Rail. Stayed at Albion Hotel. Walked in the town and on parade. The Albion is so close to the sea that our windows are splashed by the spray of the waves at high tide. Heard a woman singing Annie Laurie very sweetly in the streets.

18 May. Sunday. Wrote home and to Anne. Went a drive with Herbert round the neighbourhood.

Monday. Walked with Herbert. Caught in a shower of rain. Took a cab back to Hotel. Afterwards by Rail to Brighton. Stayed at the New Steyne Hotel. Walked on the beach and in the town and a drive. Found letters from home for us at the Post Office.

Tuesday. Walked with Herbert in the town. Purchased a garnet cross for Alice and toys for the other children. Walked in the Pavilion grounds. Went to Worthing by Rail. Dined there. Walked on the beach and took a drive round the town and returned by Rail to Brighton. Quite disappointed with the beach and neighbourhood of Worthing. Walked in the evening and shopping. Wednesday. Walked on the pier and afterwards to London by Railway.

Compared with the previous tour, this holiday in the south of England with its emphasis on seaside resorts seems to lack lustre. Nothing exciting appears to have happened – beyond watching the seasick travellers disembarking at Dover – just walking on beaches and esplanades and driving around to view the countryside. The uneventfulness of the holiday is reflected in Elizabeth's accounts, but the reason for it is not revealed until later. Bearing in mind how ill Elizabeth had been in February of the previous year prior to the birth of Ethel, Herbert was probably taking no chances with her health this year; good fresh ozone-laden air and gentle exercise were just what a lady almost eight months pregnant needed.

This time the birth was uncomplicated, Blanche was a healthy baby and in May 1857 Elizabeth and Herbert were off again on their travels, as usual starting from London.

Wednesday, 19 May 1857. To Manchester by Railway. Great difficulty in obtaining rooms. Went to several hotels and at last were accommodated at the Mosely Arms. Found it noisy and not very comfortable. Walked in the town. Found letters for us from home at the Post Office.

Thursday. Wrote home and spent the day at the Exhibition of Art Treasures . . .

On Saturday by Railway to Windermere. A young lady travelling with her lover singularly confidential to me when we were once or twice alone in the carriage. Stayed at the Birthwaite Hotel, a very comfortable house.

Sunday. Rained until three o'clock, when the mist clearing away we had a drive round Rothay and Troutbeck seeing beautiful scenery all the way. Returned to Windermere. Monday. A drive to Coniston past Esthwaite Water. Dined at the Waterhead Inn. Had carp and oatmeal bread for dinner. When in the hotel grounds I got into a boat upon the lake for a few minutes. Walked afterwards on the Old Man Mountain. Returned to Windermere. Some ladies of a family staying at the hotel sang sacred music last night so beautifully that we left our door open to hear them better. Tuesday. Drove to Ambleside. Past Dove's Nest once the residence of Mrs Hemans [the poet]. Stayed at the Salutation Hotel. Drove to Langdale Pikes and Dungeon Ghyll. Had lunch at Millbeck Farm. Left the carriage there and walked to the waterfall. The farmer walked with us, and was an amusing companion, but it was funny to see his assumed indifference when some lads passing us on their way to the waterfall rejected with contempt his offer of accompanying them as guide. Afterwards to Grassmere and Rydal. To Wordsworth's Grave and into Grassmere Church. Then to his home at Rydal, where we saw Mrs Wordsworth, an old and apparently feeble woman. Saw the different waterfalls and returned to Ambleside.

Wednesday. A drive through Kirkstone Pass to Patterdale. On the top of the Pass, our driver stopped to refresh his horses. Herbert waited with the carriage and I walked on nearly two miles before they overtook me. Went into Patterdale Churchyard to see the grave of Charles Gough. Took a boat on Ullswater to Lepilph's Tower and Ara Force. Sketched the waterfall and the Hall in the Tower. Returned to Ambleside and after dinner walked to the Stock Ghyll Falls.

Thursday. A drive to Wythburn. Lunched there. I went up Helvellyn, Herbert did not ascend but walked about Wythburn. While ascending the view was very beautiful, sometimes most extensive, but the mist closed in when near the top of the mountain. Gathered some ferns. When going down my pony fell from his leg sinking into a hole by a rock, but although my foot was hurt against the rock, I did not lose my seat. The guide with me was very alarmed until he saw the pony's knees were not hurt, and asked me not to say it had fallen. I promised, but was sorry for it, when upon again reaching Wythburn a lady waiting there for the pony asked my opinion about her taking the same ride. I said the mist was very thick, but I fancy she intended going up after we left. Went on to Keswick. Stayed at the Royal Oak. Bought chalcedony and other seals for children. Walked by Derwentwater Lake.

Friday. On Derwentwater Lake. Afterwards posted to Scales Inn. Went through Borrowdale and Buttermere. The roads difficult, but the scenery beautifully wild. Stayed at Scale Hill. [There is a possibility here that Elizabeth has slightly muddled her route.]

Saturday. Walked about the neighbourhood and afterwards posted to Whitehaven. Went through Ennerdale. The first part of the journey very beautiful. Whitehaven a dirty, disagreeable town. We stayed at the Globe Hotel. In the evening we crossed over to the pier in a boat, but the neighbourhood we had first to walk through was fearful. I never saw anything like the dirty indecency of the people.

Sunday   Waited until post time to have news from home. No letters arriving we asked the postmaster to post them on to us at York. Went by Rail to Maryport, dined there, afterwards by Rail to Carlisle. Stayed at the County Hotel.

1 June. Monday. Walked in Carlisle. Went over the Castle. Very intelligent guide who told the stories relating to the place well. Went upon the heights and ramparts of the Castle, into the cells where the Scotch prisoners had rubbed away the stone from the window when looking at the Scotch hills, and into the underground dungeons. Our guide also pointed out the prince Charles's initials, said to have been cut by himself, and the place in the wall where a closed up niche containing the skeletons of a woman and infant had been found. Went over Carlisle Cathedral; it does not interest me so much as the Castle. From the walls by the apartments of Queen Mary of Scotland I gathered some ivy. Went by Railway to Newcastle.

Tuesday. Walked in the town and went over the Castle where there is a nice collection of Antiquarian relics, and St. Nicholas Church, a nice old place with an altar piece by Tintoretto. By Railway to York. Stayed at York Hotel. . . . Walked in the city and on the walls. The walls do not surround the town, but appeared in good preservation.

Wednesday. Went over the beautiful Cathedral in which coloured glass is very rich. Copied an antique chair into my sketch book. Afterwards to the Museum, in the grounds here sketched Ruins and Etty's tomb, which is seen from the grounds. By Railway to Scarborough.

Stayed at Royal Hotel. Walked on the sands and terrace. Bought toy for Eva. Thursday. Walked in town. Bought specimens for children. Rather disappointed with Scarborough. By Rail to Muston. Here a kind of omnibus took us on to Flamborough, did not stay in the town but went on to Flamborough Head. Very wild scenery here and the people strangely uncouth. The enormous quantity of sea birds, and their cries added to the wild character of the scene. Sketched several scenes here. Rather startled after lying down to look closer down the cliffs by seeing the ground beneath was hollow underneath for several feet inwards. Fancying the earth now trembled I moved my position as gently as I could.

Dined at the Star Inn. . . . By fly again to Muston and by Railway to Hull. Stayed at Railway Hotel. Evening a drive round the town and neighbourhood until quite dark.

Friday   By Railway to Cambridge. We had intended returning home tonight, but found no train going further than Cambridge. Stayed at Lion Hotel. Walked in the College grounds and saw the Collegians boating.

Saturday   By Rail to Ipswich. Took a cab home. Found all well. Baby had forgotten me, but knew her father.

Most mothers who have left their very small children for a short period will recognise the situation in that last statement. It is almost as if the child punishes the mother for having left it by deliberately refusing to go to the maternal arms. However, despite this slight upset on her return, there is little doubt that Elizabeth had thoroughly enjoyed this particular tour. She reveals that her interest lay with areas which could offer interesting scenery and historical associations rather than the somewhat bland new seaside resorts. Her comments on Whitehaven are, I believe, a genuine expression of conditions rather than an example of affront to middle-class nicety; she was quite used to passing through the worst areas of Ipswich. The account of her lying down to look over the edge of the cliff is quite startling; one does not anticipate this type of behaviour from respectable Victorian matrons. But more important, how very human is her reaction when she discovers that the ground beneath her is extremely fragile. Was this episode and the near-miss accident on the pony confided to Herbert?

Having gone north in 1857, the next year found them travelling south-westwards. From Winchester where they shared a hotel with the German cavalry they journeyed to Salisbury:

28 May 1858. By Railway to Salisbury. Went over the cathedral – a very beautiful place, with monuments of great interest. The Council Chamber restored with great splendour and excellent taste. The man explaining its wonders to us, applied the word 'which' to persons and things alike in the funniest manner. Posted to Amesbury. On our way saw Old Sarum, and in the evening walked to Stonehenge. The desolate character of the heath was increased by the lateness of the hour and added to the grandeur of the scene. I was never more impressed by any remains of antiquity than by these wonderful monuments. The moon rose before we left the heath. Stayed· at the White Hart at Amesbury.

Saturday. Posted to Devizes, walked about the town, by Railway to Weston super Mare. Sunday. Walked by the water and a drive round the neighbourhood and to Banwell. Went over the gardens there. The caves not allowed to be shewn on Sunday.

Monday. To Barnstaple by Rail. . . . Strange old house at Barnstaple where we went for post horses. A lady here, agreeable and very handsome asked to be allowed to join us to Ilfracombe. When we arrived there she took the steam packet to Swansea. We stayed at the Clarence Hotel. The town a disagreeable place and our hotel not nice. The scenery in the neighbourhood beautiful. Walked on the heights by the sea. Sketched lighthouse on Lantern Hill.

1 June. Tuesday. Posted to Lynmouth by Combe Martin. The natural scenery beautiful, but by Lynton and Lynmouth greatly destroyed by the 'Got up for Visitors' improvements. Carriage ride to the Valley of the Rocks where we got out and walked to the heights. Places for Pic Nic parties to boil their kettles made all about here – sadly interfering with the natural grandeur of the place. Saw the Cheese Press rocks – sketched some views. To Waters Meet – a most lovely scene Lyn Cliff, and through some gardens to see cascades etc. Collected wild flowers in the lanes. Returned to Ilfracombe. Walked by the sea in the evening again. Bought shells from Barricane [a natural shell beach] for Alice.

Wednesday. By steam packet to Hayle. [A distance of over 100 nautical miles taking between 14 to 18 hours.] The day was stormy and Herbert very ill. As we approached the Cornish shore we saw many sea birds new to us about the rocks and cliffs. At Hayle stayed at the White Hart Hotel. When we arrived here after a long and fatiguing day we found the place in an uproar. The open space before our inn was taken up by a large menagerie with a noisy band of music playing before it. The hotel was lighted and its windows filled with people smoking and drinking and looking out with delight upon the fair outside. We were shown into a bedroom and after some little delay obtained a sitting room. Saw some rare china about this house. I would have tried to purchase some, but for the trouble of carrying it with us.

Thursday. To Penzance by Rail. Stayed at Union Hotel. Fair at Penzance today. We saw placards in the road announcing 'The Camels are Coming' and of course we could not escape from music and crowds. Posted to Land's End. Saw the Logan Stone rocked and walked, or rather climbed, to the extreme point of the promontory. Herbert greatly interested to see the cormorants and other sea birds, sitting on, or skimming about the rocks . . .

On the way to Land's End we saw the Druidic Stones called the Merry Maidens, the Pipers and the Nine Maidens; St. Buryan Church with its two crosses and the house called the First and Last Inn in England. But now this is wrong, as the hut where we sheltered by the Land's End rocks is a house of entertainment for travellers. Our waiter at Penzance spoke with so broad a dialect that we had difficulty to understand him.

Friday. Carriage to Marazion, and ferried over to St. Michael's Mount. Lady showing Castle at first rather grand, but became gradually more genial. Saw the pictures and curiosities in the Castle. Sketched a singular old chair in the dining room where the table was prepared for dinner. Antique silver drinking cups on the table. Into the chapel but did not descend into the dungeons, characterized by our lady guide as 'sad isn't it, and damp'. Up the dark and uncomfortable steep and narrow stairs to the top of the tower, here only our sailor guide accompanied us. He said some ladies climbed into the stone lantern or St. Michael's Chair, overhanging the precipice, that they might have their own way ever afterwards, but I did not venture upon this experiment. When we returned to the apartments below, the lady guide appeared with the visitors book and took her fee. Bought specimens for children at Penzance and by Rail to Truro. Stayed at Royal Hotel. Walked about town.

Saturday. To see Truro Museum. By coach to Plymouth. . . . We crossed from Cornwall into Devon on a floating pier, still remaining on the coach. Stayed at Globe Hotel. Had letters from home.

Sunday. Walked on the Hoe. By steamer to Saltbush – a picturesque old town, with inhabitants, particularly the women, of the wildest appearance and manners.

Monday. Walked about the town. Crossed the ferry to Mount Edgcombe. Walked about the grounds. Returned to Plymouth. By coach to Tavistock. Travelled outside. Stayed at Bedford Hotel. Nice quiet place and town. Evening had long walk by the river and past Buckland Abbey, now used as the Bedford Dairy, the Town Library etc. We posted to Two Bridges on Dartmoor. On our way we saw the gangs of prisoners from the Government settlement of Princes Town, at work on Dartmoor. From Two Bridges we walked to Wistman's Wood, as extraordinary a monument to Nature as Stonehenge of Art's. We stayed some time here, and left at last because the weather appeared threatening. The trees are as Mrs Bray called them weird looking, and the scene with its surrounding wild moorland and fantastically shaped Tors, is most impressive. I gathered oak apples from the trees and some lichen and ferns from the moss covered branches. Returned to Two Bridges and went on to Moreton Hampstead. The scenery very wild all the way – and the Tors extremely grand. Dined at Moreton and posted to Exeter. The views were now more cultivated but still very beautiful. Stopped a minute at Dunsford to see a pretty view. At Exeter stopped at the New Inn. The rain which had been falling at intervals all day, was now very heavy. Herbert went out however, and I opened the windows of the room to hear some singers practising for an oratorio nearby.

Wednesday. To Bristol by Rail. By fly to Clifton. Stayed at Queen's Hotel. Walked in town.

Thursday walked about Clifton. By Railway to London.

For some reason, the Cottons decided against an extensive tour in 1859. In May they had a weekend in Felixstowe and the following month they had another short break:

10 June 1859. On Saturday with Herbert to Lowestoft by Railway. The line has been opened this week and the management is very bad. We were detained a long time at Beccles and did not arrive at Lowestoft until 5 o'clock in the evening instead of having been there three hours before. . . . Stayed at Royal Hotel and walked in the evening. . . . Sunday. Walked to Pakefield, and in the evening walked on the pier, and went for a few minutes into a place called a Bethel where divine worship was being carried on. . . . Monday walked in the town and to Lowestoft Old Church. Returned home in the evening. The train again late.

Eighteen-sixty found Herbert and Elizabeth venturing even further afield. Leaving Washbrook on 30 May for London, they later went north. The first few items from this holiday diary appear terse, reminiscent perhaps of the type of record many of us keep. Elizabeth appears anxious to get on to the main part of the tour:

5 June 1860. To Durham. Dined on our journey at York. Stayed at Durham at Waterloo Hotel.

6th. Walked about Durham. Went over the Cathedral and Castle. Went to Glasgow. Stayed at Star Hotel.

7th. Thursday. A drive round Glasgow. Went through Kelvin Grove, rained. Went over the Cathedral.

Friday. By steamer over the Clyde to Loch Lomond, Loch Katrine, Pass of Aberfoyle, Trossachs. Callender. Some strange people on board and afterwards on the coach recited Scott's description of the scenery with the greatest excitement.

Saturday. On the Clyde and Loch Long and Loch Gail. By coach through Hell's Glen past Carrick Castle. By boat back to Inverary.

Sunday. Walked through Inverary and in the Duke's grounds. After dinner posted to Port Sonachan by Cladich and Dalmally to Oban. Lost a quantity of ferns by leaving them in the carriage.

11 June. Walked about Oban. Posted to Ballachulish. The mistress of the Inn at Conset Ferry mended my dress, and lectured me upon the impropriety of wearing crinoline. Saw Dunstaffnage Castle. Crossed Loch Etive at Conset Ferry taking our carriage with us. Posted to Sheen. Crossed Loch Creran at Sheen Ferry. Waited in carriage for return of ferry boat and made myself a pair of sleeves of some warm plaid I had purchased at Oban. Took our horses and carriage across the ferry with us. Lunched at a small inn where they could give us nothing but oatcake, milk and whiskey. All the peasant women now walk about with bare legs and feet and with only a plaid to shelter their heads.

[This custom of the Scotswomen was obviously very worrying for English female tourists. In 1854 Ann Gurdon noted in Dunkeld that: 'The poor people here as in Edinburgh look very poor as almost all the children and many of the women go about with bare feet' and again: 'all the children and some of the women go about with bare feet, even the servant girl at Frieburn, though she had shoes, had no stockings.']

Tuesday, 12 June. By post through Glencoe and back to Ballachulish. A storm of wind and rain raged during our drive making it very difficult for our horses to face the road. The scenery was greatly improved by the wildness of the weather, the mountain passes looking very grand and wild as the mists rolled through and over them and the water falling in magnificent cataracts everywhere around us. The little inn we are staying at is closely hemmed in on three sides by mountains covered with snow and an arm of Loch Leven runs before it. When we arrived last evening the beds and mattresses of the house were laid out in the road to air, and this morning we found our bedroom very wet from the rain which had fallen during the night. The storm still continuing, we thought it useless to remain, but for some time the ferry men refused to cross the

Loch as they thought the passage dangerous. At last some cattle dealers who were on their way to Fort William insisted upon being taken over, and we crossed the ferry with them. Some women with us were very frightened and prayed in gaelic for safety. When getting into the boat the wind caught my dress and I should have been thrown into the water, had not a man caught hold of me. He was dressed like a peasant but when I offered him money he angrily refused it and I shook hands with him instead. Our carriage was taken to pieces and carried over in another boat with the luggage. We then posted on to Banavie and stayed at the Lochiel Arms. I had to have my clothes dried as I had become very wet crossing the ferry.

[In her account of her Scottish holiday, Ann Gurdon makes frequent references to the efficacy of the waterproof cloaks with which she and her family were equipped.]

Wednesday. From Banavie by the Caledonian Canal to Inverness. Had a good breakfast on board. The captain of the steam packet asked one of the passengers to crave a grace and he spoke for five minutes. The trip was very charming, the scenery around beautiful and the weather fine. We were detained some time at the different lock gates, and some ladies upon deck sang several songs, remarkably well. The steamer stopped in one place to give the passengers time to visit the Falls of Foyers, a magnificent cataract of two falls. I was amused by seeing an old gentleman in full Highland dress, even wearing a skene dhu in his stocking, walking about with spectacles and carrying an umbrella in his hand. Stayed at the Caledonian Hotel at Inverness and in the evening walked in the neighbourhood and climbed upon some bricklayers scaffolding upon Craig Phadric a high hill near the town to see the views around.

Thursday. Walked in the town and went into some shops. Bought some things for children. By Rail to Aberdeen. Stayed at Royal Hotel. We crossed Culloden Moor on our way. The day was clouded and the moor looked a desolate place. We passed Nairn and Forres and many other places interesting from association. Aberdeen looked a gay busy place after being amidst so much wild scenery. Walked in the evening.

Friday. A regiment of soldiers with a good band, passed under our windows while we were at breakfast. Walked in the town. Went over the College and particularly admired the wood carving of King's College Chapel. Then to the Cathedral of St Machan, a very interesting place. Afterwards a drive round the Brig o' Don or Balgorie Bridge. Made a sketch of it. The scenery in the neighbourhood romantic and often very beautiful. In the afternoon by Rail to Perth. Royal George Hotel. Walked in the town. Bought a doll dressed as a

Highlander for Blanche. Met several soldiers in Highland dresses. The outside stairs to many of the old houses look very picturesque, and Perth like most Scottish towns abounds in remembrances of Sir Walter Scott. A statue of Sir Walter with a dog is placed in one of the streets overlooking the Tay. Walked in the Inches, some nice meadows by the river.

Saturday. . . . By Rail to Stirling. Walked round Castle. A stone seat by the side of the Castle has carved upon it 'Rest and be thankful'. The whole walk round commands beautiful views of the valley and mountains surrounding it and we lingered until it became quite dark, before returning to our hotel.

Sunday. Walked in Stirling Churchyard where there is a very beautiful tomb to the memory of Margaret Wilson and her sister said to have been drowned by the command of John Graham, Viscount Claverhouse. I believe the execution of the sentence has been denied, but the monument is very beautiful and ought to be placed in a more protected situation. The figure of an angel holding the crown and palm of martyrdom over the sisters is exquisite in design and workmanship. When morning service was over, we were shewn over the Castle and again lingered to see the surrounding views. The field of Bannockburn looks quite close to view, and our guide, a non-commissioned officer residing in the Castle told us remains of armour was still frequently dug up upon the field.

The young Ann Gurdon was much more emotional in her response to this particular area: 'We passed the village and plain of Bannockburn where the battle was fought, which though a glory to the Scotch is a shame to the English therefore the least said about it the better.'

We went over the armoury, the Chapel, the Douglas room and other places of interest in the Castle. Herbert walked in the evening. Being tired I remained at home and wrote letters. We had seen the Greyfriars Church and had walked more than usual today.

Monday. Walked in the town and purchased some memorials of the place. Looked again at both the new and old monuments – at the Ruins particularly of the Greyfriars or Franciscan Church. A great many old buildings in the immediate neighbourhood of the Castle are very interesting. To Edinburgh. Stayed at the Clarendon Hotel, Princes Street. The Scott monument stands in this street and we are constantly passing it. Drove to Holyrood. Saw the Abbey and Castle. Looked at the very many memorials of Queen Mary. Stayed a long time in her rooms which are well preserved, but not in any way restored, so that no doubts are raised in one's mind of the authenticity of the relics shewn.

Ann Gurdon, writing with the directness of youth, offers this comment in 1854; 'Proceeded on to Holyrood Palace which is as gloomy an habitation as one can conceive. We visited Lord Darnley's apartments and poor Queen Mary's which are much too small for comfort; indeed the room in which Rizzio was surprised is so small, that I can't think how so many people can have got in. . . . The Picture Gallery is a fine room, 150' by 27' broad and would make a handsome room for a ball.'

Then walked to the Abbey of Holyrood House which is quite a ruin. Some sailors from the Fleet now in Leith Harbour followed us about here until we were tired of them. Walked by Arthur's Seat, but did not attempt to climb the hill, and drove back to the new town. Bought two skene dhus or hunting knives for Bertie and Allan.

19 June. To Roslyn. Sketched in the chapel and on the road from the carriage. To Melrose by train passing a great many places of interest and castles generally in ruins. The ruins of Melrose Abbey are guarded very carefully and the guide pointed out Sir Walter Scott's favourite points of view and the most noted places of sepulture. After seeing the Abbey, and Cross in the town we engaged a carriage and drove through the Rhymers Glen to Abbotsford. We had to wait a little time while other visitors were finishing their inspection, and I looked in a closet and saw some strange grotesque figures larger than life. The attendant shewing the house was an intelligent and civil man, allowing us to linger as long as we pleased in Sir Walter's rooms, and appearing pleased to explain every relic and picture we saw. I was very pleased with a marble bust of Sir Walter and an oil painting of him. Everything looks as if he still lived in the house. His chair in the study is drawn up to the table, and adjoins the library, a very handsome room, with a large and excellent collection of books, and a roof of carved oak. In a closet joining the study Sir Walter's clothes, walking stick etc. are shewn. Every room contains armour and many works of Art. An ancient skene dhu given by Miss Edgeworth [the novelist] to Sir Walter exactly resembles the knives we purchased yesterday for our boys. The pictures are most interesting, one is of the head of Queen Mary the day after she was beheaded and another of Graham of Claverhouse. In the garden are some stone figures from 'Tam O'Shanter'. From Abbotsford drove to Dryburgh Abey. Passed the ruins of the tower of Thomas the Rhymer and the house of the Naig of Bennerside. Saw the Eildon Hills, and almost every name recalled some poetical tradition. The custodians of Dryburgh Abbey do not take so much interest as we generally find in most Scottish people in the name of Scott. I gathered some ferns near Scott's tomb, which is placed in a beautiful ruin called St. Mary's Aisle. His wife's and eldest son's tombs are also here. The ruins of Dryburgh are very extensive and many parts still remain very perfect. We went into the Chapter House, Library, Cloisters, Refectory – a very large room, kitchens, cellars and dungeons with places for torture still shewn to visitors. We returned to Edinburgh in the evening after a day of great enjoyment.

Wednesday. In Edinburgh all day. Bought a volume of Scotch songs for Alice, and other remembrances for the children. Went over the Castle, and found it quite a task to climb about the places shewn. Saw the Regalia, Mons Meg, and Queen Margaret's Chapel – a very small building well restored. While we were at the Castle two Highland Regiments were reviewed, the men look more picturesque than our soldiers, and their dress gives them the appearance of being fine men. Afterwards upon Carlton Hill, and had a long walk about the old town of Edinburgh. We could have purchased old armour very reasonably here, but Herbert did not like to be troubled with it so far from home. [An example of marital discord?] I never saw so picturesque a place as Edinburgh and although the old town is very dirty, I think I prefer its winding lanes and closes to the more beautiful streets of the new town. The gable end of the houses and immense chimneys form a remarkable feature of the place. While here we walked into St. Giles' Cathedral and saw the Tolbooth and more than one place pointed out to us for being connected with John Knox.

21 June, Thursday. Left Edinburgh and took express train to London. . . . Friday. Returned home in the evening. Found the dear children quite well.

With Alice at school in France, it was almost inevitable that 1861's holiday should be spent in the Paris area, the parents using the occasion to meet Alice and accompany her home for her vacation. This may have been their first visit abroad and one gains the impression that neither found it particularly enjoyable.

5 June 1861. Wednesday. Crossed the Channel to France from Folkestone. Had a fine passage. Stayed at the Hotel des Bains, Boulogne. Walked about the town in the evening. Thursday. To Paris. Stayed at the Louvre Hotel.

Several years earlier young Miss Elizabeth White, accompanied by her parents and sisters, made a similar tour to Paris. Her comments on this hotel give some of the background Elizabeth Cotton omits: 'We dined at the table d'hote at the Louvre – a most gigantic hotel and everything on a gigantic scale about it. I must try to find out how long the dining room was – it was very richly decorated with painting and gilding and a bust of Napoleon and two figures above the mantelpiece. I think all in marble. The dinner was seven francs a head, but I do not enjoy the French cookery which seems all sauces. I cannot think how a wholesome generation can spring from livers on such unwholesome food.'

Friday   To Fountainbleau. Called at Madame Colbrant's. Alice went with us to Hotel de Londres. Took a drive in the forest. In great pain from a stone striking my eye. Called upon M. Miaire to remove the pebble from under the eyelid.

Saturday   Walked in the park and after again calling upon Madame Colbrant went to Paris, Alice with us. Stayed at the Hotel de Lille et Albion in the Rue de St. Honore.

Sunday   To Church of St. Roch. Fete Dieu Military Mass. Afterwards to the Louvre and Tuileries Gardens. Musard's Concert.

Monday   To the Church of La Madeleine. Saw a marriage ceremony there. Drove in the Champs Elysees and Bois de Boulogne.

The weddings held in the Madeleine seem to have excited the curiosity of most English lady travellers. Both Elizabeth White and Ann Gurdon, who were in Paris in the spring and summer of 1857, remark on them. Elizabeth White saw both weddings and a funeral taking place during her visit and said she felt an 'interloper'. Her extreme Protestant views are expressed in a comment on the altar-piece of the church which shocked her by 'the fact that that altar-piece represented a woman. . . . Oh that the day may come that this land may worship the one Lord in spirit and truth, and no woman, be she ever so blessed among women, and our Lord's mother was blessed, come between our Lord and them.' Ann Gurdon, following her comment on the wedding in the Madeleine writes: 'I wish our large parish churches were left open, so that people who have no quiet homes might have somewhere, where they could meditate in peace.' Like Elizabeth White, she too was suspicious of French Roman Catholicism, ending her holiday diary with the words: 'Much as we have enjoyed our trip we are all, I think, very glad to be back in dear old Protestant England.'

Perhaps this was how Herbert Cotton felt, for Elizabeth's journal continues with its lack-lustre account:

Tuesday. To Versailles. Saw the Palace. Great and little Trianon. The park, Marie Antoinette's Dairy etc. Evening returned to Paris.

Wednesday To Boulevards. Jardin des Plants and Gobelin Tapestry. Luxembourg Gallery of Pictures. Very much pleased with the 'Appel des dernières victimes de la terreur' by Muller, etc.

13th. To Luxembourg again. Hôtel des Invalides and Tomb of Napoleon, and a drive in the Bois and Champs Elysées.

Friday. To Père le Chaise. Very tired walking about the tomb for the day was very hot. Afterwards to the Louvre. Looked at the Rubens and more modern pictures today.

Saturday. To Hôtel de Cluny, Panthéon Church, Notre Dame, Sante Chapelle and in the evening took a box at the Opéra Comique. Saw 'Le Jardiner Galant' and 'Fra Diavolo'. Very much pleased with Crosti and Madame Lemercier.

16th, Sunday. To the Church of St Roch and afterwards with Alice to the Louvre. Herbert not well from the heat of the weather.

Monday. Shopping. Tuesday. By Rail to Boulogne and crossed the channel to England. We had a rough passage and Herbert and Alice both suffered very much from sea-sickness.

Perhaps the answer to why Elizabeth and Herbert did not make further excursions abroad lies in that last sentence above. Elizabeth had indicated when they sailed from Ilfracombe to Hayle in 1858 that Herbert was not a good traveller at sea. She herself seems to have been blessed with a strong stomach. Not only were there no further visits abroad, 1861 was the last year that the couple had what we would call a proper holiday. They still had the occasional weekend away, and the visits to London continued, but even those were on a more reduced scale than previously. With the children growing up and becoming involved in so many activities, it was less easy for the parents to go away for three weeks at a time leaving a housekeeper in charge at home as it had been when the children were young.

Elizabeth, however, made a second visit to France in the spring of 1864. She and Alice accompanied Bertie who was to spend a term at a college in Melun. All three had been very influenced by the religious fervour of the Anglican Father Ignatius and by their growing friendship with the Catholic priest in Ipswich, so perhaps this time Elizabeth, at least, would be looking at France with new eyes. There is no doubt that despite her impending separation from Bertie, Elizabeth greatly enjoyed this visit. Perhaps she was more stimulated by having two young people with her rather than her elderly husband. Alice, now twenty and fluent in French, would have felt very much at home in Paris, and the seventeen-year-old Bertie who had during the last year or so spent holidays in London away from the maternal influence would have seemed quite the young man about town.

6 April 1864. Left London. Nearly too late for the train, but the Station Master opened the office for us. To Paris via Folkestone and Boulogne. Good passage across the Channel. Lunched at Boulogne. When arrived at Paris had some trouble about our luggage as we had not had time to register it at London, and we had to have our boxes examined at the Octroi. [French customs office] Stayed at Hôtel de Lille et D'Albion.

Thursday. To Church of St. Roch. Looked at the beautiful statuary group of the Magdalen at the foot of the Cross. Engaged an open carriage and drove in the Champs Elysées and Bois de Boulogne. Then to Invalides and Tomb of Napoleon. Drove to Place de Concord. Had coffee and Ices. Went to Church de la Madeleine and walked until 8 o'clock. Late dinner at Hotel.

8th. To the Madeleine and Flower Market. Through Tuileries Gardens to Pont Royal and Quais. To Hotel Cluny and churches of St. Etienne, St. Geneviève and Notre Dame. Bought wax taper at the tomb of St. Geneviève. Went into the crypt and galleries. Saw the eccelesiatical dresses and some relics at Notre Dame. Some lads assisting at the altar in Notre Dame were dressed entirely in scarlet cloth. Dined at table d'hote in our hotel, and afterwards walked. Bought print of the Blessed Virgin at a shop in the Rue de Rivoli.

9th. Went into Church of St. Roch for a few minutes. To the Luxembourg Gallery. We were too early, but the attendants allowed us to enter. Watched artists at work. Afterwards went over the Luxembourg Palace. Walked to St. Sulpice. Bought images there. Went into the church. Bertie has become tired of churches and says he likes the Luxembourg Gardens – where we stopped to see Punch – better. Took carriage to Bois de Boulogne. Saw the Emperor and court. Dined at Restaurant Valois and walked home.

Sunday. To Church of St. Roch. Lunched in the Rue de Rivoli. Drove to the Bois. Dismissed the carriage and walked to Longchamps. Stayed to see the Races. The Emperor and court there. . . . Walked home. Very gay scene all the way. An immense number of people, and some handsome carriages passed us on the road. Some of the carriages belonged to foreign embassies, and were richly and occasionally grotesquely ornamented. One in particular we noticed covered with snake skins. Quite late when we reached our hotel.

11th. Monday. By tramway omnibus to St. Cloud. Found the public not admitted to see the Palace and grounds today. Walked in the town and by train to Versailles. Stayed a long time in the grounds, especially about the Little Trianon. Had dinner at Versailles. Alice and Bertie very much pleased with a bulldog which followed us in the streets. Waited a long time in the passengers room at the station and Bertie feel asleep. By Rail back to Paris.

12th. . . . To the Louvre. Went into the Sculpture rooms and then to the Picture Galleries. Alice and Bertie very pleased with the paintings. Looked for a great many favourites. One or two had been removed. . . . Walked in the streets, and amused ourselves by going to see some cats and dogs we have before noticed. Some of the owners appeared pleased to bring out their favourite animals, but one woman was evidently suspicious of our attentions. Lunched at Tortoni's.

13th. To Boulevard des Italiens and Champs Elysées. Saw the Emperor driving. Made purchases. Called at stables, engaged a horse for Bertie to ride tomorrow. Dined at Restaurant. Laughing very much at hearing some ladies and gentlemen conversing in the next room.

14th. Walked in Tuileries Gardens and rested there while Alice went to shops for me. Felt unwell and obliged to return to Hotel and lie down for the rest of the day. Bertie told us when he came home that he had had a delightful ride. Alice and Bertie came to sit with me after they had their dinner.

Friday. To Fountainbleau. Stayed at Hôtel de Londres. Called upon Madame Colbrant. Walked to see places Alice remembered. *16th*. Accompanied by Madame Colbrant and Eugenie went to the Chateau. Saw the state apartments. . . . Afterwards called upon M. Schopin. Went with him to see the Chapel S. Antoin to look at the painting he has commenced of the Crucifixion and afterwards to his private rooms to see his finished paintings. [M. Schopin was later to marry Eugenie Colbrant.] When we returned to Madame Colbrant's the carriage I had engaged waited for us. M. George, an old man Alice had known when at school, recognised and appeared very glad to see her again. Augusta and Eugenie accompanied us a drive in the forest, Madame Colbrant placing a basket in the carriage containing lunch. When in the forest we were startled by hearing loud cries of pain, and Bertie, Alice and Eugenie left the carriage to discern what was the matter.

After some time the girls returned to say that they had found a dog caught in a trap, and so savage from pain Bertie could not release it without more assistance. We sent our driver to help and Bertie held the poor dog to prevent him biting, whilst the man unfastened the trap. Our coachman explained the trap had been set by poachers to catch the young deer, and the cries appeared so frightful from the echo caused by the surrounding rocks. While in the forest, we went through some underground places called Robbers Caves, and the man exhibiting them afterwards performed tricks with a quantity of vipers. On our return we went into a village Inn used by Artists, and containing paintings by them upon the walls, door, and furniture. In the evening walked in the park.

17th. Walked into several churches, but missed every service we wished to attend. Called upon Madame Colbrant, and saw Minna Foster who is now recovering from an attack of Rheumatic Fever. Walked in the park, saw the carp in the pond. Went a long walk in the forest. Saw Cross of Calvary and the Chapel of La Bonne Dame.

Coming home met some soldiers beating the Roll Call drum to summon their missing comrades.

Elizabeth's mention of the beating of the Roll Call must have had particular poignancy because she was now within a day of parting with her son. On the Monday, they set off by train to Melun. Here Elizabeth conducted the business relating to Bertie's entry 'as a private pupil' and was then entertained to dinner by the principal's family. '19th, Tuesday. Parted with my dear Bertie. Left him at the station with M.Kerchoff [a master] who came to see us in the morning. From Melun by train to Paris with Alice. Then to Boulogne. Arrived late and quite worn out. 20th, Wednesday. Good passage across the Channel and by express train to London. My sisters Anne and Margot at the station to meet us.'

Despite the wrench of parting, the overriding impression left by this account is of a thoroughly enjoyable holiday. Mother and children are relaxed with each other, and perhaps for the first time in many years, Elizabeth had been able to devote herself to these two without the distraction of the rest of the family.

Overall, the picture we have of Elizabeth as she travels over the years is of a woman who was undeterred by the restrictions placed upon her by clothing, who was able to face almost any situation in which she found herself with equanimity, and possessed of indefatigable spirit. If we are able to take her as a representative of the ordinary middle-class woman of her time, then we shall no longer be surprised by the spirit of those better known women of the period who were prepared to go off to remote areas of the world and endure hardship in order to pursue their own personal missions in life.

8

The World Outside

We heard the cannons firing at Ipswich for the funeral of the Prince Consort. . . . Mr de Grey sent pheasants.

Elizabeth Cotton's Diary

A modern writer of popular books asked why her stories contained little of world-shattering events or very worrying national crises, replied that it was her belief that most people were far more concerned with their own personal problems than by any major external happening. Elizabeth Cotton's diaries seem to support this view so we shall be disappointed if we expect from her a commentary on the political, social or economic problems of the 1850s and 60s. Such details can be found in any good textbook. What we do get are occasional references to events which make us suddenly aware of the background against which she was living and those other odd bits of information about everyday life which fail to find a place in history books. Although there are many occasions when reading the diaries that we are able to forget we are reliving events which took place well over one hundred years ago, there are other times when we are brought up sharply by the realisation that we now live in the age of immediate impact. Radio and TV bring into our homes events as they take place and nowhere is this more apparent than in the transmission of the news from a battlefront in some quite remote part of the world.

That this was not so in the 1850s does not mean that people were totally unaware of what was happening abroad; it just took longer for the news to arrive, and because it was reported in print rather than by sound or picture, it may have seemed more remote. The first reference Elizabeth makes to the fact that England was involved in the war in the Crimea comes in a slightly oblique way: '*23 April 1854. Wednesday was kept as a Fast Day.*'

The order for the Day of Humiliation and Prayer was signed by the Queen at Windsor on 15 April and reproduced in local newspapers:

We, taking into our most serious consideration the just and necessary war in which we are engaged, and putting our trust in Almighty God that He will graciously bless our arms both by sea and land, have resolved, and do, by and with the advice of our Privy Council, hereby command that a public day of humiliation and prayer be observed

144

throughout those parts of our United Kingdom called England and
Ireland, on Wednesday, 26 April, that so both we and our people may
humble ourselves before Almighty God, in order to obtain pardon of
our sins and in the most devout and solemn manner send up our
prayers and supplications to the Divine Majesty, for imploring His
blessing and assistance on our arms, for the restoration of peace to us
and our dominions, and we do strictly charge and command that the
said day be reverently and devoutly observed by all our loving
subjects . . . as they tend the favour of Almighty God and would
avoid His wrath and indignation and for the better and more orderly
solemnising the same, we have given directions to the most Reverend
Archbishops, the Right Reverend the bishops of England and Ireland
to compose a form of prayer suitable to this occasion, to be used in all
churches, chapels and places of public worship and to take care the
same be timely dispersed throughout their respective dioceses.

A separate order was issued for Scotland where arrangements were
made for public gatherings to take place in central locations in villages
and towns.

The practicalities of the implementation of the royal order can be seen
in the Vestry accounts for the parish of Copdock where the special form
of prayers printed for use on that day cost the parish the sum of five
shillings and threepence, and in the Ipswich newspaper report of how
the event affected the town:

In obedience to his Worship's request, business was suspended
throughout the town, not more than six shops having been kept open.
In the various churches, the opportunity was embraced of making
collections for the benefit of those wives and children of the soldiers
and sailors who may have the misfortune of being bereaved of their
protectors by the war.

The collections in each town church varied from between £10 and £25 –
quite large sums when translated into today's terms. Of the £24 collected
in one, two-thirds were assigned to the benefit of the servicemen's
dependants, whilst the remainder was to be forwarded 'in aid of the
spiritual instruction of the soldiers at the seat of war'.

When one reads the printed firsthand accounts of the haphazard
arrangements made for the feeding and quartering of the troops at this
stage in the war, one cannot help being somewhat cynical about this
worthy attempt of the Ipswich parishioners. The local newspapers also
show just how much information was sent back to England, even if it
was outdated by the time it appeared; outspoken editorials were often
highly critical of the government handling of the situation. The Ipswich

newspapers carried supplements of war news with simple but well-drawn maps of the areas where fighting was taking place, so there was no need for the vast majority of the population to be ignorant of events.

Elizabeth would have been fully aware of the progress of the conflict, but would have found it unnecessary to comment upon it unless it had affected her in some way. Hence she feels no need to mention the fatal charge of the Light Brigade. Her reminders to us of the situation come indirectly with references to battle training, for example:

> *September 1855.* . . . With Anne walked to Landguard Fort . . . Went over a Martello Tower on Friday. . . . Tuesday walked to Bawdsey Ferry . . . some wild fowl and sea birds . . . scarcely moved away from us. I expect their weariness was from terror, the soldiers at Landguard Fort having been firing heavy artillery all the morning. . . . With Herbert and Anne drove to Landguard Fort. Went over it and walked back.

Elizabeth's sympathy with the birds' plight probably echoes her own weariness from listening to the constant barrage. The reference to visiting the fort throws an interesting light on military security of the period.

The only other direct mention of the war comes in 1856 when Herbert and Elizabeth were staying at the small coastal town of Aldeborough: '4 *May 1856.* Sunday   Walked on the beach. Caught in a storm. Met Moss, who has entered the Coast Guard Service for a time, as the regular men are on other duty during war time.' This suggests that Moss was well known to them, possibly a local man they had met on previous visits. However, the 1851 census shows that the groom of their friends the Wests of Hintlesham was also called Moss, so it may have been that man or his son; either way, it suggests that there was, if not a form of conscription, at least a redirection of labour in operation.

The diaries are littered with references to the military, usually in a social aspect, but while on holiday at Winchester in 1858, the Cottons encountered a foreign regiment garrisoned there:

> *23 May 1858.* . . . Thursday.   To Winchester with Herbert by Railway. Stayed at the George Hotel. The German Cavalry are on duty in Winchester and headquarters are at our hotel. The band very noisy and the whole place in an uproar.

This comment highlights the growing concern of the government of the period for the inadequacy of barracks and billeting arrangements generally for the armed forces. The practice of quartering officers in hotels was as unsatisfactory to them as it was to the members of the public.

Mention has been made elsewhere of military reviews being offered as a form of public entertainment to inspire patriotism and support. We read too of the local Volunteers who are paraded in the grounds of various mansions in the neighbourhood. The 1st Suffolk Rifle Corps met twice weekly for evening drill and on Saturday afternoons at the Butts for regulation ball practice – another reminder of the lack of sophisticated weaponry in use then. There was no shortage of men prepared to join the volunteer service, and it was reported in 1863 that when special constables were required to deal with an emergency in Ipswich, the majority of the three hundred who turned up to be sworn in were members of the Volunteers.

Elizabeth offers no personal opinions upon the war and its progress, but that is not to say she did not hold any. For the most part her life was touched by the military only in so far as there were military men to put on races, perform plays at the theatre or provide the band playing in the background at the numerous charity bazaars and fetes held in the town.

It is a widely held view that Queen Victoria and her family provided role models for middle-class life. Elizabeth was born in the same year as the queen and like her she called two of her children Alice and Bertie. The two women enjoyed a similar taste in literature, art and social events, and there are occasions when reading Queen Victoria's correspondence with her eldest daughter, one hears echoes of something Elizabeth might have written. However, there are no indications that Elizabeth was an ardent royalist. She betrays no emotion, beyond a hint of surprise touched with amusement when:

> 2 *June 1857.* By railway to York. Stayed at York Hotel. I was rather surprised by a gilt crown being the ornament of our rooms here. Even the bed had a large crown upon it. When we left our bill was headed 'Prince Albert Rooms' with the explanation that the apartments had been taken by the Prince when in York.

Prince Albert is mentioned again in relation to his death and the following extracts exemplify the impact national events have on everyday life as well as showing the speed with which news was communicated:

> 15 *December 1861,* Sunday. To St Lawrence Church, Ipswich. The liturgy as usual named the Prince Consort, but in the evening heard he had died yesterday. . . . Monday At home. Herbert came home in the evening. Rea sent us a present of Stilton cheese. . . . 17 *December* To Ipswich. Purchased mourning. Boys with me. . . . 23 *December.* Monday Walked with Evelyn and Blanche to Hintlesham. Heard the cannons firing at Ipswich for Prince Albert's funeral. Mr de Grey sent pheasants.

The Cottons' participation in a later royal event at a local level strikes a familiar note: '*10 March 1863*. Tuesday. The Prince of Wales married. To Ipswich with Herbert and the children. Saw the Procession and in the evening Fireworks. A wretched day.'

I presume the last remark refers to the weather, although the *Ipswich Journal* makes no reference to rain in its glowing report of the celebrations which started with children from all the parish schools and Sunday Schools assembling on the Cornhill to sing one verse of the National Anthem. Speeches and the enactment of dramatic pieces were followed by combined singing. Then the children were marched off through the town to the Arboretum for the ceremonial planting of the Prince's Tree and an explanation as to the significance of the day. They then processed by a different route back to the town centre from where they were dispersed to various large halls for tea and cakes. While the young people were treated to cake, five hundred and twenty of the 'aged poor' were dined in some splendour at the Corn Exchange. At nine o'clock in the evening all the interested onlookers made their way to the Docks where, against the backdrop of the Orwell, Ipswich tried to emulate the type of firework display that was being staged upon the Thames.

Elizabeth was not, however, sufficiently interested in royalty to wish to see the Prince and Princess of Wales when they visited Ipswich later that year, which was probably just as well as the Princess failed to come, much to the disappointment of those who did turn out, causing the comment: 'Popular as HRH deservedly is, there were blank looks about him for a time. The truth was that immense preparations had been made to see the heir to the throne and the future Queen of England – and to have them seen . . .' The report continues with an attempt to justify the reason for the royal lady's absence: ' . . . Consider what the Princess of Wales has done! She has within a few months travelled from Denmark, gone through the ceremony of a Royal Marriage and led the season to its close. Does she not require rest? Probably solitude has charms for the illustrious lady of which she little dreamt six months back in her young life. . . . the sense of being constantly an object of enthusiastic attention lured for exposure from place to place, may generate the reflection that loyalty after all is a thing of little worth when it is so very intrusive.'

When Elizabeth encountered royalty at close quarters it brought the rather terse comment: '*3 June 1868*. Went to Horse Show. The Prince and Princess of Wales being there, the crowd was very great and troublesome.' On the other hand, she does appear genuinely excited at seeing the French monarch. Perhaps it was the very middle-classness of the British royal family which made them appear mundane in contrast to the French:

9 April 1864. Saturday. . . . Took carriage to Bois de Boulogne. Saw the Emperor and court. Sunday . . . walked to Longchamps. Stayed to see the Races. The Emperor and court there. Obtained places opposite to the Royal Stand. . . . To Boulevard des Italiens and Champs Elysees. Saw the Emperor driving. . . . Bertie told us when he came home that he had had a delightful ride in the Bois de Boulogne and had seen the court party several times.

Often it is during her travels that Elizabeth meets people who are connected with major developments, for example:

June 1858. By coach to Plymouth. We travelled outside, and had some agreeable companions. They were Americans connected with the Atlantic Telegraph, and one lady, Mrs Field, a Frenchwoman married to an American was a most amusing person.

This may have been Elizabeth's first encounter with citizens of the United States, and she obviously enjoyed meeting them, according them the accolade of being 'agreeable'. This extract serves to show that slow travel by coach could be both physically and mentally tiring, especially if one were stuck for hours with those who were 'disagreeable', and it also emphasises the gulf between the old and the new; the lack of a rail link between Truro and Plymouth meant that old fashioned modes of travel were still in operation, yet it was now technically possible to send a telegraph message across the Atlantic to America. It is likely that Elizabeth's travelling companions were in some way linked with the problems that had been encountered with the submarine cable. The *Suffolk Chronicle* for 11 September 1858 states:

The condition of the Atlantic Telegraph is unaltered. Signals continue to be received, but they are too uncertain and faint to be intelligible. Occasionally an entire word is given, but never anything approaching to a sentence. The experiments may lead to the belief that the injury is near the coast – probably within two or three miles. The strong portion of cable manufactured expressly for the shore has now been shipped from Plymouth for Valentia [Island in Ireland] and will be substituted immediately on its arrival in place of the ordinary wire, which however well-adapted for undisturbed depths, is totally inadequate to resist the liability to accident on a rocky coast.

The Cottons do not seem to have availed themselves of the internal telegraph system, but they were occasionally in receipt of such transmitted messages: '15 *November 1867.* With Alice to Ipswich Station. When there received a Telegram from Henry Page to stop Alice going to Dulwich upon account of the sudden death of his sister Mrs Hall.'
Elizabeth did however, make great use of the postal service, and the speed at which letters were exchanged is impressive. In 1866, there was

a move to suspend the Sunday delivery of letters in rural areas, a suggestion so outrageous to her that: '14 *August 1866*. Wrote to the Editor of 'The Times' about the non delivery of letters on Sundays.'

Alas, her letter was not selected to add to the lively debate which took place within the correspondence columns of the newspaper during that month. The question of Sunday postal deliveries, which had already been withdrawn in London, had its roots in both economics and religious attitudes. The Postmaster General maintained that wages would have to rise to cover the seven-day delivery service. This was refuted by one correspondent, a curate from a village near Tunbridge Wells, who drew attention to the fact that his local postman, whose daily round covered a walk of twenty miles, had had his wages cut by one shilling a week after an agreement that a Sunday delivery was no longer required. On the other side, religious pressure groups were campaigning for 'the day of rest' for the postmen and a general move towards the strict keeping of the Sabbath.

In areas outside London, the PMG had set up a compromise procedure; he would discontinue the Sunday delivery if he was petitioned to do so by six sevenths of the recipients of Sunday mail. Naturally, those areas where the Sabbatarian movement was strongest were the first to lose the Sunday post. It was this use of petitioning which stirred up most of the *Times* contributors. A gentleman from Leamington Spa said that the town was threatened with the withdrawal of the Sunday service because 'a few strait-laced people had memorialised the PMG' – an event which had occurred while he was unfortunately away from home. He voiced his concern for the impact this move would have on the vast population of Leamington who were largely invalids and friends of invalids; the delay to letters for American visitors because the mail from America usually arrived in England on Saturday, and most harrowing, for the poor widow who is prevented from receiving 'the solitary letter from her soldier or sailor son over the sea' which she could only answer on her leisure day. He concluded that 'if people do not choose to read their letters, by all means let them lie unopened, but they have no right to deny me the privilege of seeing mine'.

Another contributor reported that the town of Faringdon in Berkshire had reached the solution that only those who petitioned against the delivery should not receive one. The battle of words waged on, bringing suggestions for the introduction of a shilling surcharge for the Sunday delivery from one, and a uniform rule for all country post offices from another. There was a denunciation of clergymen who deprived a working-class village of its Sunday post – 'The rich man it does not affect; he can send for his'.

The day after Elizabeth wrote her letter, she would have read in her morning newspaper one from a country parson who rather neatly summed up the religious argument; he pointed out that had he not had the opportunity of getting his letters fetched from the post town he would not have received until Monday morning the new prayer ordered to be read in all churches on that Sunday.

It was again while travelling, this time by train from Scotland, that Elizabeth heard at first hand the experiences of someone caught up in the craze which had fired the imagination of thousands throughout the land, including the Queen and Prince Albert:

> *21 June 1860.* Left Edinburgh and took express train to London. Two very agreeable ladies travelled with us, one a Lady Anderson who appeared in great sorrow for her sister, the other a most amusing woman, Mrs Turton. She introduced herself as the wife of the Colonel of an Indian Regiment. Mrs Turton believes in mesmerism and gave us an account of some singular experiences she had known when visiting celebrated mediums.

Franz Mesmer (1733–1815), a doctor, believed that health depended on the free flow of energy throughout the body. He developed a system based on the use of magnets to achieve this energy flow, and for a time enjoyed tremendous success in curing patients through what he termed 'animal magnetism'. However, in the 1780s he was discredited and branded as the 'biggest quack of the eighteenth century'. Nonetheless his name lived on to be misapplied to both hypnotism and spiritualism. A French follower of Mesmer had realised that the magnetic healing techniques used often induced a somnambulistic state during which some patients appeared to have exceptionally heightened perception leading to a form of clairvoyance. Furthermore, those in an advanced state manifested the ability to diagnose disease in others.

Parallel with this, the Mesmer techniques introduced into the United States developed into trance-like states in which subjects claimed to be able to hold discourse with the dead. In Britain both hypnosis and especially spiritualism enjoyed tremendous popularity among the respectable middle and upper classes.

In 1872 the Revd. Francis Kilvert noted in his diary that he had attended a demonstration of what we would now call hypnosis:

> Then began the mesmerism. A number of men came up on the platform . . . They were placed in a semi-circle on chairs sitting with their faces to the wall and their backs to the audience. A young lady went to the piano and began playing low soft dreamy music. The Mesmerist passed between his victims and the wall and after making a few passes over their faces and arms and looking intently into their eyes he soon had eight out of the ten prostrate on the floor in

mesmeric sleep. . . . One by one he raised them up. . . . then he bade them look at the stars and they all stood with their ghastly faces turned up gazing steadfastly at the ceiling. Suddenly he assured them they were cocks and commanded them to crow and flap their wings. Instantly they flapped their arms violently and crowed in every key . . .

There followed a variety of demonstrations and Kilvert concludes his account: 'He, the Mesmerist, asked the lads if they had ever seen him before or had any collusion with him and in the face of the audience they openly denied knowledge of him. It seems they were all well-known young men from the town. The lads said they were perfectly aware all the time what they were doing, but they had no power to resist.'

That was the type of 'mesmerism' which was being reproduced for public entertainment in halls and theatres throughout the country. What Mrs Turton had described to her travelling companions were spiritualist seances. Elizabeth mentioned that Lady Anderson was in great sorrow for her sister who, we may assume, had recently died. It was probably to bring some comfort to the grieving lady that Mrs Turton had raised the topic of communication with the dead and thus the conversation had flourished. It is again an oblique reference which makes us aware of a current situation, here in connection with Mrs Turton's husband, a colonel in the Indian Army. In the same way that we hear nothing from Elizabeth about the battles of the Crimean campaign, neither do we learn anything of the various troubles in which Britain was engaged in India. Yet from her reading of *The Times*, which we know was the daily newspaper at Amor Hall, she would have been fully conversant with what was happening there; she would doubtless have followed, for example, Dalhousie's negotiations in 1855 with the king of Oudh who was eventually deposed at the beginning of 1856. Having read of the king's treatment of his subjects, it is no wonder that her attention was caught by: 'The jewels worn by the king were of enormous size and lustre' when she had seen the deposed monarch and his suite at the theatre in London in December of that year.

Although perhaps somewhat sceptical of the mysteries of the mind, Elizabeth was very interested in scientific matters generally. She attended meetings of the local archaeological society, visited sites of special interest and helped her sons to identify and form a mineralogical display. On occasions, a small note in the diary reveals an event which is quite spectacular. This is true for the entry for the week beginning 12 September 1858 which reads: 'Monday. . . . Evening. Saw the Comet.'

While recording that she saw the comet, Elizabeth fails to impart that the phenomenon she was fortunate enough to see was one that none of us have had or ever will have the opportunity to witness – a comet whose estimated period is two thousand years. It had been discovered three months earlier, on 2 June 1858, by Donati in Florence, when it was of magnitude 7½, rather below naked-eye visibility. The *Suffolk Chronicle* reported on 11 September:

> During the last few days the comet has rapidly increased in brightness, and on Sunday evening, when the sky was very clear, was fully as conspicuous to the naked eye as a star of the fourth magnitude. The tail is very distinct, forming, with the somewhat brilliant nucleus, a pretty telescopic object. The brightness of the comet will be constantly on the increase during the present month. It will be found about 10 degrees above the NW horizon at 8 o'clock in the evening.

It was during that month that the comet developed its distinctive curved tail. On the 30th it passed the closest point to the sun and reached its peak. On 2 October the head of the comet outshone Arcturus, the brightest star in the northern hemisphere, and the tail, both a curved dust one and a straight one of ions, extended over 25 degrees. At its maximum the diameter of the nucleus was around 2000 miles. It remained visible to the naked eye until the end of the first week in November, and was finally lost telescopically on 4 March 1859. When Elizabeth and her family stood out in the garden on that Monday evening around eight o'clock they were looking at something which had last been viewed from earth well before the birth of Christ.

The family's interest in politics is reflected only in references to the local elections:

> *1 May 1859.* Ipswich Borough and County Elections this week. Great excitement in Ipswich. . . . *25 July 1866.* To Ipswich shopping and called for Herbert who had gone to see a County Election. There was no contest. . . . *18 February 1867.* Election at Ipswich. Mr Corrance returned. . . . *24 November 1868.* Herbert and boys went to Nominations of County Elections. . . . *27 November.* County Elections.

As a member of the rural community, Herbert would have been eligible to vote in the County elections. The very fact that Elizabeth mentions when the elections are held shows her interest in such matters. Similarly, she was open minded, as she showed when in Sheffield she stopped to listen to a man who was: 'haranguing a cluster of persons upon their political rights. Both he and his listeners appeared in earnest.' Of politics and politicians on a wider scale, her only reference shows a hint of annoyance: '*27 October 1865.* Friday To Ipswich. Shops closed for the burial of Lord Palmerston.'

Occasionally Elizabeth does provide a glimpse of practices which, like the latter, have changed. For example: '2 *October 1863*. Wrote to Rea Nelson and sent her the votes we have collected for the candidate she wishes to get in to the Idiot Asylum.'

Rea Nelson was her unmarried middle-aged cousin, sister of the James who caused all the family upsets. Miss Nelson fits our stereotype picture of a woman of good works, and on this occasion she was seeking help for one of her protégés, in all probability a child. The fact that Elizabeth uses the term 'Idiot' rather than 'Lunatic' suggests that the child in question was severely mentally handicapped, perhaps suffering from cerebral palsy. Beyond the Workhouse and the few hospitals founded by ancient charities, the only institutions available to care for handicapped people were those run privately. The expense of such asylums was often well beyond the means of the family concerned. Thus it became the practice for a patron to take up the case and enlist the support of others to donate regularly towards the sufferer's upkeep. This then gave the donors voting rights in the management of the institution concerned. Rea had spent a day at Amor Hall during August and sufficiently stirred Elizabeth's compassion for the cause for her to go round her friends to gain their 'votes'. Occasionally such appeals for votes appeared in the local press. One pitiful case concerned the attempt to place the nine-year-old son of a schoolmaster in an asylum – pitiful because the advertisement revealed that there was also a seven-year-old child in the family who was similarly handicapped.

On a much lighter note there is a reference to bureaucracy which we have come to take for granted: '7 *May 1864*. A letter from Margot asking me to obtain a certificate of her birth. Called upon Mr Stokes the clergyman of St Stephens for it.' Nowadays we would apply to the Registrar for a copy of a birth certificate, but Margaret had been born before the registration of births had become a legal requirement. Thus it was necessary for Elizabeth to obtain a copy of the record of Margaret's baptism from the church where the ceremony had taken place. This small entry does not prepare us for the later revelation that Margaret is about to depart for Australia.

The diaries also give us developments in the fads and fancies of the period, and none is more detailed than the interest in photography. By the 1860s there were a dozen photographic artists established in Ipswich, but Elizabeth had given her allegiance to one by 1855:

30 September 1855. Saturday. To Ipswich. Had photographic portraits taken of Alice, Bertie and Evelyn by Mr Cade. . . . 7 October. Monday Called for photographic portraits. Herbert being very pleased with the pictures of the children wished to have Eva's portrait taken and we took her to Mr Cade's but the attempt was a failure from her extreme restlessness.

The delightful vignette of paternal pride in the family acts as a reminder of the length of time that was required for the exposure and the necessity to remain absolutely still may explain: '10 September 1860. Monday. The boys and Eva had their portraits taken . . . Tuesday. The boys had their portraits taken again.'

By 1861 it was becoming fashionable to send photographs not only of oneself and members of the family, but also of other people, particularly actors and actresses, to one's friends: '3 May 1861. Anne sent me a photograph of Faust and Marguerite. . . . 16 November. Letter from Anne with picture of Mrs St. Hervey. . . . 5 December. Letter and photograph of herself and Edward from Arabella. Letter and photograph of Mr Fechter from Anne.'

An even more interesting development followed with: '7 February 1863. Saturday. To Ipswich. Met Bertie [from school]. Went with him to Mr Stokes' Photographic Rooms to have his dog's portrait taken.' And two months later, 'To Ipswich with children. Had the pony's photograph taken by Mr Stokes.'

One cannot help marvelling at the ingenuity of Mr Stokes in tapping the market for animal photography. One wonders if this was his speciality, or if he also practised human portraiture, in which case, did he have separate studios for his diverse clientele? Certainly, when Elizabeth had her own photograph taken the following month, she again patronised the familiar Mr Cade, as did Alice in June of that year, and Margaret in the next year when she had her picture taken prior to her departure for Australia, to give to Elizabeth as a keepsake.

Quite why Mr de Grey, who saw Elizabeth regularly, should want to present her with his picture, we can only guess. Possibly such offerings were considered as tokens of friendship, which accounts for those given by other people, like Father Kemp for example. All these photographs were not necessarily placed in frames for display, but rather in albums which could be browsed over at leisure, and offered for the interest of visitors. Twelve album portraits could be had for half a sovereign, and the albums themselves, often beautifully ornate, cost anything from 4/6d. upwards. Elizabeth had to buy a new one for herself in 1866, and the next year she gave one as a present: '3 December 1867. Evelyn and Blanche spent the day at Ipswich Convent. Lady Superior's Fete Day. Sent a Photograph Book to her.'

By 1866, it had become fashionable to have one's photograph taken in costume:

26 September. Rea sent me a photograph of her husband taken in Highland Costume. . . . 30 March 1867. To Ipswich with Herbert and Bertie who was dressed as a rough fisherman to have his portrait taken in character by Mr Smith the photographer. His disguise was so complete several persons we know passed him without recognition.

If only we knew whether Elizabeth actually walked with Bertie to the photographer's or if he reported later that he had passed unacknowledged by acquaintances. Whatever the truth of the matter, Elizabeth obviously enjoyed the episode, again showing a strong sense of humour, and perhaps a desire to shock. Bertie too, enjoyed 'dressing up' for on another occasion, his mother reports: '*13 November 1864. Sunday.* . . . Bertie mystified Miss Rope and amused us very much by making up in the character of Capt. Fitzgerald.'

For a while Elizabeth and her friends and relations joined in a fashion which has enjoyed frequent revivals, that of collecting autographs: '*12 February 1860.* Letter from Edward and autographs. . . . *8 October 1861* Anne sent me some autographs. . . . *24 September 1866.* Mr. Kemp sent me some autographs.'

However, as far as Elizabeth was concerned, this particular fashion was not of consuming interest to her. Far longer-lasting was the interest in reading and the Cottons bought and read new books as they appeared. The books (list appended, p. 197) which Elizabeth mentions display a catholic taste, and embrace those which we now deem classics as well as many which have long faded into oblivion. Elizabeth belonged to the town's subscription library which provided those books she did not wish to buy, but by the 1860s there was a rival to the established bookshops in the town in the form of the railway bookstall. Elizabeth frequently seized the opportunity when travelling or merely visiting the station to meet a train, to purchase the latest bestseller like Mrs Oliphant's *Salem Chapel* from the station kiosk.

From 1864 a new development in reading habits is mentioned: '*24 March 1865.* . . . read magazines to Herbert.'

This form of entry recurs, often for a Sunday evening. Apart from mentioning on one occasion that she read from French periodicals which her brother had sent, we are not told which magazines were favoured but the choice was wide; *The Cornhill Magazine*, *Fraser's Magazine*, *Punch*, *Household Words*, *The Illustrated London News* and *All the Year Round* having the largest circulation. The scale of religious publishing of all types was enormous with the *Christian World*, *Leisure Hour* and the *Christian Herald* leading the field.

While Elizabeth's reading matter was probably a reflection of that of the country as a whole, her comments on agricultural developments must necessarily apply only to those areas which were involved in cultivation. By the time her diary starts in 1854 mechanisation of some aspects of farm life had become accepted, but from George Ranson we learn something of the earlier antagonism that greeted such progress. His reaction probably echoes that of other farmers:

29 January 1844. Last night three alarming fires took place all about the same time in the parish of Ardleigh, Essex. The work of some wicked and vile incendiary. . . . *30 January.* A Fire broke out at Mr Ansell's of Wenham about half past 6 o'clock in the evening of yesterday. Everything burned down except the house and a malting. The act of a villain, and I am sorry to say there does not appear any clue to finding out these horrible fires. I think my own opinion is it is done by some idle set that is out on purpose to alarm the country. Everything remains in mystery. . . . *24 February.* The country is getting into an alarming state about these terrible fires and no cause can be assigned for it. . . . *29 February.* A fire last night at Offton; a horse burnt worth £100 thoroughbred, entire horse, heifer, sow and pigs and fat hog. . . . *15 April.* A dreadful fire again this evening at Cornard, appeared to be set on fire 2 or 3 places; 54 sheep burnt, 68 injured so much obliged to be slaughtered, 54 pigs burnt, 17 weaned calves, about 100 cwt of beans, 200 of barley and 2 barns, 4 stacks, about 400 cwt. of wheat and buildings. Estimated loss £3,000; very distressing and destructive fire.

Ranson's farm escaped such attention, and after this last entry there are no further references to arson in the region. However, he had also become mechanised: '*16 March 1846.* Threshing out a stack of barley by machine damaged by the wet weather during harvest.'

With Ransomes and Sims of Ipswich being described as the largest maker of agricultural implements in the kingdom, and Richard Garrett of Leiston producing steam engines, it was inevitable that Suffolk farmers would take to the modernisation available. The novelty of such things that we have come to take for granted can be seen from some of the entries that Elizabeth made regularly from 1859 onwards: '*20 November 1859.* With Eva and Blanche to see Steam Threshing of a stack of wheat.' However, Herbert seems to have held back on further innovations since Elizabeth notes: '*7 August 1865.* Walked with children to Belstead. Saw Mr Harwood's men cutting wheat with a reaping machine.'

The farmers might introduce machinery to the farms, but it was often difficult to persuade the workers to accept them. When they did, there could be a problem with safety. The local papers are full of grisly details of the accidents which befell careless operators. Apart from fatal accidents to the men, steam threshing could also be responsible for dangerous fires. An early example of a jingle to assist in safety precautions appeared in the *Ipswich Journal*: 'High wind blowing!/ No steam threshing./ But whatever weather happen/ Let the funnels have a cap on/ And if your men want extra beer/ They should not have it till the field is clear.'

Elizabeth often mentions the occasional minor accident which occurred among the workers at Amor Hall, and with most of them she coped very well. She would, if necessary, go herself to Ipswich to fetch medical assistance, and she considered it part of her role to visit the sick or injured in his home, making sure that the man and his family had all they needed. However, one episode caused her great distress. It may be that it was occasioned by too much of the strong brew provided at harvest time, or possibly it was a personal dispute between the two concerned. Again this is one of those dramas about which we wish we had more information:

> *20 August 1868.* Bertie came in hastily to tell us he feared Walter Whalley had been murdered in the harvest field by a man employed to help the other labourers. Very frightened by this and by the distress of the poor child's father and mother when I went to their cottage. Herbert sent for a doctor to attend Whalley and had Grimwood arrested. I was taken ill and did not leave my room again for the rest of the month. It proved afterwards that Whalley was not seriously injured and the prosecution was given up.

We can imagine the emotional impact that this event had on the village as a whole, but it also reveals two pieces of information, one that Walter Whalley was young enough for Elizabeth to refer to him as a child, so he might well be anywhere between 10 and 12, and the other is the practice of hiring extra labour to assist at harvest. Farming records show that a separate contract was struck between master and men for the harvest period. Walter was the son of one of the Cottons' regular employees, living in a tied cottage, and it is likely that he had recently been taken on as a permanent member of the work force. Grimwood, on the other hand, was a casual worker. This may have been the cause of the argument, Grimwood resenting a youngster in full-time employment while he had to rely on whatever he could find. Two other points emerge; that Bertie was working in the fields with the men, and that, shocked though she was, Elizabeth immediately took it upon herself to be either the bearer of the ill-tidings or comforter to the parents. This was one of the few occasions when Elizabeth was unable to cope with the after-effects of an event. Her narration suggests that she suffered a minor nervous breakdown. Hardly surprising perhaps, for this was the second time that year that the village had had a tragedy to discuss: '*14 April 1868.* Tuesday. To Ipswich with Herbert . . . When I returned home heard that G. Clarke one of the villagers had been found drowned in the stream in our meadows. Went to see his poor wife who was in terrible distress.'

This event reached the pages of the *Ipswich Journal*, for a coroner's inquest was held locally the day after the event. It was disclosed that George Clarke, who was a 26-year-old farm labourer, had risen at five in the morning and gone to the stream to fetch water for his wife to wash with. The report does not state if Mrs Clarke raised the alarm when her husband failed to return with the water, but evidence was given that during the afternoon a villager had gone to the brook that ran across the road by the toll-gate where he had observed a hat and a pail on the bank. Then he found the body in the water. Since the deceased was known to have fits, a verdict of accidental death was recorded.

Distress was to overtake the Cottons themselves the following year when the farm was hit by another widespread outbreak of what Elizabeth called the Cattle Plague. This had been recurring intermittently for years, as George Ranson noted:

> *22 October 1845.* Melton Bullock Fair. A very short supply of Beasts, a great quantity could not reach the Fair in consequence of the disease amongst them, poor things, they were in a very sad state with sore feet, scarcely able to stand. The disease is called the Murrain; the best remedy I think, is to give each 1½lbs of Epsom and keep them dry and warm.

During the late winter and early spring of 1866, the disease had become so widespread that again the nation was called upon to offer up concerted prayer:

> *7 March 1866.* Wednesday Afternoon attended Copdock Church. Humiliation Service for the Cattle Plague. . . . *9 March.* Allan went to meet the hounds but found the Hunt postponed because of another Fast Day for the Cattle Plague.

On 3 November 1869 the cattle disease rinderpest, broke out at Amor Hall. Simultaneously, a horse was taken ill and to make matters worse, so was Herbert. Elizabeth was torn between a loving concern for her husband and the practical impact the outbreak would have on the farm. Her diary entries indicate a woman who crosses easily between the boundaries of working wife and middle-class lady:

> *8 November 1869.* Allan and I sat up all night attending to remedies for the horse, as our men were sitting up with it. . . . *9 November.* With Herbert and at night sat up with Alice and Allan to help the men with the horse. . . . *10 November.* Our poor horse died.

In the same way that Elizabeth fails to give details about food, so too is she a poor recorder of weather patterns. Since her diaries were accounts of the daily life of the family rather than analytical reports of her time, she mentions the weather only in so far as it affected their activities. As the wife of a farmer we might have expected her to comment on what conditions were like at harvest time, for example. Yet, if we look at the year 1860, she makes only one reference to what the farmer Rope, of Blaxhall, called 'the wettest and coldest summer to this time [15 August] I ever remember.' On the 23 July Elizabeth went:

To the Chauntry to see Review of Rifles. Fanny, Emily, Alice and our boys with us. The rain fell in torrents all day and when we returned home our clothes were perfectly drenched, but I think the children enjoyed the absurdity of the scene and did not heed the discomforts.

In fact we read on a number of occasions that Elizabeth and her family were 'perfectly drenched' but this seems to have been accepted as part of normal everyday life.

Similarly, in 1863, Elizabeth offers no detail of the summer; we are left to assume from the number of times she mentions she is 'in the garden' or 'on the river' or playing croquet that August that year was reasonably warm. It was unfortunate that on the 26th, when the family went to Felixstowe, it should have been: 'Very nice in the morning upon the beach. Rained in the afternoon and all the way home.' Yet according to Mr Rope, writing in his farm journal on the 28th, it was: 'The finest harvest I ever knew – all brilliant weather except a few hours one day when men were obliged to leave the corn for the turnips.' Putting the two accounts together, we know that it was on the 26th that Rope's men had to leave the cornfields.

In 1859 the immense heat and drought of the summer led to a temporary suspension of Parliament because of the unbearable stench rising from the low level of the Thames. Elizabeth encountered this for herself and for one used to farmyard and stables she offered the very delicate comment: '7 July 1859. Evening walked in the Temple Gardens and found the scent from the river very annoying.'

There are several references to the first snowfall of the winter, but only rarely did this prevent the family from getting from one place to another. On the whole, icy weather was greeted with joy as it meant skating was possible either in the flooded farm meadows or on the ponds and lakes in neighbouring gardens. One of the first purchases Elizabeth mentions in the earlier diary is a pair of skates for Bertie during the early winter of 1859, when she does volunteer several comments upon the weather and its consequences:

27 November 1859. . . . Weather snowy and bad all week. . . .
4 December. . . . This has been another week of bad weather. . . .
11 December . . . Severe frost all week. . . . 18 December. Thursday. Started with Miss Betts and Alice to take a drive, but our horse not being able to stand upon the ice, we had to leave the cab upon the road, while the horse was taken to the Blacksmith's to have his shoes

roughened. Walked to Copdock Hall. Called upon Mrs Marshall. Afterwards to Ipswich in the cab. To shops etc.

East Anglians will long recall the October of 1987 when hurricane-force winds wreaked havoc. One hundred and thirty years before Elizabeth witnessed something similar, albeit on a much smaller scale:

4 October 1857. Thursday. We drove to Bawdsey, intending to take a boat on the Woodbridge river, but quite a hurricane of wind came on preventing our leaving the little inn where we had put up the chaise until 6 o'clock in the evening when we returned to Felixstowe to dinner. Two of our umbrellas were broken up like egg shell when we held them up as some defence against the wind. The sea very grand.

The unpredictability of the English climate is summed up in her comment: '*22 May 1859* In the garden and with the children during the week. Some days very cold, on others so warm that we sat for hours out of doors.'

Dickens's awesome Mrs Pardiggle listed among her many activities that she was 'a School lady'. So too, it would appear, was Elizabeth, at least for a short time. By the mid-nineteenth century most rural villages, Copdock and Washbrook among them, had a school set up and maintained by 'The National Society for promoting the education of the poor in the principles of the established church'. The local vicar was responsible for overseeing that the children were indeed instructed fully in the liturgy and catechism of the Church of England, but other pillars of the church and community were encouraged to visit the school to see that all was as it should be. In some areas, it is said, this gave the ladies – and gentlemen too – the opportunity to mark out likely future servant girls. An exceptionally fine seamstress, for example, might well be worth engaging for the household, and many young boys were given their first chance to make an addition to the family income by finding employment out of school hours as 'boot boy' in a big house. While we may imagine that Mrs Pardiggle, with all her smug brood in tow, would poke and pry in corners as well as examining the children rigorously on their religious knowledge, I like to think that Elizabeth's interest in her local school was of a more benevolent nature.

18 March 1860. Monday. With Margaret called upon Mrs Shepherd. She asked us to see the school and house, which has been enlarged and newly furnished with elegance and with great luxury as well as comforts for the girls. . . . *29 October*, Monday Miss Ransome and Miss Rix spent the day with us. Called at the Rectory and went to the Church and the School.

From various old school log books it is clear that it was customary for ladies to bring their visitors, and children, to see the work of the school. '5 February 1861. With Blanche to Village School. . . . 11 July To School Fete at Copdock. . . . 16 July. . . . To Village School.'

There are no other references to the local school, but it may have been an interest in education which prompted Elizabeth's first visit to the Convent at East Bergholt where she was shown the schoolrooms and the dormitories. Later she became a regular visitor to the various performances presented by the pupils of the convent school in Ipswich, and on one occasion she entertained some of the girls to tea at Washbrook. It is possible that this was not just a social visit, the girls may well have come for a 'farm visit' or a natural history practical lesson – we tend to think that such things are a feature of modern education.

With all the odd references to some item like placing the children's money in the Savings Bank, or that she 'heard Miss Bacon the new singer Father Kemp has engaged in his choir' – which makes us look anew at the composition of the Catholic church choir at that period – Elizabeth provides us with a wide range of events and trends of the world around her, mostly unconsciously, since to her they were simply part of her everyday life.

Bound up with the world outside the home and her life in Suffolk is Elizabeth's relationship with her extended family through whom she is brought into contact with the fashionable trends in London. From these relations we learn odd details about how money was invested, the provisions made for dependants and the roles played by different members of the family group. Davidoff and Hall in *Family Fortunes* point to the importance of the 'family network' in many spheres of life during the first half of the nineteenth century. Elizabeth's diary for 1854–63 bears this out, but her second diary shows a decline in its influence as the older members die and the brothers and sisters develop their own dynasties.

Initially, one cannot help seeing the occasional resemblance to Galsworthy's Forsyte family. In the space of sixteen years we are presented with four generations. There are the uncles John and George Nelson with their connections with the inn-keeping and coach business and Elizabeth's father, James Haxell still running his side of the business in Ipswich up to his last illness. Elizabeth's own generation included her brothers Edward and Arthur and their wives and her sisters Anne, Rebecca Page, Kate Nelson and Margaret. Then came the Cotton children and their cousins and by the time the diaries end the continuing line in the children of Emily and Fanny Page.

Uncle George Nelson is a shadowy figure about whom we learn little from the pages of the diaries beyond his concern for Herbert Cotton's eyesight and that he was frequently present at John's home when the family met. From various wills it emerges that George had pretensions to grandeur. When John made his last testament in the 1830s he described his brother as the holder of the Saracen's Head Inn in Friday Street in the city of London. However, by the time George made his own will in 1850 he described himself as 'gentleman', a designation which was again applied in 1857 when he witnessed John's renunciation of the role of executor to James Haxell's will. By then George was living in Duke Street off Grosvenor Square, but he also had a country house at Chadwell where Elizabeth once spent an enjoyable Sunday walking with her uncles in the garden and meadows until quite late in the evening before they all returned to London. George's primary concern in his will was for the welfare of his sister-in-law Mary, wife of Robert Nelson. He instructed that she should receive the income from £500 invested on her behalf, for her 'sole use'. In making a bequest to his brother-in-law, Haxell, we are able to deduce that Elizabeth's mother had died before 1850. Haxell did not live to receive his legacy, but his children did benefit: '31 *January 1867*. Letter to say Uncle George died yesterday. . . . 20 Aug. Received a legacy left me by Uncle George.'

To John Nelson fell the patriarchal role. It was to his house that the Cottons went on arrival in London. The proximity of the Bull Inn in Aldgate to the Great Eastern Railway terminus may have had something to do with it, but even so, John was visited several times during each stay in London. John was only a few years older than Herbert, and between them existed a friendship which was greater than that brought about simply through a marriage relationship. Possibly it was of much longer standing; it may even have been responsible for the meeting between Herbert and Elizabeth. The two men exchanged gifts, Herbert sending the first game of the season to John, John sending the barrel of oysters at Christmas. As both men entered their mid to late sixties, we read of Herbert staying with John while Elizabeth goes off alone to carry out her religious devotions in various London churches. When the news comes to Washbrook that John is ill, it is Herbert who goes immediately to see him. John had remained at the Bull with his mother, eventually bringing a wife to join the household. She had died childless during the 1840s leaving mother and son to continue providing a base for the family, and during the early 1850s a home for Anne and Margaret Haxell. The stability of that base was rocked when John died in 1868: '25 *July*. Letter from Anne to say my poor Uncle John died at six o'clock yesterday morning.'

Sad though the passing might be, John was in his seventies, and his death had been expected. What had not been anticipated was the news which came next: '28 *July*. Telegram from Edward to ask me to join him in contesting Uncle John's Will, if, as he fears, the property falls to James Nelson. To London with Allan.'

There is nothing quite like the disposal of a deceased relative's estate
to stir up a good family squabble. Elizabeth's brothers and sisters in
London had quickly discovered that there was likely to be trouble and
that a united front was called for. Hence Edward's unprecedented step
of summoning Elizabeth's aid by telegram. Elizabeth had not intended
to attend the funeral, but she went immediately to London. If Herbert
was unable to go with her, one might have expected Bertie, as the elder
son, to accompany her, if she needed to be accompanied. Instead she
took Allan. The logic behind this is clear when one remembers that
Allan was training to be a solicitor:

*29 July. My poor Uncle's funeral. The Will was read afterwards. It had
been made a great many years and no one named in it is now living.
James Nelson claimed the Freehold. Henry Page consented to act as
Administrator for the interest of the rest of the family. . . . 31 July. A
letter from Henry Page to say he believed the property of my uncle
would be divided fairly.*

This is another occasion when the brief details would merit a dramatic
scene. It has a familiar ring; we have all watched such enactments in
period films. The clan gathered; Edward and Arthur Haxell, Rea and
Henry Page, Anne, Elizabeth and Allan and the villain of the piece,
James Nelson – cousin and brother-in-law. Poor sister Kate, his wife,
where did her loyalties lie? Imagine them as they sat through the
reading of the last Will and Testament of John Nelson which runs to six
pages of very closely written legal verbiage, yet gives a great many
details regarding holdings and capital. The trouble was that John had
not revised the document that he had so carefully made in 1835. At that
time, apart from his coach business, he had owned a farm of 74 acres
with horses and stables at Great Burstead, another at Leyton and had a
major interest in an inn and the lands around it at Stamford le Hope, all
in Essex. Furthermore, he held the leases of several properties in
Aldgate. He also had monies loaned out on various mortgages. He had
instructed that £4000 was to be invested in 3% Bank of England stock to
provide for his widow's lifetime. He had shown a liberal attitude in so
far that in the event of his widow's remarriage, the income was to
remain hers for her sole use. After her death the estate was to be divided
equally between his brothers Robert and George and sister Rebecca
Haxell. He also stated that any outstanding loan to James Haxell was to
be cancelled and considered by James as a gift.

Quite why there should have been any problem over the final settlement is difficult to see, for John clearly stated that if his brothers and
sister predeceased him, their share was to go in equal portions to each of
their children on attaining the age of twenty-one. Daughters were to

have sole use of their money, their portion being given them on marriage if that came before reaching twenty-one. George was childless, so that left the estate to be divided between the children of Robert Nelson and Rebecca Haxell. Perhaps James Nelson felt this to be an unfair distribution since there were more Haxells than Nelsons. The copy of the will does not reveal what the value of the estate was by 1868, neither is it known if John had retained his farming properties. With the decline of the long-distance coaches he would no longer have needed the stabling facilities they afforded. A codicil made several days after the original will stated that John had just purchased £1000 worth of Bank of England stock, so that was probably intact and may have been added to over the years. Although Henry Page had volunteered to act as administrator, it was to his wife that power of administration was eventually granted. Nothing more was heard on the subject until: '6 *January 1869.* Received £200 from James Nelson.' Since James had originally claimed the freehold of The Bull, it may be that he wished to maintain the business and so paid out the rest of them on valuation.

The death of John must have had most effect on Anne who lost his companionship and was now in danger of losing her home. In many respects, Anne was mother-figure to the rest of them, taking over the role previously held by her grandmother. She was a prolific letter writer and it is often from what she relates to Elizabeth that we learn what is happening to the others. It would be easy to cast Anne as the stereotype 'spinster aunt'. When we meet her in the first entry of the diary she was in her early forties and fulfilling a benevolent role: '1 *January 1854.* . . . On Friday the 6th. Anne sent a Twelfth Cake to our children.'

A year later she is again in an accepted role, acting as travelling companion to the young Page girls for a visit to Washbrook. After a week she returns to London, this time with three charges for Alice is going to stay with her cousins. When she brings Alice back Anne remains at Amor Hall for a month during which the impression is gained that Anne fitted easily into the household as a member of the family rather than a guest who had to be entertained. She comes again a few weeks later with other members of the family for the christening in July of her god-daughter, Ethel. A month later it was to Anne that the grieving Elizabeth turned for comfort and support after the baby's death. She accompanied Elizabeth and the children to Felixstowe and remained with the family until mid-October. Although the different members of the family used Anne to escort their children when travelling, there is never any suggestion that she should be called upon to take over the running of a household while her brothers and sisters took a holiday. Anne was an independent woman with a life and friends of her own. We learn that she was fond of music and art, and since it was with her that Elizabeth attended her first Roman Catholic service, we deduce she was also interested in religious matters. She made two long visits to Washbrook in 1860 and 1861, but thereafter Elizabeth's contact with her was either by letter or in London.

In 1857 Anne appears to have handed over the role of travelling companion to nieces to her sister Margaret. She, being much younger than the others must have seemed more like an older sister than an aunt to the Cotton children. When she visited she played games with them, joined them for rides and generally exuded life and vitality. During the period of the first diary we see her relationship with Elizabeth deepening thus making her departure to Australia in 1864 much harder for Elizabeth to bear. There is no indication as to what prompted this move; even if she were going out to join her brother George, it was a momentous decision for a woman of thirty to undertake such a long and arduous journey on her own. Elizabeth noted that Margaret joined the ship, *La Hague*, at Plymouth on 1 August 1864. On 20 January 1865 came the long awaited 'letter from Margaret. She is quite disappointed with her first experience of Australia.' It may have been a conscious effort to understand the way of life that Margaret was now leading that led to Elizabeth reading aloud to Herbert in May 1866 the very popular novel *The Hillyards and Burtons* by Henry Kingsley.

Thereafter, for the next four years, letters went back and forth between Australia and Washbrook, and then came the news: '*30 January 1869*. A letter from Margot to say she is engaged to Mr Mills of Yandilla, Darling Downs.'

Elizabeth must have been responsible for placing the announcement of the marriage in the local newspaper when confirmation of the event arrived in November:

> On 2nd. Sept. at Yandilla, Darling Downs, Queensland by the Revd. Joshua Jones, James Checkley, 3rd. son of John Mills, esq. of Checkley, Parramatta, NSW to Margaret Nelson, youngest daughter of the late James Haxell of Ipswich.

Closest in age to Elizabeth was Rea and as we have already noted, both she and brother Edward provide us with examples of the upwardly mobile middle classes. Having moved from central London to Dulwich Henry was able to lead the dual life of a city businessman and countryman indulging in the gentlemanly pursuit of shooting. The Pages went abroad for their holidays; Elizabeth mentions a letter from Rea, 'giving an account of her tour of Switzerland' and later that she and Henry are 'travelling extensively in Germany'. Although visits between sisters tail off after 1864, Elizabeth maintains a close relationship with her nieces after their marriage.

Edward, who branched out from being a wine merchant into the hotel business, also followed the pattern of separating family and business by buying a country house, first at Gerrards Cross and then at Kingsbury. Initially this was to be for use at weekends and during the summer, but as time passes it is evident that Arabella and the two children spent more and more time there. In 1867, Elizabeth was somewhat put out to find her sister-in-law not at her London home, and indirectly gives a glimpse of another middle-class custom: '23 *June*. Sunday. . . . Left cards upon Edward and Arabella. . . . Monday Called twice upon Edward. Arabella not yet returned.'

Elizabeth's relationship with her sister Kate is more tenuous. They keep in touch by letter with news of Kate's confinements, her children's illnesses and Kate's own bout of rheumatic fever, but there was not the same frequency of interchanging visits:

> *11 Sept. 1859*. Wednesday A letter from Kate saying she intends with her husband driving from London to stay with us next Saturday . . . Kate and James came on Saturday evening having driven to Chelmsford on Friday and the remainder of the way today. . . . Sunday. At home with Kate. James went to church with Herbert and the children. Monday to Felixstow with Herbert, Kate and James. The day beautifully fine . . . Tuesday. To Ipswich with James. Kate started with us but wished to return . . . James left early on Thursday.

There is an underlying sense of tension here created in part by the implication that the Nelsons invited themselves and that all was not well with the couple themselves. Although Elizabeth does bring herself to use his Christian name, her first reference is the very formal 'with her husband'. The visit has none of the gaiety which was there the following month when Edward and Rea and their partners came to stay. For them there were visits to the races and the theatre; dinner parties both at home and with friends and excursions to places of interest. Additionally for the men there was shooting. As often happens in close-knit families, one of the visitors must have reported back to James and Kate what a splendid time had been had at Amor Hall. This upset James so much that Elizabeth received:

> another letter gross insult from James Nelson who, we imagine angry at not having shared the pleasures of our party during the Race Week, has ever since behaved to us in the most insolent manner. I have not retaliated upon him, but will not if possible read another letter from him.

Despite the occasional meeting of the two parties concerned at the home of others the rift was not repaired until: '25 *May 1863*. James Nelson

wrote an apology. Answered him and said we wished to be friends.'
The overall impression gained from the first diary is that the family
was a united one which enjoyed being together as much as possible.
However, the years between 1864 and 1869 show a falling off in the
exchange of visits and, to a large extent, the correspondence between
them. Elizabeth's interest was centred on the activities of her children
and her ever-increasing commitment to religious affairs. Visits to London tended to be short, often just for a day as she became more involved
with what was going on locally. Her new friends who shared her beliefs
began to take the place of the brothers and sisters who in turn were
developing their own life-styles.

As a footnote to Elizabeth's relationship with her extended family can
be posed the question of how truthful was she in what she wrote. I
believe that she reported events as they appeared to her with a natural
personal bias. However, I have proved that she did not tell all. For my
own amusement, a graphologist was asked to examine specimen pages
of the diaries. The assessment of her character confirmed my own, but
included the comment that the subject was concealing something, 'a
skeleton in the cupboard – a mad uncle perhaps?' How close this was to
the truth was revealed by that chance encounter with the old newspapers mentioned in my Introduction. On the 2 May 1861, Elizabeth
noted that Anne had informed her of the death of their brother James,
but what she did not write was that a few months earlier James had
appeared in court in London charged with falsifying two cheques. He
had changed two pounds on each to twelve. The *News of the World* for 21
October 1860 devoted almost half a column to the case. Which would
have been worse for her, the discovery that her brother was guilty of
fraud or that he should be declared insane? His surgeon who had
known him for twenty-two years testified to his respectability but
affirmed:

I have not the slightest hesitation in saying he is of unsound mind,
and not responsible for his actions. I should have no hesitation in
signing a certificate of lunacy authorising his detention in an asylum.
Yesterday he chased his wife round the room with a couple of pokers
in his hand and she was obliged to be locked up in the coal cellar for a
considerable time to escape his violence. He is labouring under the
strange hallucination that he is about to realise a large fortune in a
short time, and he goes out without the slightest discretion taking up
public houses, and sending workmen into them to fit them up. . . .
The Lord Mayor requested the officers to take him to the Union in St
Mary Axe, and to treat him with all possible kindness. – Prisoner:
Thank you, Sir; but I am not going to any Union. You have no power

to take me there. – The unfortunate man was then conveyed to the London Union.

It is strange that James who had been a successful auctioneer should, in his deranged state, have tried to revert to the family tradition of inn-keeping. However much Elizabeth might wish to keep this information buried, local people would have known of it. The Ipswich newspapers were in the habit of taking interesting stories from other papers and the Haxells were well known in the town. I can only assume that the random papers that came my way were preserved because their con-tents held something of particular interest to their original reader, and that it was the Haxell case rather than anything else which led to the saving of the inner pages of the only copy of the *News of the World*.

With the middle-class emphasis on respectability, how did Elizabeth and her family cope with the scandal? There is nothing in the diary to indicate that her life was altered in any way; nor did she suffer social ostracism during the weeks immediately following the report for she continued to make calls upon her friends and they to visit her. Neither was it necessary for her to confide the information to her diary for she had Anne staying with her at the time and they would have been able to discuss fully the implications of James's misfortune. And if she did deliberately hide this episode from her journal, and possible future readers, who can blame her for showing a very human reaction to an event which she would rather remained 'in a cloud'.

9

Religion

. . . if you have three services on Sunday and domestic prayers at home, you do very well.

Framley Parsonage Trollope

'1 *January 1854*. Sunday. To Washbrook Church with Herbert, Alice and Bertie.' From this, the opening entry of Elizabeth Cotton's diary, we could conclude that we are about to have proof of the generalisations about Victorian religious practices, for it is one of the most widely held views of the period that family life was severely restricted by religious observances. We have read of family prayers being held night and morning at which attendance was obligatory for each member of the family as well as all the domestic staff. We know that families marched to church at least once every Sunday to endure tedious services with sermons of inordinate length and that what was left of the day was given over to 'suitable' pastimes which, in the main, consisted of children learning the Epistle and Collect for the day and the reading of religious works for the family as a whole.

As with all generalisations, it is possible to find examples which show that this was not true for everyone. That it was not so for the Cotton family is, I suggest, not unique, for they were leading lives very similar to those of others who moved in their own sphere. According to W.J. Reader's *Victorian England*, 'Religion, especially non-conformity, lay at the heart of Victorian middle-class life'. The Cottons and most of their friends and relations were firmly rooted in the Church of England, and they, far from veering to the evangelical branch as Reader suggests most of the middle class did, became caught up, as we shall see later, in the High Church movement. Initially, their religious observances were coloured by where and how they lived. The two villages of Copdock and Washbrook each possessed its own parish church. Copdock had a large building situated in a fairly central position, while Washbrook had a much older and smaller building on the edge of the Amor Hall farm some distance away from the main village.

When William the Conqueror carved up England, he gave a large slice of East Anglia, including Washbrook, to his kinsman Odo. A later heir granted the village to the abbey at Aumerle in Normandy. Amor Hall, a corruption of Aumerle, was for a hundred years or so the home of the Norman monks who acted as bailiff to the abbot. In due course the area reverted to English ownership and from the seventeenth century Washbrook and adjoining Copdock were in the hands of a Norfolk family which took the title of Walsingham. As often happened on English estates, the landowners held the right to appoint the clergy to the parishes which made up their holdings. At a time when it was accepted practice that the estate and its revenues passed to the eldest son, leaving the rest of the family to exist on whatever small incomes came their way, supplemented perhaps by a commission in the Army or Navy, the ownership of a family church living provided a way of ensuring that at least one of the younger·sons had a secure income and home, provided he was willing to take Holy Orders. Thus it was that in 1837, at the age of twenty-seven, the Revd and Honourable Frederick de Grey, a younger brother of Lord Walsingham, became vicar of Copdock and rector of Washbrook, the two parishes having long before been combined into a single living, providing enough income for the vicar to employ a curate to assist him.

The clerical income derived from the tithes that each tenant farmer was obliged to pay to the church, and since in many cases the parson was in effect the representative of the landowner, it meant that those dependent on the landlord for the means to a livelihood remained adherents to the Church of England. Although a Dissenting chapel had been in existence in Washbrook for generations its supporters were very largely those whose jobs were not likely to be jeopardised by turning away from the established Church. Naturally Herbert Cotton, as the major tenant in Washbrook, supported his parish church, setting an example to his workers and their families.

Being held by an absentee landlord, the twin parishes lacked the traditional squire. Although the Cottons and several others farmed on quite a large scale for those times, and held a social position above the mass of agricultural workers, it was the Revd de Grey who exercised the role closest to that of squire. He was the local magistrate and the final arbiter in both lay and church affairs – and one of the principal players in the story of Elizabeth's life while she was at Washbrook. He obviously considered the Cottons to be socially acceptable in so far as he visited them both formally and informally, occasionally dining at Amor Hall, exchanging books with them and even bringing visiting members of his family to take tea with them. However, it is in relation to de Grey that a very strong side to Elizabeth's character emerges. She was never willing to kowtow to him, as perhaps others in the parish did, and it was perhaps from her that he heard things he did not like. As we shall see in due course, she was more than a match for him.

From the diary we learn much about the religious observances of the day as they affected Elizabeth, and the various movements within the Church of England itself. In the early stages we have no inkling that

Elizabeth's interest went beyond the token Sunday attendance at church. She makes no reference to family prayers being held or that Sunday was kept as a particularly quiet and reverential day. She does not attend church every Sunday even though Herbert does, nor is there any compulsion upon the children to attend regularly, and it is not until the boys start at the Grammar School that there is any mention of the traditional learning of the Epistle and Collect for the day when it became part of school homework. Frequently, Elizabeth's entry for Sunday simply reads, 'At home'. In the early years this may be followed with the information that Mr Martin spent the evening with Herbert. The Cottons also entertained on Sundays, usually members of the family or very close friends, and when they were away they went to dinner parties and enjoyed entertainment in the form of music and dancing.

The Queen herself wrote to the Princess Royal in 1859: 'You know I am not at all an admirer or approver of our very dull Sundays, for I think the absence of innocent amusement for the poor people a misfortune and an encouragement of vice.' It was belief in innocent entertainment which led Elizabeth to allow freedom to her children. '27 July 1862. Sunday. To church. With children afterwards. Let them take off their shoes and play in the garden stream.' One cannot believe that this could be performed with the decorum and sobriety one associates with a dreary Victorian Sunday.

One of Elizabeth's endearing qualities is her honesty;

14 August 1859. With Herbert and children to church. The curate's son, Mr C. Paglar kept us waiting half an hour for the service to begin. The day stormy. . . . *2 October.* To church with Herbert and the children. Mr Paglar preached to collect subscriptions for the Propagation of the Gospel. A few pence over 14/- only collected – and quite a scramble after the people, who were hurrying out of church to obtain that. . . . *18 December.* At home. Herbert went to church with the children and after waiting half an hour for Mr Paglar, returned home again. . . . *29 December 1861.* Started to walk to church. Found the day so cold, returned home. . . . *30 April 1862.* With Herbert to Choral Meeting at St. Matthews Church, Ipswich. Music too loud and harsh.

The last is an example of personal opinion conflicting with a glowing press report. It is also an example of parochial support, for the choirs of Washbrook and Copdock joined with eighteen other choirs, totalling 267 for the afternoon's choral service. It was estimated that over twelve hundred people, with the Revd de Grey among the many clergy, attended to hear both the choirs and the sermon preached by Lord Arthur Hervey. Elizabeth makes no comment upon what she thought of his lordship's discourse on Psalm 150, verses 1–6.

Initially her interest in churches was an intellectual and artistic one. As far as the latter was concerned, she found much in church architecture and decoration to provide material for her many sketches, as did many other women of the time. We also, from the pages of the diaries, particularly the shorter second one, learn something of the mid-nineteenth century movement for restoration which made many of the parish churches of England into the buildings with which we are familiar. As early as 1844, George Ranson reported in his diary:

22 December. Opened Sproughton church again today. The church has been thoroughly renewed, cleaned, pillars scraped and restored. Pulpit and desk removed, new fireplace, stove I mean, placed. This has been done by subscription from landowners and occupiers of the Parish. The chancel also is altered, benched out under Mr Gould's direction and his expense; the body of the church done . . . for £125.0.0. . . . and altogether looks very well, indeed a very nice improvement.

Ranson was commenting on his own parish church, Elizabeth made a point of looking at others:

5 March 1863. Thursday. With Alice to Ipswich. Went with Mrs Walton Turner and Mrs Miller to St. Lawrence Church. First service of re-opening after restoration of church. . . . *14 January 1864.* To the re-opening of St Mary le Tower Church, Ipswich after partial restoration. . . . *10 June.* Went to see Stoke Church. It has been nicely restored but the east window looks like a carpet. . . . *14 September 1865.* Mr de Grey called to show us the plans for the restoration of Washbrook Church. . . . *26 November.* To Washbrook Church. Last day of its being used for Divine Service before restoration. . . . *2 December.* Saturday. With little girls to Washbrook Church. Made sketches. Mr de Grey joined us there. When the workmen were taking down the plaster of the ceiling we found the remains of the original boarded roof of the nave. The wood had been painted a bright vermilion with black stars upon it. Under the plaster of the walls we found the remains of fresco painting. . . . *6 April 1866.* Friday. To Washbrook Church to choose seats we wish to have. Selected the stalls in the north wall, and wrote to Mr de Grey. . . . *22 April.* Washbrook Church re-opened for Divine Service. The Holy Sacrament given in the morning. Afternoon Mr Hales-Tooke preached.

The entry about choosing seats in church recalls the custom of the wealthier classes paying a rental for the privilege of sitting in the same place for every service. To have two services on the same day was unusual at Washbrook, but this was a very special occasion, and therefore one to mark by the celebration of Holy Communion for the sacrament was not given on a regular basis. The afternoon service had special significance too, since the preacher was the landlord of the village, who had no doubt contributed largely to the restoration costs.

Intellectually, Elizabeth showed curiosity about theological questions and other people's religious observances. As ever in the fashion, in 1862, just after its publication she sent her sister-in-law, Arabella, a copy of *Hymns Ancient and Modern*. Similarly she read aloud to Herbert that most controversial of books at the time, Bishop Colenso's theories on the first five books of the Old Testament. Colenso, who for a time was bishop of Natal, found that during his missionary work among the Africans he had been forced to reconsider many of the accepted interpretations of the Bible stories.

Curiosity too guided her into other religious establishments: '12 June 1859. Sunday. Walked to Pakefield, and in the evening walked on the pier [at Lowestoft] and went for a few minutes into a place called a Bethel where divine worship was being carried on.'

17 May 1857. Sunday. With Herbert to Woolwich. Heard Music at Catholic Chapel. . . . *22 Aug. 1859.* Sunday. In the morning with Anne and Margaret to the Roman Catholic Chapel at Southwark. A Grand Mass in honour of the Assumption of the Virgin performed. The music very beautiful indeed. After the service was over, a Catholic lady introduced us to Mr Griffiths, a priest, who went with us over the Cathedral. Some good sculpture and fine architecture. A bronze crucifix, life size, given by the widow of Napoleon 1st. . . . *26 October 1862.* With Herbert to St George's Cathedral, Southwark.

While trying other forms of service than those of the established church, Elizabeth still conformed sufficiently to ensure that her children were confirmed at the correct time according to the fashion of the period:

20 May 1860. Saturday. Mr de Grey examined Alice about her preparation for Confirmation. . . . *8 July.* Thursday. To Sproughton Church with Alice who was confirmed by the Bishop of Norwich. . . . *21 October 1863.* Wednesday. Herbert went to Orford. Morning attended Confirmation Service at St Margaret's, Ipswich. Bertie and Allan confirmed. Mr de Grey had examined the children but as he did not attend the service, I asked Mr Berresford of St Margaret's to help us, and he passed my boys with his own parishioners. Evening with Alice, Evelyn and the boys to hear a lecture given at Ipswich by Ignatius upon Monasteries.

There is implied criticism of the Revd de Grey for failing in his duty to present his own confirmation candidates to the Bishop but more interesting is the account of how the evening was spent. What is not revealed openly is the growing rift between Elizabeth and the vicar over what he considered to be dangerous practices.

At the beginning of 1863, the older children, that is, Alice who at 18 perhaps should no longer be classed as a child, and Bertie and Allan, now 15 and 14, started attending church in other parishes:

4 January 1863. Sunday. At home. Afternoon Alice and Bertie to Belstead Church. Herbert took Allan and Evelyn to Washbrook Church. . . . *1 March.* Sunday At home. Bertie with his father to Washbrook. Alice and Allan to Sproughton Church. . . . *8 March.* Morning Washbrook Church Evelyn and Blanche with me. Afternoon Alice, Bertie and Allan went to Hintlesham Church. . . . *12 April.* Ada West spent the day here, and in the evening went with the boys, Alice, Fanny and Emily Page to Claydon Church. They heard a clergyman calling himself Brother Ignatius and dressed in a Monk's robes preach. . . . *31 May.* Evening to Claydon Church. Brother Ignatius asked us to walk round Mr Drury's grounds with him.

There are a number of books which deal with the life of Ignatius and the impact this extraordinary man had for many years on the religious life of a vast number of people in mid-Victorian England. Briefly, Joseph Leycester Lyne, who was admitted as a deacon into the Church of England but never ordained as a full member of the clergy, felt he had been called to re-establish the Benedictine Rule within the Church of England. His aim was to found a series of monasteries and convents with a third order for lay people where the ancient Rule and rituals of the past might be upheld. Many of his aspirations were echoed by the High Church Oxford Movement in this country and in similar movements throughout the world, but his appeal was much more widespread in that it was less intellectually founded. He was, by all accounts, what nowadays would be termed a charismatic preacher, and many from all walks of life were inspired to follow him in pursuit of his dream.

Within the Church itself some of the clergy in the Eastern Counties were adopting High Church rituals, among them the Revd George Drury, of Claydon near Ipswich. When Ignatius had first projected his Society for the Love of Jesus, Drury had declared his sympathy with the idea. In November 1862, Drury invited Ignatius to preach at Claydon, where the services were celebrated with a degree of ritual severely frowned upon by Dr Pelham, the very Low Church Bishop of Norwich. While he was at Claydon, Ignatius floated the idea of establishing a monastery in Ipswich, the cost to be underwritten by sympathisers in the town and surrounding area. Drury introduced Ignatius to two prominent local High Church professional gentlemen, Benjamin Lillistone Gross and William Batley Jackson, who were to be trustees of the project. Ignatius, at the time only twenty-six and full of confidence, wrote enthusiastic letters to all the nobility of Suffolk to enlist financial support, but to little avail. Gross and Jackson also met with little success and in due time had to report that the Ipswich supporters had been unable to raise either enough funds to hire the proposed venue for the monastery or guarantee the first year's expenses. Still fired with personal enthusiasm for the cause, Drury suggested that Ignatius and the three brothers who formed the community should take over one wing of his large rectory at Claydon.

Ignatius's mission in Claydon, which began in earnest on Shrove Tuesday 1863, brought mixed reactions. By the time the Cotton children attended a service on Easter Sunday, opposition as well as support was growing. Under the headline 'Forms and Ceremonies at Claydon Church' the *Ipswich Journal* reported:

> Public service was conducted on Easter Sunday with an extravagance of form and ceremony such as is scarcely ever seen except in the Roman Catholic Church. The result seems to be the attraction of a large number of persons, drawn together by curiosity, but the mode of conducting the worship does not appear to be in accordance with the feelings of the large body of parishioners, who are attached to the Church of England.

Just how strong the opposition was Elizabeth was to find out at first hand:

> *14 June 1863*. Sunday. Morning to Washbrook Church. Evening to Claydon. Mr Drury and Brother Ignatius protected us from some drunken mechanics. Ignatius preached in the schoolroom after service in Church. . . . Monday. Herbert wrote to thank Ignatius for his kindness last evening. . . . *22 June*. Monday. A letter from Ignatius. Wrote to the Bishop of Norwich for Mr Drury.

Elizabeth describes the mob of angry protesters as drunken mechanics, and there may be some truth in her assessment, but there was also widespread feeling among the members of the Low Church evangelicals that what they were seeing and hearing in Claydon was but a short step to the Church being caught up in the snares of Roman Catholic practices.

The bishop, who had for some time been very worried about the 'goings-on' at Claydon, ordered that Ignatius should not preach in the church; thus the congregation removed to the unhallowed confines of the village schoolroom to hear him. It was to support Drury in his running battle with the bishop that Elizabeth took it upon herself to address Dr Pelham. Drury's side of the controversy was stated in a letter to *The Times* on *26 September 1863*: 'Three or four years ago a correspondence took place between the bishop and my solicitor about the vestments, rites and ceremonies in use here, and it ended by the bishop allowing them to remain.'

However, before then, Elizabeth had her reply from the bishop by return of post. She does not relate his lordship's comments but, bishop or not, events continued at Claydon, events which were reported nationally via *The Times*:

29 June 1863. St Peter's Day, a High celebration took place with Ignatius leading the village children singing a kyrie adapted from bits of Mendelsohn's Elijah, the Sanctus and Benedictus from Mozart's 2nd and 12th Masses, the Agnus Dei and O Salutaris. After Choral Evensong black robed Benedictines carried banners during an outdoor procession. Acolytes in scarlet cassocks and lace trimmed surplices held crucifixes and candles, one boy waved a smoking censer. The church was packed to suffocation.

Such papistic ritual was enough to rouse one stalwart of the Low Church brigade, a wealthy landowner, to offer £1000 to anybody able to 'destroy the hornet's nest'. It was from reactions such as this that rumours flourished that many of the protesters who mobbed Ignatius's meetings were in fact fuelled by free beer and small financial inducements. Some felt so strongly that on one occasion Ignatius was actually seized and carried off to be placed on a bonfire that had been prepared for his dispatch. Fortunately, he managed to release himself before this barbarous act could take place.

Undeterred by all this, Elizabeth was wholeheartedly behind Drury, and Ignatius with whom she was regularly exchanging letters and listening to all he had to say: '*5 July 1863*. Sunday. To Claydon Church. Ignatius walked with us. . . . *19 July*. To Claydon. Ignatius walked with us. Met Mr and Mrs Mark Wade and Miss Wade.'

She attended church at Washbrook only once during July so perhaps that is why the Revd de Grey thought it was time he should exert his influence: '*20 July 1863*. Monday. To tea with Mr de Grey. Met Mrs Garnier, Miss Garnier, Mr Paglar, Mr Rouse and the Marshalls. Miss Garnier and Alice played and sang in the evening.' This is the first time in ten years that the Cottons had been invited to attend what was virtually a select private evening party at the vicarage. The fact that his relations, the Garniers, were staying with him, gave de Grey the excuse for the occasion, but social though it might be, it is noticeable that the vicar had brought in his reserves in the form of the curate, Mr Paglar and Mr Marshall who was a churchwarden.

If it was a ploy to get Elizabeth safely back into the fold, it did not work, for the following Saturday Elizabeth and Alice were off to Ipswich to attend a lecture given by Dr J.M. Neale, warden of Sackville College, East Grinstead, on the subject of Sisterhoods. This time they had Herbert's company, he, she tells us, coming directly from the market in Colchester to meet them at the Lecture Hall. From the newspaper report of the meeting which was chaired by the mayor, Mr Bacon, we are given a list of the notable people who attended. Among the clergymen was a certain C.J. Kemp, described as 'a Roman Catholic priest'. Two familiar names among the laity were Messrs Gross and Jackaman, Ignatius's backers. Dr Neale had come to talk about the Sisterhood at East Grinstead, an Anglican nursing order which sent its members anywhere in the country to care for those with serious infections. It is likely that young Alice was particularly influenced by the opening remarks made by the mayor, which give a very masculine attitude to the place of Victorian womanhood:

There must be, and there are, many women – earnest minded religious women – weaned from all special ties and family duties, ready to devote themselves to works of charity and piety, and these institutions are fitted, by systematic prayer and discipline, to exercise a beneficial influence in such cases.

The meeting was said not to be well supported, which is borne out by the fact that the retiring collection amounted only to £5.

The following day, Elizabeth was again at Claydon to attend service in the church and the lecture given afterwards by Ignatius. She was by now thoroughly caught up in the High Church ritual:

4 *August 1863.* Tuesday. At home. Sent altar candles to Mr Drury. . . .
13 *August.* Thursday. In the evening to Claydon Church. Ignatius preached a farewell sermon before going to Scotland. The choral service beautifully sung by Ignatius. Some people attacked the School House during the lecture and Mr Drury was thrown down and injured by a stone.

Ignatius was not leaving the area for good, merely taking a holiday for the sake of his health. Elizabeth and the children continued to divide their religious attendance between their home parishes and Claydon, the latter conveniently holding evening services. The Sunday before Bertie and Allan were to be confirmed marked a turning point: '18

October 1863. Sunday. Morning to Copdock Church. Evening Claydon Church. Herbert went with Alice, the boys and myself. Ignatius introduced us to Brother Anselm. Lecture after service in the schoolroom. Collection for replacing robbery of Crucifix etc.'

This was the first occasion that we hear of Herbert actually joining them at a service and lecture at Claydon. That plans for the Suffolk monastery were to go ahead is revealed in the mention of Brother Anselm. He, Charles Walker, was to be the Prior of the Claydon establishment. Further, the mention of the robbery of church furniture points to the unabated antagonism towards the High Church movement itself and Ignatius's mission in particular which had now reached major proportions in the area.

At the end of September, the Revd Drury had informed the public through the press that 'Mr Lyne [Ignatius] has not preached or officiated in my church since he was inhibited about three months ago', which neatly skirted the fact that he had preached in the Schoolroom. Throughout October and November a series of lectures and sermons was mounted in Ipswich by the evangelical faction of the Church of England with titles like: 'A Scriptural Duty in Critical Times'; 'Christ the Only Priest, Altar and Sacrifice'; 'The Tendency of Extreme Ceremonialism to Promote Superstition, check True Devotion and Dishonour the Holy Ghost'. The local papers carried advertisements for these as well as those promoting the *Church Standard*, a weekly magazine for 'sound Protestant Christian principles.' Similarly, within the correspondence columns of the *Ipswich Journal* the opposition waged their war of words against Ignatius. The strength of feeling of how dangerous Ignatius was thought to be by some is best summed up in a letter which appeared on 10 October 1863 from the Revd Francis Maude of Trinity Parsonage, Ipswich:

I see by your last that 'Ignatius' has again resumed his offensive attacks on the Protestant religion. I am not about the enter into the controversy, but beg you will alow me to say a word on the matter as it affects myself and many others similarly placed. It is this; when I have done with the 'Journal', I send it into my kitchen, where its pages are curiously searched by manservant, maidservant, labourer and anyone else of that class who may happen to be in the house at the time. Up to the present I have done so with the assurance that nothing in its columns is unfit for eyes and ears of such parties and have always had the satisfaction of feeling that while its contents offer amusement for all, it never embraces matters of a mischievous tendency. Now, Mr Editor, I am not going to put myself into a passion, or hold out any horrible threat of excommunication against you, but . . . if that young man is to be allowed a space in your paper to dissemi-

nate his abominable doctrines of Romish supremacy and a sealed
Bible, when I have read all I want I shall have the necessity of putting
it under the grate or keeping it under lock and key.

The Revd Maude, besides disclosing a paternalistic attitude to his
household staff, gives a slight clue as to Ignatius's methods of preaching
and the content of his message in the reference to 'passion' and 'horrible
threat'. All this opposition to what Maude called the 'abominable doctrines of Romish supremacy' vented itself at the beginning of November
in violent attacks against the members of the Roman Catholic population
of the town, on that most significant of days in the history of the
Catholic and Protestant struggle, the fifth of November. Elizabeth
writes:

5 November 1863. Thursday. Riot at Ipswich caused by a person calling
himself Baron de Camin who had been lecturing against the Anglican
and Catholic Churches. Mr Turnock's and Mr George Bacon's windows broken by the mob, and also windows of the Catholic religious
houses . . . Friday   Riot continued at Ipswich. The house of the
Catholic clergyman injured and several private houses . . . Saturday
To Ipswich. Drove round the town to see the mischief done. Special
constables are being sworn in today . . . Sunday   Edward Foster
came to breakfast [from Ipswich] and told us the rioters were stopped
last night from doing more mischief. Rose Foster came, and went with
us in the evening to Claydon. Found the church closed and Mr Drury
told us the Ipswich mob had threatened to destroy his property
tonight, and he wished us to hasten home for fear we might meet the
rioters. As we returned throught the village we saw the Dissenters
Chapel at Claydon lighted and were told Mr Lynge, an Ipswich Low
Church clergyman was addressing the people against Mr Drury. *10
November.* A letter from Ignatius to say he was going to leave Claydon.

From the Ipswich Journal we can fill in some of the details Elizabeth
omits. Andre Massena, 'Baron de Camin', who was touring the country,
was booked to give a series of lectures at the Temperance Hall. The first,
held on Thursday 29 October had passed without incident but that
arranged for the Friday was billed as a men-only occasion, and during
the course of it de Camin professed he had once been a Roman Catholic
monk. His revelations were said to have been of a prurient nature and
were accompanied by scurrilous remarks about Mr Kemp the local
Catholic priest. This angered some of the audience which included
soldiers from the Ipswich Barracks who happened to be from the 18th
Hussars, an Irish Catholic regiment. Fighting broke out. As a result, the
mayor, Mr Bacon, tried to put a stop to the meeting scheduled for the

following Tuesday, but he could not persuade the owner of the Temperance Hall, a prominent Dissenter, that it was necessary. Thwarted, the mayor took the precaution of having police in the audience which now included a very rowdy element. When the eager crowd turned up for the lecture on 5 November, they found their way into the hall was barred by twenty policemen. Undeterred, de Camin addressed the assembly outside in the street, whipped the crowd into a frenzy and many of the rabble went on the rampage into the centre of the town where they carried out various attacks. For some reason, the meeting planned for the following night was allowed, but to the bitter disappointment of the troublemakers this turned out to be no more than a dreary historical lecture. To alleviate their frustration, those seeking excitement set out to attack the house of the Catholic priest.

One might have expected that all this disturbance and brushes with unruly members of the labouring classes would have been sufficient to deter a forty-four-year-old middle-class mid-Victorian lady from pursuing her religious ideals. Far from it: '6 December 1863. Morning Belstead Church. Evening to Catholic Church.' Herbert and Elizabeth then went off to London. During the two Sundays they were there, they attended a church where the preacher was the Revd Bellew. Elizabeth fails to name which church this was, so we can only assume that the Revd Mr Bellew was of the High Church persuasion, or possibly even a Catholic. One wonders if part of her motivation in going to the Catholic church in Ipswich was to show her support for Mr Kemp who had been the subject of the November riots.

22 December 1863. Tuesday. Returned home . . . A note enclosing an account of Christmas Mass at Catholic Church . . . 23 December With Alice called for advertized tickets at Mr Kemp's. Invited upstairs and met Mr Kemp. He asks us to go through his house into church to avoid the crowd on Christmas Eve. . . . 24, Thursday. Evening to Midnight Mass at St Pancras Church. Mr Kemp came to us there. . . . 25 December. Friday. At home.

The first diary ends on 31 December 1863, leaving Elizabeth in a buoyant mood, having given a dinner party for her close friends: 'While we were talking we suddenly heard the church bells striking up to ring in the New Year, and we opened doors and windows and all our friends shook hands and congratulated each other on the new year.'

That volume, containing the record of the years 1854–63, had only one complete page left in it, so it was time to start another and in some ways, the opening of a new book coincided with the beginning of a new era in the life of Elizabeth and her family. Alice is now a mature young woman; Bertie and Allan left the Grammar School to undertake their further education; the two younger girls are happily settled at school and Elizabeth's own attitudes and way of life are changing too. Freer now from the many restraints of motherhood and domesticity, she does not settle to a quiet decline towards old age, she throws herself instead into new activity much of which is directed towards the Church:

> *7 February 1864.* Evening to St Pancras Church with Bertie, Evelyn and Blanche. Mr Kemp came to us and shewed us the Chapel of Our Lady. . . . Began etching from 'Procession to Crucifixion' by Gustave Dore. . . . *Palm Sunday.* My children went with me to St Pancras to see the Blessing of the Palms. Afternoon read 'The Monastery' to the children. . . . Easter Sunday. To St Pancras with children to hear High Mass.

This last entry must have had repercussions. It was established custom within the Church of England that confirmed members should take the sacrament of Holy Communion on Easter Sunday and we may be certain that it was given at either Washbrook or Copdock, if not at both, on that day. That the Cotton family had not attended would have been noted by all the parishioners. It most certainly was by the vicar. '23 *April 1864.* Mr de Grey called and behaved in a most ill bred manner, because we have occasionally attended other Church Services and I would not promise to cease knowing our Catholic friends.'

This must have been a stormy encounter. Elizabeth defines de Grey's manner with that most scathing of Victorian attributes of being 'ill bred'. The scion of a noble family, he had failed to behave as a gentleman should. It is tempting to suppose that he had blustered and bullied in his attempt to recapture her allegiance to his flock, yet by all accounts he was a mild-tempered man. Possibly he cast a slur on the reputations of her new friends. Whatever he did, it was the wrong way to appeal to Elizabeth. The genes of her grandmother Ann Nelson, who had with-stood fierce business competition and threats, were firmly imbedded in Elizabeth. She was always prepared to take a bold stand on those matters in which she considered she was right, even if it left her out on a limb. She considered herself as an independent individual with the right to choose how she should think and act, and like many, when told not to act in a particular way was likely to become even more ardent in the forbidden cause.

In de Grey's defence we can argue that he was doing what he saw as his duty in trying to save members of his congregation from making this dreadful mistake of becoming ensnared by Catholicism. We can also offer the excuse that as a bachelor he was inexperienced in the best way of appealing to a woman's better nature. However, in the months that followed it would appear that the vicar behaved in a manner which was becoming neither to a gentleman nor a clergyman.

5 October 1864. To Stratford St Mary with Herbert to call upon Mr James Josselyn and heard Mr de Grey had interfered most unjustifiably in our private affairs. Called upon Mr de Grey for an explanation. He said he would atone for the past if we would be friends with him.

The vicar had been guilty of gossiping about Elizabeth's religious activities not just within the twin parishes but further afield to the leading families in neighbouring areas. It is perhaps only those who live in small rural communities who can fully understand both the effect and influence a vicar can have, even today, to stir up feelings of intense animosity or loyalty. Victorian literature, in particular the works of George Eliot and Trollope, is full of it. Incensed by what she heard at Mr Josselyn's, we can imagine her back straightening into a ramrod as she demands that Herbert drive her there and then to 'have it out' with de Grey. Attacked on his home ground, entirely unprepared for the onslaught, de Grey capitulated. The Sunday following, Elizabeth compromised by attending her parish church in the morning with Herbert but going with the children to the Catholic church in the evening.

In June 1864, Elizabeth had found yet another facet of the Roman Catholic way of life to interest her, and it may have been this that sparked off de Grey's careless talk to others.

7 June 1864. To Bergholt. Called at the Abbey. Met Mr Rogers who is the clergyman of the abbey and is the same we once heard preach for Mr Kemp at St Pancras. He introduced us to the Abbess who was very kind and walked through the grounds and shewed us the Convent schoolrooms, dormitories, etc. The Abbess invited us to lunch with her and when we left gave me a bouquet of flowers.

While Elizabeth was fighting her own personal battles the High/Low Church arguments still continued in the area: '*8 June 1864.* To Claydon. Saw the church. Several monuments in the chancel had been destroyed by order of the Bishop of Norwich.'

Ignatius had left his incipient monastery at Claydon and gone to Norfolk where he moved into new premises at Elm Hill in Norwich. He returned to Ipswich in June, however, to give a lecture:

16 June. Evening with Alice, Margot, Evelyn and Blanche to Lecture Hall, Ipswich to hear a lecture given by Ignatius. He wears his hair almost quite shaved off and looked ill and very altered. He came to see us after the lecture and I introduced Margot and Blanche to him. Ignatius told us he was sometimes quite frightened at the great success he has met with at Norwich.

One might be excused for thinking that there was a very special empathy between Elizabeth and Ignatius, that he singled her out from everyone else. This would not have been the case; his talk with her would probably have been short and similar in content to the many others with whom he had established friendly relations. There is a danger too, of thinking that her religious fervour was connected with a pre- or actual menopausal state, or that she was unknowingly physically attracted to this dynamic young man. Without doubt, Ignatius did have a powerful appeal to women of all ages, and we should recall, that it was Alice who first attended his services. Elizabeth nowhere gives a physical description of Ignatius, beyond this comment on his hair and altered appearance. Had she been sexually attracted by him, we might expect a detailed portrait of him, instead, we have to turn to a man to provide this. It was six years later in 1870, that the Revd Francis Kilvert encountered Ignatius at Llanthony in Wales where the final Ignatian monastery was established. Kilvert had met Ignatius's brother Clavering Lyne and his parents:

Mrs Lyne brought up Father Ignatius and introduced us. He struck me as being a man of gentle, simple, kind manners, excitable and entirely possessed by the one idea. His head and brow are very fine, the forehead beautifully rounded and highly imaginative. The face is a very saintly one and the eyes extremely beautiful, earnest and expressive, a dark soft brown. When excited they seem absolutely to flame. He wears the Greek and early British tonsure all round the temples, leaving the hair at the crown untouched. His manner gives you the impression of great earnestness and single-mindedness. Father Ignatius wore the black Benedictine habit with the two loose wings or pieces falling in front and behind, two violet tassels behind, the knotted scourge girdle, a silver cross on the breast, and a brazen or golden cross hanging from the rosary of black beads under the left arm. . . . After luncheon we went up to the monastery again and Mr and Mrs Lyne, Clavering and I each laid a stone in the wall. We had to go up a ladder on to the scaffolding and hoarding. Each of us 'walled' our stone for the benefit of the masons. I laid a stone at the particular request of Father Ignatius.

If this is the unbiased description of one man by another, who can blame the ladies for being captivated by him. Incidentally, although Ignatius's compulsion to encourage people to lay individual bricks in the walls of his monasteries was a symbolic gesture of their support, his act of 'blessing' bricks in other places caused storms and additional work for builders. When he was in Suffolk, Ignatius had been inspired to bless a brick as it was being laid in the wall of a house in the course of erection. When the vicar of the parish was informed of this outrage, he commanded that the wall be dismantled in order to remove the offending brick.

Whatever private feelings Elizabeth may have had for Ignatius, she mentions him but once more: '16 June 1865. Sunday Walked in St James Park [London]. As we drove through the City we saw a crowd of people round St Martin's Hall waiting to hear Ignatius preach.'

In the same way that Elizabeth's life had changed somewhat, so too had her friends. Some of the ladies with whom she had been on visiting terms were mothers of the boys' schoolfellows. Inevitably, once the bonds of school were broken, some of these. acquaintances were dropped, not deliberately perhaps, but because the mutual interest no longer existed. Furthermore, Elizabeth now had the new circle she met at St Pancras church along with others who held the same High Church views as herself. Among these was Mrs Burrell, wife of the perpetual curate at St Mary Elms in Ipswich to whom she entrusted the further education of Bertie and Allan. The Burrells were to become regular participants in the Cottons' social activities and excursions.

19 October 1864. Called for Mrs Burrell who accompanied Alice, the boys and myself to the Convent at Ipswich. Saw the ceremony of Taking the Veil. One young lady took the black veil. Four others took the white veil and two lay sisters also took the white veil. Mr Kemp came to us and invited us to lunch with the Bishop of Northampton at the Convent. We declined.

The ritual and dramatic quality of conventual life obviously held a fascination for Elizabeth as it did for many women at that time, but that she retained a balanced view can be demonstrated: '24 *April 1865*. With children to St Mary's Abbey, Bergholt. Saw the Abbess, Dame Agnes and Father Rogers. Father Rogers said Fanny [her niece] would make a charming nun. She answered him "CATCH ME" at which we all laughed.' If this was a coy invitation from Fanny or a rather pert reply is open to interpretation, either way no one seems to have taken it seriously.

Back on her home territory Mr de Grey had kept his promise to atone for his past mischief by involving Elizabeth very much in the plans for the restoration of the church at Washbrook, which we have already noted. He made a final gesture of goodwill by sending her a personal gift: '23 *April 1866*. Mr de Grey sent me his photograph and the key of the Church.'

Elizabeth seems to have worked out a compromise which may have appeased de Grey. Each Christmas from 1864 onwards she both designed and executed the floral decorations for Washbrook church. From her brief hints and details from other sources we know that these decorations would have taken the form of garlands and streamers made of evergreens. She worked hard on these, on one occasion sitting up very late into the night to finish them, but although she made a token appearance at the parish church, most of her devotions were at the Catholic church, though she still had not taken the final step of being received into the faith:

> *25 December 1866*. Christmas Day. Morning to St Pancras with Alice and Bertie. Service very long, having Benediction after High Mass. Rather late at Washbrook Church. . . . *25 December 1867*. To St Pancras in the morning with Bertie and Blanche. Mr Kemp asked us to his house to meet Father Wallace and the Moores, but had to hasten home to attend Washbrook.

Elizabeth's birthday followed Christmas Day and was often used when the children were small as the day for general present giving. In the first diary, Elizabeth never mentions what she receives on her day, but this changes in the later diary; three presents in particular show how far she and Alice have gone along the path of ritual worship: '*26 December 1865*. Alice gave me a statuette of the Blessed Virgin and Child. . . . *1866* My Birthday. Alice has worked me a cushion for my devotional chair with fleur de lis upon a blue ground. . . . *1867* My birthday. Alice's gift a beautiful crucifix.'

Where, in the earlier diary, we would read of Elizabeth walking or driving to Ipswich to make calls on her friends Mrs Allen, Mrs Foster and Mrs Turner, we now find her making regular social calls at the East Bergholt convent where she seems to have established an extremely informal relationship with the occupants. One of the most endearing items in this diary paints a delightful picture: '*4 March 1867*. Monday. Afternoon with Alice and Blanche [now aged ten] to St Mary's Abbey. Blanche took her guinea-pig to show the nuns who were very much amused with it. Saw the Abbess with Dame Agnes and several other nuns. Sister Frances took the little pig into the kitchen to feed it.' Here, surely, is neither a religious fanatic nor yet an austere Victorian mother?

As we have already heard, nuns did not exist only within the Roman Catholic church. In 1857 Sisters from the Anglican Convent of St Margaret at East Grinstead had formed a community, the Sisterhood of St Mary the Virgin, in Ipswich. Here they found ample work to do among the occupants of the many overcrowded tenements, offering what relief they could to the destitute, nursing the chronically sick and running a school for the children. Most of the sisters came from well-to-do middle-class families, many were imbued with the ideals which led Florence Nightingale and her nurses to the Crimea, all were dedicated to serve others, to find a purpose in their lives. Despite criticism from many quarters, it was recognised that the Sisterhood did a great deal to alleviate the suffering of the poor and fulfilled an essential role not catered for by any other agency. This particular community did not survive for more than a year or two, and perhaps it was to rekindle interest that Dr Neale, who was chaplain of the mother-house, came to give his lecture on Sisterhoods in 1863. As we know, Elizabeth and Alice attended this meeting, as did the Revd George Drury.

One might have thought that following his experiences with Ignatius, which left him not only out of favour with the bishop but also heavily out of pocket, Drury might have had his enthusiasm for the monastic movement somewhat dampened. Not so, for in 1866 he was behind the establishment of a small community of Benedictine nuns in Claydon. Miss Mary Ware, who at least had financial funds at her disposal, bought a large house in the main street of the village which she conveyed to Drury for use as a convent, becoming herself the superior of the order. The primary aim of the convent was to provide education for all children of the parish. After Ignatius and his monks, this would seem innocent enough, but more trouble was to arise:

22 April 1867. Monday. Mr Rowland and Mr Edward Rowland called. They told us Mr Drury was to be attacked this evening. Bertie drove to Claydon Rectory to warn Mr Drury who took precautions against the danger. He introduced Bertie to the Superior of the Convent.

The reason for the proposed attack was a personal one. A wilful daughter had had the audacity to leave her father's home and join the Sisters. The irate father, accompanied by a band of his labourers, planned to remove the girl by force. Since this piece of news was related to the Cottons by the Rowlands of Akenham which adjoins the village of Claydon, we can assume that it was common gossip in the villages. We can imagine the twenty-year-old Bertie driving furiously to Claydon like a latter-day Paul Revere to bring Drury the news. Thus the convent was prepared when the assault came and the subject of the rescue mission very sensibly hid herself upstairs. When one of the raiders attempted entry by breaking the kitchen window he was repelled by Drury who emptied the contents of a basin of cold water in his face. The incensed attacking party then made an onslaught on the front door with sledge hammers, and having gained access, two of them held down Drury while the others ransacked the house in their search for the girl. The distraught young woman was dragged off to be promptly put under restraint in a lunatic asylum for nearly a year. She obtained her freedom on the death of her father, whereupon Sister Theresa returned to the convent.

Did Elizabeth crave excitement in her life, or was it again the case that what she saw as the injustice of a situation made her offer support for the cause? The week after this event: '29 April 1867. Monday Morning with Alice to Benedictine Convent at Claydon. Saw the Mother Superior.'

She and Alice continued to divide much of their time and religious energy between St Pancras and Claydon. While Elizabeth still visited the Catholic convents at Bergholt and Ipswich, Alice was becoming increasingly involved with the Claydon Sisterhood:

28 August 1867. Alice went to Claydon to stay with Sister Mary at the Convent. . . . 31 December. Alice went to Claydon to help nurse Miss Drury who is ill with Rheumatic Fever at the Convent. . . .4 January 1868. A letter from Alice . . . With Herbert to Ipswich, Blanche with us. Had luncheon at the White Horse. With Blanche drove to Claydon to see Alice. Met Mr Drury and Sister Mary at the Convent. Drove back to Ipswich for Herbert. . . . 5 January. To Claydon Church. Called at the Convent for Alice who accompanied me to church and returned to be with Mary Drury afterwards. . . . 10 January Ill from neuralgia attack. . . . 12 January. Sent for Alice . . . 30 January. To Claydon Convent. Met Mr and Mrs Drury. Left Alice with them. . . . 14 February. Alice came home.

We might deduce from this that Alice was treading a path which would lead her to join the Sisters, but there is ample evidence that she was still leading a very active social life. She continued to ride regularly with her brothers, particularly Bertie, she attended parties and dances, often returning home in the early hours, and she made regular visits to relations in London. Nonetheless, she did reject an offer of marriage, whether from aversion to the gentleman who offered or to the idea of matrimony in principle we are not told. In fact, Elizabeth gives us no clue whatsoever that any such proposal is in the offing.

'7 October 1867. Letter and photograph from Mr Harvey . . . 8 October. Wrote to Mr Harvey.' These entries appeared to have no particular significance. Mr Harvey had not been mentioned before; he was never listed among those present at any gathering Elizabeth attended or held at her home, and she was meticulous in recording such things. The sending of a photograph suggests there is some form of friendship involved but nothing further is heard of him until:

21 June 1868. Sunday. With Alice and the boys spent the day with Father Kemp. Attended Mass and Vespers. Met Mrs Last who with Alice and Allan went to Tower Church in the evening. Afterwards Music and singing. When we returned home found Mr Harvey had called and dined with Herbert and had asked permission to pay his addresses to Alice. She declines to accept him.

And there the matter ends, leaving us to ponder on all the unanswered questions this episode evokes. While Alice was obviously allowed the freedom to make her choice in this matter, it becomes clear that another member of the family is also free to choose the direction her life should take. Elizabeth usually states those who accompany her to the Catholic church, and conspicuously absent on most occasions is Evelyn. She, of all the children, must have inherited her mother's artistic talent, and although both she and Blanche received private tuition in woodcarving as part of their artistic education, we learn, in passing from Elizabeth, that Evelyn has progressed to actual studies at the Ipswich School of Art. We have seen earlier that Eva was the 'different' one of the children, and perhaps for that reason, she failed to become swept along with the High Church fervour of the rest. Possibly she was too involved with her art to embrace other causes, or it may be that she enjoyed a special relationship with her father, for on the rare occasions that Elizabeth mentions Evelyn's church-going it is to note that she attended the parish church with Herbert.

By 1868 Elizabeth was expending much of her time and energy on the Catholic Church, though she still owed allegiance to the Church of England, albeit mainly to the High Church wing of it. Possibly she saw no dichotomy in this.

24 February 1868. Mr Kemp sent me two wax candles he had blessed at the Feast of Candlemas. . . . *Ash Wednesday* With Blanche to service of Receiving the Ashes at St Pancras. Had breakfast with Mr Kemp. . . . Sunday With Herbert to Holy Communion at Washbrook Church. . . . *20 March.* A letter from Father Wallace to ask me attend to Funeral Mass at St Pancras. Went to it.

12 May 1868. A letter from Father Wallace asking us to attend St Pancras today but stayed home to meet Dr Bartlet who came to see Evelyn. Alfred Allen called to ask Bertie and I to be sponsors for him as he wished to belong to the Church of England. . . . *13 May.* With Bertie to St Mary Elms, Ipswich. Met Mr Burrell there and Alfred Allen who was baptised by him. Bertie and myself stood sponsors for him.

7 June 1868. [During a visit to London] To the Jesuits' Church alone. The singing very good. . . . *19 June.* Friday. Had the choir of Washbrook Church here to spend the afternoon and evening. The children had tea and supper. Played in the garden and meadows, and had music and singing in the evening. They appeared to enjoy themselves very much.

Since Elizabeth possessed a great love of music and she makes such frequent mention of the music she heard in Catholic churches, this may have been what had initially drawn her to that form of worship.

In 1869, she achieved a minor triumph in bridging the gulf between her friends of different religious persuasions:

6 January 1869. An evening party. Mr de Grey, Mr and Mrs Sanderson, Miss Waller, Mrs William Bruff, Miss Bruff and two brothers, Mrs Elliston, her son and daughter, Lucy, Belle and Margaret Meadows [friends and riding companions of the boys], Mr and Mrs Dawson, Mr Harry and Grace Meadows, Mr Rowland, Mr Notcutt, Mr B. and E. Edwards, Mr Allen, Count de Ronsee, M. Wackernsai, Mr Thomas etc. forty five persons altogether.

Quite how de Grey responded to finding himself rubbing shoulders with the Count de Ronsée and M. Wackernsai, the French Catholic pupils of Mr Kemp and the Ipswich Catholics like the Sandersons and Bruffs we are not told. The very fact that he accepted the invitation shows that he must have become reconciled to the situation, and doubtless among the forty-five present there were local families who were well known to him and safely Low Church.

Immediately before this grand social occasion, Elizabeth had again exhibited that trait of hers of going contrary to advice and putting herself at risk:

29 December 1868. A letter from Father Kemp to say Father Wallace is ill at the Convent with Scarlet Fever. Called upon Mr Kemp and went with him to see Father Wallace. Evening went with Alice and Blanche to Claydon Convent to assist at village party. . . . *30 December.* To see Father Wallace. Met Dr Bartlet at Convent. . . . *31 December.* Thursday A letter from Father Wallace to say Dr Bartlet considered it unsafe for me to visit him for fear of taking infection home to the children. . . . Saturday. Called at the Convent. Saw the Superior. Father Wallace better.

In her continuing search for enlightenment in the field of theology, Elizabeth and the children had in October 1868 joined the 'large and highly respectable audience' for a lecture given by E.F. Brewster, Esq. of

White Notley Hall, Witham in Essex on The Second Coming of Our Lord. According to the *Ipswich Journal*,

the lecturer, in his introductory observations, dwelt at some length upon the fact that the whole of prophetic Scripture must be received and taken as it was found. There could be no possible doubt upon anyone's mind, upon reading the 20th chapter of the Apocalypse that there were to be two resurrections; the one to take place a thousand years before the general resurrection, of a select number of the saints, who would fulfil the prophecies of the Psalms and rule the earth in righteousness. The Devil would be chained up, and there would be no sin; angels would descend upon the earth, and in fact, it would become a sort of Paradise, and the Church Militant would become the Church Triumphant.

What the *Ipswich Journal* does not report is the audience reaction, but we do have that of at least one:

26 October 1868. Evening with children to lecture by Mr Brewster. After hearing him for a short time found the lecture so stupid we could not remain, so walked to the White Horse for our carriage.

If Elizabeth joined a general exodus, was the instigator of one, or marched her family out in solitary protest, we are not told. Neither do we know at what point of the lecture she left. Did she wait to hear that 'the first resurrection was at hand' or was it when the lecturer stated that he would reserve all the proof for his doctrine to a further lecture that she felt she had heard enough?

With her new-found Catholic inspiration, Elizabeth becomes much more our accepted idea of the Victorian lady of good works. Within her home village she had naturally undertaken to help the poor and needy, but now her range was extended:

19 March 1868. With Alice to Ipswich to enquire the character of a servant. When driving through the Rope Walk [a very overcrowded area] a little child fell under our carriage and was hurt. Called to see her. Child's name Jane Shepherd. Gave her mother some money and sent the child to be seen by a surgeon. . . . *20 March*. Funeral Mass at St Pancras. Went to it and afterwards called to see Jane Shepherd.

10 November 1868. To Ipswich. Called upon Mrs Gaye for Father Wallace to tell her of a child requiring baptism in Mr Gaye's parish. . . . *11 February 1869*. To Ipswich. Called to see Mrs Hawkins and Mrs Smith, poor Catholics. . . . Sent Mrs Hawkins a flannel jacket. . . . The second Superior, Mother Ann from the East Grinstead Sisterhood called. Father Kemp came to say goodbye before he leaves Ipswich and stayed the night. Mary Drury sent us some tatting to trim dresses we are making for a Bazaar to which the Lady Abbess has asked us to contribute.

However caught up she might have been in her religious fervour, Elizabeth still retained the ability to make a balanced judgement: '*4 October 1865*. A girl named Agnes Ellis called upon me to ask assistance and said Father Rogers had sent her. Wrote to the Father Kemp to enquire into the truth of her story. . . . *6 October*. Mr Kemp wrote to say Agnes Ellis is an impostor.'

It is very obvious from both diaries that Elizabeth was unstinting in her generosity and hospitality. There are numerous references which show her care and concern for others; she rushes to comfort the distraught wife of one of the farm labourers who has had an accident and continues to call taking gifts with her. Such acts she would have performed without thinking. Once, when she herself was making the long walk into Ipswich she encountered a poor woman who had been overcome with fatigue and in her compassion she stopped a passing carter and paid for the woman to be conveyed to her destination. I doubt she even considered the parallel with the parable. She visited her friends when they were sick, taking luxuries for them, and seemed entirely to disregard her personal safety when, for example, she visited the Walton Turner family, most of whom had contracted typhus while in Felixstowe.

Her home too, was always open and she was quick to respond to requests for hospitality:

9 December 1868. Father Kemp called and stayed to dinner. Father Harper came to see Mr Kemp and a messenger following him from Father Wallace to say Miss Kemp had fallen in a fit. Father Kemp returned home and Father Harper stayed with us. . . . *10 Dec*. Miss Kemp very ill and her brother asked me to invite Father Harper who is in delicate health to remain here.

The Catholic priests seemed to spend a great deal of time at Amor Hall. Perhaps the opportunity to escape from the bustling and overcrowded area in which they lived and worked to relax in the countryside and enjoy the lavish hospitality the Cottons offered was too much to resist. Perhaps too, they enjoyed talking with a woman who was both widely read and possessed a lively intellect.

As in most places in England at the beginning of the nineteenth century, the Roman Catholic population of Ipswich was very small. A French emigré Abbé had established a small chapel on the edge of the town which catered mainly for those few families who had adhered to the old faith and the occasional Irish regiments quartered in the Barracks. In 1860 a convent school and orphanage was opened in conjunction with the chapel, but the decision was taken in 1861 to build a new church in the centre of the town to work among the poor and the expanding number of immigrant workers who had settled in Ipswich. The building of the railway had brought in many Irish Catholics, many of whom had stayed to help run the new system, among them Elizabeth's new friend Mr Bruff who was both an engineer and Station Manager at Ipswich. Did it ever strike her as ironic that she should become so closely acquainted with a representative of the institution which had destroyed her father's business?

The church of St Pancras was still very new when Elizabeth commenced attending in 1863. Father Kemp was appointed as the first priest in charge, dividing his time between there and the original chapel to which he had been appointed in 1854. Two or three years younger than Elizabeth, he was a Suffolk man and had, like John Henry Newman, found his way into Catholicism via the Oxford Movement. This too had been the path of Father Wallace, an Oxford MA who joined the staff at St Pancras following a fairly recent conversion. It is a measure of the work of these two and Father Rogers, who was a curate as well as chaplain to the East Bergholt convent, that the estimated Catholic membership of sixty in 1861 had risen to around four hundred by the early 1870s.

It is likely that Kemp's and Wallace's Anglican background gave them common ground in their discussions with Elizabeth, but sadly for her, the very close friendship which she and the boys had established with Kemp was to be lost:

18 March 1869. To Ipswich with Herbert. Took Blanche to carving lesson. Subscribed £5 to Testimonial for Father Kemp. . . . *21 March.* A letter from Father Wallace asking us to attend Mass as it would be the last time Father Kemp would officiate in his own church. Went with Alice and Blanche. Lunched with Father Kemp. He gave me a palm he had blessed yesterday.

Following Kemp's resignation Elizabeth tended to worship most often at Claydon church where Alice's loyalty lay – and within the bounds of the established Church. However, both of them still took much interest in the two convents at Ipswich and Bergholt. The Abbey had become very much a place to show her visitors from London in much the same way that in days past they had been taken to view the historic Helmingham Hall. Alice still went off to spend days at a time with the Claydon

Sisterhood, which is where she was at the beginning of November when disaster struck both the farm and the occupants of Amor Hall. On and off throughout 1869, Herbert, who was as old as the years of the century, had had periodic bouts of ill health. On 3 November at the same time as he fell ill yet again, the 'Cattle Disease' broke out on the farm. The next week or so found Elizabeth in her dual role of loving wife and deputy in the running of the farm dividing her time between sitting with Herbert and staying up at night with an ailing horse.

The doctor visited Herbert again on the 12th and 13th, but on the 16th Herbert must have felt well enough to go to Ipswich, but this proved to be but a temporary remission in his illness:

> *17 November 1869.* Mrs Gross's children came. Sent them away as Herbert was very ill. Dr Bartlet came and advised him to keep in bed. Father Rogers came and stayed the night. Mr de Grey called. . . . *18 November.* Doctor came. Father Wallace came and stayed the night. *19th.* Next day Father Wallace and Father Rogers left. They came into my husband's [room] to see him.

Elizabeth's usually meticulous handwriting shows stress here and one entry merges into another as it has not done for many years, and she omits the word 'room'. The following day the doctor ordered a nurse to help care for Herbert and the situation had become serious enough for Elizabeth to send for Bertie who had, just a month before, gone off to begin his medical studies.

Now, if ever, Elizabeth needed the support of her religious faith and she was not disappointed in the succour offered by the clergy from the Catholic Church:

> *25 November 1869.* Dr Bartlet came and Father Wallace.
> *26 November 1869.* Father Wallace sat up tonight with us and Dr Bartlet came several times.

There was no entry for the 27th.

> *28 November 1869.* My dearest husband died at eleven o'clock at night. Father Wallace was with us.

The final entry in the second diary records that Herbert was buried on Friday, 3 December 1869. He was interred in the churchyard at Copdock beside other members of the Cotton family.

10
Postscript

When Elizabeth Cotton made the final entry in the diary for 1869, she had come not only to the end of that volume, but to the end of a way of life that had been hers·for twenty-six years. In his will, Herbert left everything to her, expressing the hope that if she so desired it, the lease on Amor Hall would be renewed for her life and that she would appoint an agent to run the farm for her. Since Herbert had been on very friendly terms with the landlord, there would have been no problem concerning the lease. However, Elizabeth chose not to remain at Washbrook.

Until any further diaries of Elizabeth Cotton come to light, the only record that exists of her later life in Ipswich, where she made her home, is to be found in the portfolio of her artwork. In the early part of the 1870s she set herself the task of illustrating 'A Suffolk Legend', the strange story of Grace Pett whose death in 1744 was recorded as having been caused by spontaneous combustion. The wife of a fisherman, Mrs Pett was reputed to be a witch responsible for an outbreak of sheep plague in a village near Ipswich. The farmer's wife sought the aid of a 'doctor' who provided her with an incantation and instructions for a ritual burning of a sacrificial sheep. In order to carry out the horrific live roasting of the animal it was necessary to tie its feet together, and at the end these were all that remained untouched by the fire. The circumstances surrounding Grace Pett's death which occurred around the same time were equally macabre. The lady had fallen asleep in her living room following a celebration to mark the return of a daughter from abroad. There was little evidence of fire damage to the room, even a paper screen was unscathed, yet of Grace Pett all that remained were her feet and hands. The legend grew over the years and it was the verses composed on the subject which inspired Elizabeth to illustrate them in her own way. Many of the scenes are etched and she drew on her own experiences, for example for the scene depicting the field of sheep, she included one of their flock at Washbrook. For the scenes of the farm, she journeyed to the actual location that she might have the details correct. The verses are carefully inscribed and around them are borders of intricate patterns. The whole work, which she had bound, would have made an immensely commercial publication, yet Elizabeth presumably executed it for her own satisfaction.

During the 1880s she was constantly recording old buildings in the town in carefully drawn sketches, often returning to a picture to note when the house concerned was demolished. On one of the drawings, Elizabeth added a quick sketch of the carved overmantel of a fireplace. The importance of this is that she added the date on which it was made – 13 May 1891, so we know that she was still in Ipswich at that time. Perhaps it was to escape the rigours of an East Anglian winter that she went to Naples; perhaps she was already in ill health. We do not know if she made the journey alone, but certainly Bertie was with her at the Pensione Sabelli, Palazzo Bellocchio, at Posillipo, Naples, when she died on the ninth of January 1892 aged seventy-two. She was buried two days later in the old British Cemetery.

Elizabeth Cotton's Reading List

The following are the books which Elizabeth mentions she is reading to Herbert. In some cases it has been impossible to identify the author.

1854–1863

Travels in Bolivia	
Roughing it in the Bush	Mrs Moodie
Adventures of Mr Ledbury	A.R. Smith
A Faggot of French Sticks	Stead
Christie Johnson	Charles Reade
Pride and Prejudice	Jane Austen
Pursuit of Sport in Foreign Lands	H. St. John
The New Timon	Edward Bulwer-Lytton
The Fortunes of Nigel	Sir Walter Scott
The Newcomes	William Makepeace Thackeray
David Copperfield	Charles Dickens
Fishing and Shooting Scenes in Sweden and Norway	
Cranford	Mrs Gaskell
Peveril of the Peak	Sir Walter Scott
Esmond	Thackeray
Rambles in Cornwall	
General Bunce	T.E. Hook
Peg Woffington	Charles Reade
Waverley	Sir Walter Scott
Little Dorrit	Charles Dickens
The Ingoldsby Legends	R.H. Barham
The Dead Secret	Wilkie Collins
The Life of Charlotte Brontë	Mrs Gaskell
Sporting in Africa	Capt. Drayton
The Falcon Family	Marmion Savage
The Bloomer	
Harry Coverdale's Courtship	Francis Smedley
Dark and Fair	Jarnac
The Interpreter	

Notes on Fishing	
White Lies	Charles Reade
Guy Livingstone	G.A. Lawrence
Deerbrook	Harriet Martineau
Tancred	Benjamin Disraeli
History of England	Knight
Dr.Thorne	Anthony Trollope
The Warden	Anthony Trollope
A Good Fight	Charles Reade
Dombey and Son	Charles Dickens
Sword and Gown	G.A. Lawrence
Sporting	H. St. John
A Tale of Two Cities	Charles Dickens
The Virginians	William Makepeace Thackeray
The Bertrams	Anthony Trollope
The Woman in White	Wilkie Collins
Love Me Little, Love Me Long	Charles Reade
Framley Parsonage	Anthony Trollope
The Old Shikari	
The Siver Cord	C.W. Brooks
Lovel the Widower	William Makepeace Thackeray
What Will He Do With It?	Bulwer Lytton
Adam Bede	George Eliot
Market Harborough	G.J. Whyte-Melville
Hypatia	Charles Kingsley
Orly Farm	Anthony Trollope
The Pentateuch	Bishop Colenso
Make Your Game	Sala
No Name	Wilkie Collins
Ravenshoe	Henry Kingsley
Barren Honour	G.A. Lawrence
North America	Anthony Trollope
Cruising on Wheels	C.A. Collins
Arrow Flight	
Mildrington the Barrister	P. Fitzgerald

1864–69

Salem Chapel	Margaret Oliphant
House by the Churchyard	J.S. Le Fanu
Verner's Pride	Mrs Henry Wood

The Monastery	Sir Walter Scott
The Small House at Allington	Anthony Trollope
The Rosea Pass	
Elsie Venner	D.W. Holmes
Capt. Clutterbuck's Champaigne	
Maurice Dering	G.A. Lawrence
The Gordian Knot	C.W. Brooks
The Struggles of Brown, Jones and Robinson	Anthony Trollope
Lindisfarne Chase	
Can You Forgive Her?	Anthony Trollope
Bella Donna	P. Fitzgerald
A Box for the Season	Charles Clarke
Armadale	Wilkie Collins
Our Mutual Friend	Charles Dickens
The Hillyars and Burtons	Henry Kingsley
The Church and the World	
Sans Merci	G.A. Lawrence
75, Brooke Street	P. Fitzgerald
The Last Chronicle of Barset	Anthony Trollope
Land at Last	E.H. Yates
Archie Lovell	J.S. Knowles
Story with a Vengeance	Reach
Lady Audley's Secret	M.E. Braddon
Sooner or Later	C.W. Brooks
Silcotes of Silcote	Henry Kingsley
Sweet Anne Page	Mortimer Collins

Bibliography

SOURCES

Unpublished Diaries

Elizabeth Cotton	1854–63	Property of M. Tyler.
Elizabeth Cotton	1864–69	Property of A. Copsey.
George Ranson	1842–48	Property of A. Copsey.
Isabella Brett		
Ann Gurdon		In Suffolk Record Office.
Elizabeth Rope		
Elizabeth White		

BOOKS AND NEWSPAPERS

Brown, A.F.J., *Essex People 1750–1900; From their Diaries, Memoirs and Letters*. Chelmsford: Essex Record Office, 1972.

Glyde, John, *The Moral, Social and Religious Condition of Ipswich in the Middle of the Nineteenth Century*. Ipswich: J.M. Burton, 1850 (facsimile edition), Wakefield and London: S.R. Publishers, 1971.

Gray, I.E. and Potter, W.E., *The History of the Ipswich School 1400–1950*. Ipswich: Ancient House Press, 1950.

Kilvert's Diary 1870–1879. Ed. William Plomer. Harmondsworth: Penguin, 1982, (One-volume selection first published by Jonathan Cape, 1944).

Haxell, E. Nelson, *A Scramble Through London and Brighton*. Bath: Lewis, Sons & Tyte, 1884.

Pipe, Richard, *Copdock: A View of the Parish*. Private publication, 1977.

——, *Copdock Walkabout*. Private publication, 1982.

——, *Washbrook Walkabout*. Private publication, 1982.

Southwold Diary of James Maggs, Vol. 2, 1848–1876. Ed. A. Bottomley, Woodbridge: Boydell, for Suffolk Record Society, 1984.

Thompson, Leonard, *Old Inns of Suffolk*. Ipswich: Ancient House Press, 1950.

Tricker, Roy, *Anglicans On High*. Private publication, 1988.

Wilson, P. and Cox, E., *The Waller Story*. Victoria, NSW, private publication, date unknown.

The Ipswich Journal.

The Suffolk Chronicle.

BACKGROUND READING

Adburgham, A., *Silver Fork Society 1814–1840*, London: Constable, 1983.

Allen, D. Elliston, *The Victorian Fern Craze: A History of Pteridomania*. London: Hutchinson, 1969.

Anson, P.F., *Building up the Waste Spaces*, Leighton Buzzard: Faith Press, 1973.

Bates, A., *Directory of Stage Coach Services, 1863*, Newton Abbot: David & Charles, 1969.

Bovill, E.W., *The England of Nimrod and Surtees*, Oxford University Press, 1959.

Brander, M., *The Victorian Gentleman*, London: Gordon Cremonesi, 1975.

Briggs, M.S., *The English Farmhouse*, London: Batsford, 1953.

Calder, J., *The Victorian Home*, London: Batsford, 1977.

Calder Marshall, A., *The Enthusiast*, London: Faber & Faber, 1962.

Cannell, B.G.A., *From Monk to Busman*, London: Skeffington, 1935.

Churton, E., *The Rail Road Book of England, 1851*, London: Sidgwick & Jackson, 1973.

Copeland, J., *Roads and Their Traffic 1750–1850*, Newton Abbot: David & Charles, 1968.

Davidoff, L., *The Best Circles: Society, Etiquette and the Season*, London: Croom Helm, 1986.

Davidoff, L. and Hall, C., *Family Fortunes*, London: Hutchinson, 1987.

Fawcett, T., *The Rise of English Provincial Art*, Oxford: Clarendon Press, 1874.

Fletcher, R., *A Victorian Village: Richard Cobbold's Wortham, 1860*, London: Batsford, 1977.

Fulford, R., ed., *Dearest Child – The Private Correspondence of Queen Victoria and the Crown Princess of Prussia, 1851–1861*, London: Evans, 1964.

Gillis, J., *For Better For Worse: British Marriage, 1600–the Present*, Oxford University Press, 1985.

Malster, R., *Ipswich on the Orwell*, Lavenham, Suffolk: Terence Dalton, 1978.

Martin, E.W., *The Secret People: English Village Life after 1750*, Phoenix House, 1954.

Matz, B.W., *The Inns and Taverns of Pickwick*, Cecil Palmer, 1921.

Mercer, E., *English Vernacular Houses: A Study of the Traditional Farmhouses and Cottages*, London: HMSO, 1975.

Mingay, G.E., *Rural Life in Victorian England*, London: Heinemann, 1976.

Moore, K., *Victorian Wives*, London: Allison & Busby, 1985.

Reader, W.J., *Victorian England*, London: Batsford, 1964.

Stanley, L., (ed.), *The Diaries of Hannah Cullwick: Victorian servant – 1854–1873*, London: Virago, 1984.

Vicinus, M., *Independent Women: Work and Community for Single Women*, London: Virago, 1985.

Watson, F., *The Year of the Wombat: England 1857*, London: Gollancz, 1974.

FICTION

Dickens, C., *Bleak House*

——, *The Cricket on the Hearth*

——, *Pickwick Papers*

Eliot, G., *Scenes from Clerical Life*

——, *My Lady Ludlow*

——, *Middlemarch*

——, *Felix Holt*

Scott, Sir W. *Peveril of the Peak*

Trollope, A., *John Caldigate*

——, *Travels in Australia*

——, *Doctor Thorne*

——, *Framley Parsonage*

——, *The Vicar of Bulhampton*

Index